'Not many people could tell the fascinating story of these three Mighty men of God in Welsh history as Geraint Fielder has done. His book is a significant contribution to our knowledge of the Forward Movement in Wales in the generation just before Dr. Martyn Lloyd-Jones heard its appeal for evangelists and left London for Aberavon.

The Joshua brothers and John Pugh were deeply involved with the early evangelistic drive of the Movement, and with the powerful visitation of God in the 1904 revival. Geraint Fielder sets out Seth Joshua's penetrating analysis of the distinctions between evangelism and revival and the peculiar dangers of days of revival. He was particularly concerned about the subjectivism which was evident is so many areas of the church's life at this time. The book is full of relevance for our own times. Welsh readers will not need to be encouraged to read it. Non-Welsh Christians will be the losers if they don't.'

Eric Alexander

'Those who are concerned about the state of the church and society must read this book to see how God can change everything through men and women whom he has called by his grace and to whom he has given the grit and gumption to carry out his work. It is a well written story that warms the heart, and took me right back to Sandfields, Aberavon.'

Lady Elizabeth Catherwood

'What a great, and true, story this book tells! It is a thrill to read of the "Grace, Grit and Gumption" that so characterized the exploits of three remarkable men in reaching out with the Gospel to the English speaking labouring classes of South Wales over 100 years ago. Times and circumstances change, but lukewarm discipleship, uninspired ministry, and respectable orthodoxy can never achieve such victories for Christ, whether then or now.

For me, living church history of this sort is uniquely able to rekindle the fires within, in order to be "flat-out" for Christ and His kingdom, in the time that remains, as they were.

Mr Fielder is a shrewd and honest scribe whose wise judgements give the reader confidence to learn from the few mistakes made as well as the many triumphs won.'

Dick Lucas

'This is a story that had to be told. These are men who should live in the hearts and minds of a new generation. Their devotion to Christ, their compassion and their indomitable courage stand as both a rebuke and an inspiration. There were giants in the land in those days. May their example breed others such as they in our generation too.'

Peter Lewis

GRACE, GRIT
AND
GUMPTION

The Exploits of Evangelists
John Pugh, Frank and Seth Joshua

Geraint Fielder

The Evangelical Movement of Wales

CHRISTIAN FOCUS

Geraint Fielder has been part time minister at Highfields Church, Cardiff since 1987. A former President of UCCF and author of two books on its history. Has spoken at Spring Harvest and Word Alive and was a regular broadcaster for nearly twenty years. Interests – family adventures with Mary and four children!

ISBN 1-85792-500-9

First published in 2000
Revised and expanded edition
published in 2004
by
Christian Focus Publications,
Geanies House, Fearn, Ross-shire
IV20 1TW, Scotland, UK
and
The Evangelical Movement of Wales
Bryntirion, Bridgend, CF31 4DX, Wales, UK

www.christianfocus.com

Cover design by Alister MacInnes

Printed and bound by
MacKay's of Chatham

Contents

INTRODUCTION: BEELZEBUB TAKES A KNOCK 11

1. THE CLOCK STRIKES FOR PUGH 17

2. THE DRINKING DENS 23

3. THE JOSHUAS AT NEATH 39

4. GLASGOW, CARDIFF AND THE FORWARD MOVEMENT 61

5. GRACE, GRIT AND GUMPTION 85

6. POVERTY AND PROSTITUTION 103

7. SETH – WALES FOR CHRIST 113

8. THE FULL TIDE OF REVIVAL 121

9. REVIVAL REPERCUSSIONS 139

10. A GREAT VICTORIAN and his loyal lieutenant 153

11. 'SAINT FRANCIS OF NEATH' 179

12. THE RETURN OF SETH 185

13. POSTSCRIPT AND PRELUDE 203

APPENDIX 1: Edward Davies, Llandinam 215

APPENDIX 2: Temperance 221

A CENTENNIAL APPENDIX: Burning Hearts 225

BIBLIOGRAPHY 241

NOTES 243

INDEX 265

Dedication:

To the churches of my youth:
Caersalem, Tabernacle and Penyrheol Hall, Gorseinon.

To the church of our marriage:
Heath Church, Cardiff.

To the churches of my ministry:
Whitefields's Presbyterian Church, Abergavenny;
Highfields Free Church, Cardiff

Acknowledgements

The impulse that produced this book was provided by two lectures I gave at gatherings of the Evangelical Movement of Wales – one to the Bala Minister's Conference and the other as the Aberystwyth Annual Conference's Historical Lecture, both in 1996. There have been a dozen or more further occasions when I have been invited to give the lecture in various parts of South Wales and each time was encouraged to 'get it published'.

My own searching has brought a lot of additional material to the light, but much of the story of the Joshua brothers and John Pugh has already been told by T Mardy Rees, F. R. Hist.S, *Seth And Frank Joshua – the Renowned Evangelists*' (1926) and Howell Williams, *The Romance of the Forward Movement* (1946). Sadly these books have long been out of print and unobtainable, so I have sought to recraft and rewrite sections of them and quote extensively from them.

Several friends have helped form this book. I wish to thank Alun Ebenezer of Gorseinon for introducing me, first, to a 1945 newspaper article on Seth and Frank Joshua and then to books in Welsh on John Pugh, again long out of print. I am grateful to others for translating the books for me – in particular Nerys Davies, along with Ceinwen Elias, Gwyneth Samuel and John Phillips. Mrs Shirley Edwards of Neath introduced me to Mr Vernon Mills who passed on his personal recollections of Seth Joshua's ministry in the 1920s. Helpful corrections, criticisms, suggestions, information and encouragements have come from Eric Alexander, Dr Oliver Barclay, Roger Brown, Lady Elizabeth Catherwood, G. Wyn Davies, Martyn Fielder, Graham Harrison, Dr Carl Henry, Joy Horn, Peter Lewis, Dick Lucas and Dr David Wright.

This thrilling, at times heroic, story of three evangelists, who, by God's grace, can be accounted great among any of that calling, has been largely lost to the memory of Christians in Wales and is virtually unknown to a wider Christian public. The task of writing it has been a happy one and has helped revitalize my Christian commitment. May reading it do the same for others.

Abergavenny, 1999.

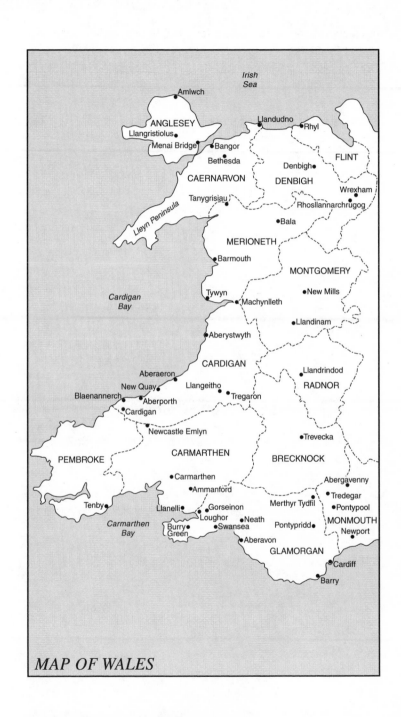

MAP OF WALES

Introduction

Beelzebub takes a knock

One Saturday morning in May 1891, in the unchurched and sprawling industrial area of East Moors, Splott, Cardiff, two men could be seen putting up a large tent. The older man of forty-five, John Pugh, was unused to swinging a sledge-hammer and he had lumbago for a month. The younger man, Seth Joshua who was in his early thirties, was adept at the job. Just as they finished, one of the rough characters of the area passed by. He was curious as to what was going on.

'Hello, guvnor, what is this, a boxing show?'

'There is going to be some fighting here,' said Seth.

'When are you going to start?'

'Tomorrow morning at 11 am.'

'Tomorrow's Sunday.'

'Well, better the day, better the deed.'

'Who's on?'

'I've got to take the first round.'

'Who's with you?'

'He's a chap called Beelzebub'

'Never heard of him. Who's he?'

'O he's a smart one I can tell you. Come tomorrow morning.'

'I'll be there.'

'And strange to say, he was there,' said Seth. 'When I had given out the first hymn, "All hail the power of Jesus' name" he knew he had been caught. Beelzebub went over the ropes all right, for the chap was converted that very morning'.[1]

Those tent meetings on Sunday, May 5, 1891, were the beginning of a great surge of evangelistic activity to reach the unchurched working classes in Cardiff, most of whom were by now unable to understand Welsh. For the previous twenty years, before he came to Cardiff, Pugh, as we shall see, had laboured with exceptional success in ministries in English-speaking churches in the new mining towns of Tredegar and then Pontypridd. Those years from 1872 to 1891 showed him that the Welsh-speaking evangelical churches of that time, secure and successful in rural areas and country towns, and still warm with the afterglow of the 1859 revival, were getting seriously out of touch with a new urbanized generation growing up in the mining and seaport towns because most of that generation were monoglot English in speech. Untouched as many were by Christian influence, and thrown into living conditions that were primitive as regards amenities and dangerous to health, they were raw and rough in their ways and increasingly under the social scourge of the day, 'the drink'. When Pugh moved to Cardiff his passion to reach the unreached led to the tent evangelism in East Moors. This joint initiative with Seth Joshua soon developed into what became known as the Forward Movement of the Calvinistic Methodist (Presbyterian) Church of Wales. It was an attempt to face and tackle the deep divide that was growing up between the churches and the rapidly changing social patterns of ordinary folk.

The world in which Pugh lived was a booming coal and railway building age. The entire Welsh coalfield was absorbing population, much of it young, able-bodied, working men, at a rate without comparison in the United Kingdom, and indeed was, for a while, a magnet for immigrants surpassed in the world by the United States alone. Cardiff became the largest coal exporting docks in the world. It had begun with the sinking of coal pits in village areas all over what became the South Wales coalfield. These villages had had a closely-knit, Welsh-speaking identity. When more houses were built to meet the inrush of men to man the mines, new chapels soon followed, retaining their Welshness. Eventually however, as the immigrant population took over, the valleys became anglicized in speech. Though there had been plenty of personal ungodliness in the old village communities they had not been beyond the reach of the moral and spiritual influence of the chapel. But now the drinking clubs and betting shops became rife and took over. The local chapels and their traditional activities, all wrapped up in the Welsh language, did not touch these new needy but tough types. At first the bulk of immigration had come from rural Wales, bringing with them their cultural legacies in the chapels. Then increasingly newcomers arrived from England (and Ireland), uprooted from any religious background they may have had and hurled into a harsh, unchurched urban environment, destined to reject the old Welsh chapel based values.

The critical point for our story, and Pugh saw its implications early on, is that the English-speaking chapel in Wales was still a rarity in the late 1880s. The advent of English-speaking immigrants caused much heartsearching among the Welsh-speaking community. Some said the church should 'function in the Welsh language exclusively'. Others saw this was not consistent with the history of Welsh Calvinistic Methodism. The English leaders of Methodism – Whitefield, the Wesleys, the Countess of Huntingdon and others – had often been present in gatherings in Wales during the early days of the eighteenth-century reawakening. When the hearers could understand it, Howel Harris would preach in English as he accompanied Whitefield on their South Wales tours. One hundred and fifty years later, the tide of immigrant irreligion that was engulfing the urban areas of South Wales, would only be met by evangelism in English. However, as late as 1899 the Home Mission reported that an Atlantic passage in winter was not as stormy as the Calvinistic Methodist transition from Welsh to English.

Standing tall and massive in front of the former coal exchange on the Barry seafront is a statue of David Davies.[2] In front of the imposing Cardiff Civic centre, alongside that of David Lloyd-George, stands one of John Cory.[3] Davies and Cory were two of the entrepreneurs responsible for South East Wales industrialization and the resulting massive social changes. They were the builders of Barry Docks and, as coal owners in the Valleys, its main coal suppliers via their own Taff Vale railway. Within twenty years Barry grew from a village of less than 100 people to a busy seaport of over 30,000. In 1913 it surpassed Cardiff for a while as the world's greatest coal exporter. The Davies family and Cory will appear in our story as Christians supportive (in the Davies' case, massively so) of Pugh's vision of bringing the Christian message to the anglicised families whose men worked in docks and mines.

That vision was born in the heart of the son of a railway builder, John Pugh, of New Mills, Montgomeryshire, who lived from 1846 to 1907. Bilingual and born near the English border he was equipped by background to bridge the two language communities. It is important to say that Pugh was never one of those who thought Welsh an inferior language, best dropped if the Welshman was to throw off his supposed inferiority. He was a bilingual Welshman whose missionary heart bled for 'the stranger in their midst' who did not know Christ. In his attempts to reach them he showed himself to be a doughty fighter, obstinate, determined, a man of steel, but also tender and compassionate – a soul of emotions which could frequently break out into tears. First he, and later the Joshua brothers Seth and Frank, quite independently of each other at first, went out to the street corners and public houses of places like Tredegar, Pontypridd, Neath, Cardiff and Barry and saw the unreached drawn and won for Christ.

Our Lord's words in Matthew 22:9-10 were lived out in the ministries of Pugh and the Joshuas and were crucial in Pugh's calling as we shall see. 'Go to the street corners and invite to the banquet anyone you find. So the servants went out into the streets and gathered all the people they could find, both good and bad and the wedding hall was filled with guests.' Their mission was primarily to those neglected by any Christian influence and concern – a challenge to any generation, and once more a challenge to today's as we see a burgeoning underclass. It is also a virile boost to spiritual morale! We can't copy the past. But we can be stirred by these men to live out that text in our context. In a recent correspondence Sir Glanmor Williams, formerly Professor of History at the University of Wales in Swansea, says, 'These excellent men of the Forward Movement put us all to shame.'

The Three and the Thirty

We launch into the background and then the early story of a vigorous and courageous evangelistic adventure. It is a tribute especially to three men of God – John Pugh, Seth and Frank Joshua – who were gospel beacons in their age and whose full-stretch labours have not received the attention of history that they warrant. As men of resurrection power their memory deserves to be raised from the dust so that their spiritual life will motivate us once more. These three men we shall occasionally call 'The Three'. They served their Lord as did the famous 'three mighty men' of King David as recorded in the Old Testament. By the death of John Pugh they had been joined by the 'Thirty' – the number of evangelists then serving the Forward Movement. No scripture describes more appropriately the spirit and exploits of these men than when the Spirit of God came upon one of 'The Thirty' of King David, as recorded in 1 Chronicles 12:18:

> We are yours, O David!
>   We are with you, O son of Jesse!
> Success, success to you,
>   and success to those who help you,
> For your God will help you.

The story of the Three who became also the Thirty is a romance of faith in a harsh world of social deprivation, sometimes shameful poverty. It began without a following, in a borrowed tent, on a piece of waste ground. Yet in fifteen years it built forty-eight well-equipped centres seating 43,080 people, had 6,896 born again members, 1,056 on probation, 10,763 Sunday School scholars and 22,000 hearers.

Happily, some of these statistics have names and faces. They will enter our story from the ruins of their raw backgrounds. They will remain in our hearts as joyous recruits for Jesus. But first we trace the hand of God in the young lives of 'The Three'.

CHAPTER ONE

THE CLOCK STRIKES FOR PUGH

The years of preparation

Pugh's father, also John, was a strong disciplinarian and a deeply convinced Calvinist. His mother Ann was a very loving and learned lady. They made sure their boy grew up under the sound of the gospel. When he was a teenager the family moved to Pembrokeshire where his father was a builder of bridges on the Tenby-Pembroke railway project, in charge of a raw crowd of navvies who moved with their work as the lines were laid. He left elementary school to become an assistant to his father. John was full of vigour and 'Go' – more inclined to be active than a reader. He also had a bit of an image and was regarded as quite a trendy dresser. He sported a white waistcoat and gold chain together with a white hat, which he wore at an angle. Surrounded by the rough characters of the railway building era he became sidetracked into aping their habits and began to spend a lot of his free time at the local tavern. For sheer amusement he started to give some old women money for drink and enjoyed the sight of them getting drunk.

However, an old aunt had got him to promise to read a portion of his Bible every day. He began with Genesis and kept going. One morning he got to chapter 39 which tells of the determined attempts of the wife of a high ranking Egyptian officer to get Joseph into bed with her. He was arrested by Joseph's words, 'How can I do this great wickedness and sin against God?' It helped set his moral sights for life. Forty years later a student recalls his sharing this with a team of young men in a Forward Movement campaign in Cardiff.

Some time later at the age of nineteen, on a Sunday afternoon far too stormy to make the long walk to Sunday Bible Class, his mother gave him a copy of the Welsh Calvinist Methodist magazine *Y Drysorfa*. With the wind howling outside he settled down to read. He read it from cover to cover and never forgot the sermon on Revelation 1:17: 'And when I saw him I fell at his feet....' That sermon remained a strong tower all his days and gave him a sense of the majesty of God. His Welsh-language biographer writes:

> As he began to read, the truth began to lay an increasingly stronger hold on him. He began to tremble and shake. Like the young William Williams, Pantycelyn, who became a leading hymn writer of the eighteen-century revival, he felt he was caught by a summons from above. He saw himself as a guilty creature before God and he was forced to his knees to beg for forgiveness. Here he was at last, his feet free from the fetters, a new creation in Christ.
>
> His fellow workers soon realized an important change had taken place in his life. On Monday morning, one was heard to comment about the strangely sober John who obviously had something serious on his mind. It became apparent that the greatest change possible had come over him – he had enlisted under Christ's banner.[1]

One of the first things he did was to sign the pledge to refrain from intoxicating drink. It evidently being a factor on his conscience, he quickly sought out the women whom he had got drunk for his own amusement, asked their forgiveness and prayed with them.

A background factor to his conversion had been the ministry of two gifted university students not much older than Pugh. One was the young Oxford scholar Thomas Charles Edwards[2] who, during his summer vacations, went to minister among the railway navvies at Tenby. The other was the promising David Lloyd Jones, son of John Jones, Tal-y-sarn, one of the most renowned ministers in nineteenth-century Wales.

'I well remember David's visit to take temporary charge of the navvies' mission in the absence of T C Edwards over 42 years ago,' wrote Pugh in 1905. 'Though I was not yet a professing Christian, the deep impression he left on me and others was indelible. I never missed one of his sermons and heard him preach his first sermon in English at Bethesda, Tenby.'[3] Pugh saw at first hand the nervousness this switch of language produced in the young preacher. But he was one of those determined to bridge the gap with the monoglot English-speaking navvies for the gospel's sake. His lack of freedom over his message can be judged by his comment to Pugh's father before going out to preach – 'I must act the parson tonight and read my sermon.'[4] These men of high intellectual calibre became Pugh's life long friends and stalwart supporters of the Forward Movement's drive to evangelize among the non-Welsh speaking. Pugh acknowledged the influence in his conversion of their vacational campaigns in Tenby. He was twenty when he joined Begelly Presbyterian Church.

He discovered straight away that conversion meant, not only personal awakening to God and the assurance of salvation, but also the emergence of a passion for the salvation of others. This new love was born within him on the day of his conversion – 'a love not so much for humanity in the mass, as for men, women and children'. It never left him. He lost no time in putting into practice the words of the chorus he loved to sing later:

> If Jesus has found you,
> Tell others the story.

He was a born leader and soon gathered young people and held open air meetings in the Tenby area. He had no intention then of the ministry, but open air preaching was to be the first article in the Forward Movement plan of campaign. After ten years of working as a contractor, and after long periods of prayer, he decided in 1869 that God was calling him to the ministry and entered Trevecka College under Principal Howells. Pugh was twenty-three-years old. Trevecka was the preparatory college in South Wales for those training for the Calvinistic Methodist ministry. Its origins lay in the eighteenth century when it had been the home of Howell

Harris, and the base of a Christian community centre and also a training college supported by the Countess of Huntingdon, visited often in her day by the leading figures of the eighteenth-century revival in England and Wales. John was to show a deep sense of identity with these eighteenth-century models of 'highways and hedges' evangelism.

He was no mean student, even a prizeman in some subjects. But from the start he was marked out among his fellows as a real evangelist with popular gifts. At one sermon 'crit' class, where a student is asked to preach before his peers, the principal asked Pugh to comment on his fellow student's sermon. 'Polished and elegant, but I hope our brother is not going to preach that sermon to any congregation, for it has one fatal defect – it will never save a single soul.' It highlighted what was to be his life's longing. His first test came in Tredegar where, after ordination, he went to his first pastorate in 1872.

The influences that drew Pugh and Tredegar together illustrates the shifts in population movement that was so deeply affecting religious life. Between 1869 and 1872 many young men moved from rural Pembrokeshire in search of work in the new mining town of Tredegar. Among these were four brothers named Badham, previously members of Begelly Calvinistic Methodist church near Tenby, who had known Pugh in his wilder, unregenerate days, but were thrilled to hear the soundly-converted theological student preach in the churches around Tredegar. They were among the few who established the Tin Chapel in Tredegar, a rather drab and uninviting place, and approached Pugh to pastor them. Pugh had a longing to work among his former friends. It so strongly captured his heart that he cut short his college course so that he could take up the call. As Pugh settled to the demands of his new calling his friends took care to find him relaxation. They enjoyed many a game of quoits together, which at that time was one of the favourite outdoor games of the mining areas.

'Meet you at the clock'

It was approaching 7 pm on a Tuesday evening in August 1872. Down the main street of Tredegar marched a young man of athletic build and handsome face, a swing and rhythm in his step. He had the distinguished presence of a leader of men. He cheerfully greeted passers-by and burst into a peal of laughter. He crossed the street to the Town Hall clock at the centre of Tredegar and stood alone, looking around and waiting....

It was now a month since John Pugh had come to this busy mining town at the head of one of the South Wales valleys. As he took the services in the Tin Chapel he was aware of the crowds thronging the streets outside, uncared for and without God and hope in the world. The tragedy of the masses passing by outside hurt him. As he agonised over it he seemed to hear the command, 'Obey your Master's marching orders – "Go into the highways and hedges, and compel them to come in, that my house may be full".'

A minister once expressed his chagrin at his congregation's failure to bear witness in these words – 'As one skeleton said to another in the museum, "If any of us had guts we'd get out of here".' John Pugh had the 'guts', or the 'grit' as he called it. He helped save his denomination from a museum mentality at a time when the adventurous vitality of earlier generations was settling into respectable orthodoxy. Pugh led by example. He got 'out there'.

'Go into the highways and hedges' seemed a clear call from the Lord. From that moment he was a conscript of the Lord for a new adventure. 'If the people would not come to the church to hear the gospel I must take the gospel to the people.'[5] His deacons and his young friends were timid about open-air worship. They did not encourage him. But within the first month he invited his congregation to an open-air service at the Town Hall clock at 7 pm Tuesday.... And that is where we find him.

7 o'clock came and went as he stood alone amidst the passing throng, equipped with what he called 'his double barrelled gun – his Welsh and English New Testament.' Then, across the road came six women from the church to join him: 'Never have I been disappointed by Christ-possessed women,' he later said. 'I'll sing a hymn,' he told them – 'you join in the chorus'.[6]

> I hear thy welcome voice
> That calls me, Lord, to thee

he sang, his voice filling the square in days before the petrol engine drowned out even the uplifted voice in the street. They joined in the chorus:

> I am coming, Lord,
> Coming now to thee.

This to us is an old, well-loved, invitation hymn. But that choice shows in its way the nature of his evangelism, old message – new presentation. The hymn had been composed that very year (1872) in America and had been included in Sankey's 'Sacred Songs and Solos' during his English campaigns. Pugh was open to new ideas, eager to be in touch with what was going on among Christians and non-Christians. Having sung, he then prayed. It was God's help above all he was after. 'When I opened my eyes, after being on the mount with God, a crowd of men and women stood before me gazing in amazement into my eyes.' At the sound of the hymn some of the drop outs who hung around the spot were amazed at this intrusion into their territory. His message, betraying the hard experience and realism of his earlier work among railway navvies, started like this:

'Boys, they tell me that you are an awful set here, and that you were in the habit of throwing rotten eggs and mud at a dear old minister who used to stand up here and tell you of Jesus and his love. I am not afraid of anyone in this crowd, but I am awfully afraid of myself, for if any of you should insult me and I lose my temper, I should surely mark that man.' A roughish-looking collier championed Pugh and demanded that he be given a fair hearing. 'Go on, youngster; I'll stand by you. The man who insults you will have to reckon with me.'[7]

The urge and dynamism that later became the Forward Movement, and destined to reach tens of thousands of people, was prefigured under the clock at Tredegar that evening. Pugh had begun his quest of the unreached masses for Christ.

CHAPTER TWO

THE DRINKING DENS

Tredegar 1872–81

When Pugh began to fulfil that calling and show his popular gifts of evangelism under the clock at Tredegar there was much prejudice to overcome. He was opposed by many in the churches. He was called a 'Ranter'. He was charged with lowering the prestige of the denomination (a denomination that had arisen in the field preaching of the Methodist founders!). He was quoted a misapplied scripture, that he was 'casting pearls before swine' by preaching to loafers! In every age, including our own, orthodoxy can seem sadly blind to God's own initiatives.

But scepticism was not to have the final word. This attitude ceased one memorable Sunday during a visit to the town of two men – Rev. Edward Matthews, Ewenni,[1] perhaps the most esteemed minister in Wales at the time, and Pugh's old Principal at Trevecka, William Howells. At their suggestion Pugh preached at 8 pm that Sunday from the steps of the clock. Matthews arrived with all the Welsh deacons in his train. 'As the Spirit of God moved upon the crowd I could see the principal's countenance lighting as though transfigured and tears flowing over Matthews' cheeks.'

At the close of the preaching, Matthews came up to me and, putting his two hands on my shoulder, he closed his eyes and said:

'God bless you, my boy. I am thankful that Howell Harris is not dead. I never felt myself such a sinner as I am now, for had I and others done this in our life, Glamorgan and Monmouthshire would not be in the grip of the evil one.... You are the true Methodist.... This is what made Welsh Wales what it is today and this is what must transform Glamorgan and Monmouthshire' (the main English speaking areas).[2]

Soon the Tin Chapel proved too small. Pugh turned to the temporary expedient of renting the Temperance Hall. A large percentage of the newcomers attending were previously unchurched youngsters. He got through to them. There was nothing of chapel sombreness about him. 'The negatives of the pulpit will never move the negatives in the pew,' he used to say. He was a breath of new life, and though intensely aware of the alternatives of heaven and hell, and the seriousness of the message he handled, he drew others by his good cheer. A fellow student once said of him, 'He summoned us all unto daylight and bade us fling all melancholy aside.'

Within four years Park Place, Tredegar, seating up to 700 people was built. The builder was Pugh's father. During Pugh's ministry in Tredegar hundreds professed conversion and the membership rose from 16 to 400+, with a Sunday School of 450 adults and children. There were clear signs of the power of God among the coal-mining people. Eventually calls to other churches came in thick and fast. But with a time of economic depression hitting the valleys Pugh decided to stick with his people and see it through.

Marriage

One Sunday Pugh was away preaching at Moserah Calvinistic Methodist Church near Abergavenny, when he was introduced to Mary Watkins, the daughter of a prosperous farmer of Pentre Farm, Raglan. Pugh's daughter, Ann, has left us her mother's memories of the family reactions:

> I believe that I heard my mother say that my grandparents did not look very favourably upon the attentions which the young minister payed to their daughter. They prophesied an unhappy future for her if she paid little heed to what she would bring upon herself in marrying

a Calvinistic Methodist minister. Her life would be one of hard labour and obscurity. [He was, after all, minister of a tin chapel on a cinder heap, and they might well have been showing no more than a natural, parental, protective interest!] They explained that they had no personal objections to young Mr. Pugh, but marriages were not made in heaven but rather here on the hard soil of earth where income etc. needed careful consideration. In reply he had argued the promises of the Bible that 'all these things' would be added to those who sought first the kingdom of God and cast all their care upon Him.[3]

As in most things Pugh prevailed! At twenty-nine he married her at Abergavenny. Mrs. Pugh was, in later years, to be a something of a household name among women in Cardiff and wider Wales. Her daughter pays tribute to the way God so fitted them for their later work which depended so much on the gifts of the wife.

My mother was a woman of intellectual ability and a suitable partner for a man of my father's capabilities. She was a strong character, a woman of personality and considerable bravery. She was an influential person, but her forcefulness was tempered by a great kindness and a warm heart. She loved the Master and served her husband for His sake and took pity upon the people who his ministry sought to save. They stood together, sharing each other's joy, not sparing any effort to fulfil the task which they set before themselves in life.[4]

Pontypridd (1881–1889)

But much of that story was yet to dawn. After nine years at Tredegar Pugh eventually thought the time was right for a move to Pontypridd. He bade farewell to a church that was now a living gospel light at the Heads of the Valleys. He was almost beginning again. The English cause was small, meeting in a large school room. His experience at Pontypridd was to further reinforce his awareness that the church was losing touch with the English-speaking, industrial classes, partly because of a passive lack of initiative.

The year that Pugh moved to Pontypridd, 1881, was the year of national census, the year of the Welsh Sunday Closing Act, and the first year of D. L. Moody's mission visit to England.[5] The census showed that the booming mining area of the Rhondda

Valley, which was within the Pontypridd district, had expanded dramatically in population. The main developer of the Rhondda coal field, David Davies of Llandinam, and his son Edward were, like Pugh, Methodists. Pugh's growing concern for the spiritual welfare of industrial workers and their families, many of whom were Davies' employees, was soon to bring their paths together, a partnership reinforced by their concern to see English used as a medium of evangelism.

At Pontypridd, Pugh saw at first hand the appalling social consequences of rapid, unplanned-for immigration of people from rural areas of Wales and England.[6] One of the first challenges he resolved to face head on was the drink problem. In the hard, unyielding grind of life and the overcrowded, uncomfortable and often insanitary conditions which was home for so many, the public house (and also, for different reasons, its great rival, the chapel!) could appear cheerful, warm and attractive. The counter attractions of leisure opportunities were often non-existent. 'Drowning your sorrows' seemed the lone option of escapism for many even though it took its nemesis of violence and misery. The recent passing of the Welsh Sunday Closing Act[7] in 1881 was a sign of the immense influence of the Welsh Chapel in the nation's life and showed how many wanted to preserve Sunday from the freer attitude to drink taking hold in the urban areas. But in itself, of course, it never could and was never intended to solve the growing drink problem.

Pugh soon discovered that there was a square near the Pontypridd railway station called 'The Tumble' around which clustered an array of seventeen pubs. The drinkers called themselves the Tumble Gang. It was notorious enough a spot to be called 'a little hell'. He yearned to bring Christ to people, many of whom seemed to be on the edge of ruin. Within weeks of his arrival he again informed his church leaders of his intention to go open air in that neighbourhood – not an easy prospect for conventional chapel goers. On a Saturday evening he turned up at The Tumble. This time neither man nor woman joined him. The impetuous side to his nature made him impatient of others' delay. But of his courage and his compassion for people without Christ, there is no shadow of a doubt.

As he wandered into the square alone he saw a gang of two dozen rough-looking men who were discussing a coming fight. It took some nerve to go up to them, interrupt their conversation, and tell then what he intended to do! At first he was told to withdraw, 'but he held his ground resolutely, leaning his back against the wall, and as he did so, the divine protection over him became so apparent that no one dared touch him.'[8]

'I purpose preaching on this spot this evening, but I don't see any saints to stand by me, only some poor sinners like myself – for once I belonged to your school, but I've given up knocking men about. I've taken to fighting the devil and his imps. Will you stand by me, for I'm a stranger here?'

'We don't mind, sir,' came the reply.

'Thank you. Will you please form a ring.'

He broke into song and then preached – a straight gospel message, but laced with humour and lit up with homely illustrations. He knew how to draw listeners in the open air. His direct and unconventional approach simply captivated the crowd.

'Some of you may not have Sunday clothes, for the slaves of the devil do not have such things... but if you come to Christ He will give you a new heart and then will come the new clothes and the new furniture and the new home – "old things will pass away. I will make all things new." But until these new things come men, come to the Hall and come in time and take any vacant seat that you see and like, for we do not keep seats for any favourite or any big swell and his family.'

He was set on breaking the traditional barriers of formality and never had a doubt or hesitation in his mind that he was applying the great commission of Christ, and that in so doing the world was his parish. The open-airs at the Tumble, right among the people he most longed to reach for Christ, went from strength to strength. It roused vigorous opposition. This was mainly engineered by the union of the seventeen pubs. It was a rare contest. One Sunday the publicans sent a drunken man into the circle during the service. But the contest was not without its touch of comedy. To counter Pugh's powerful lungs they hired a Town Crier to raise his voice

and ring his bell in competition. Pugh must have won for they
then hired a brass band. Pugh knew his limits. He waited. Then,
'when they got puffed I preached'. These plots backfired and
aroused public sympathy for Pugh. In 1882 a local journalist
(Awstin) described Pugh as 'a friend of the public and not of the
publican'.

Gospel Temperance

Pugh's colourful but dedicated efforts to counter an escalating cause
of violence and misery prepared the people of Pontypridd for the
Temperance Mission of January 1882. It was called the 'Blue
Ribbon' campaign because those who professed conversion to
Christ were encouraged to wear a blue ribbon on their clothing as
a sign of total abstention. John Pugh became a strong champion of
temperance because he saw too much heart-breaking evidence of
its power to ruin, not just individuals but families. It was a society
where there were no State financial safety nets for rescuing families
from poverty. Self inflicted poverty caused by excessive drinking,
where literally it could be food and furniture that was sacrificed,
impelled him to share the gospel's liberating power to save, so
that ordinary mums and dads might turn from excess and give the
family a new start. During the 1870s the temperance movement in
Britain had become more and more linked to gospel campaigns.
This had received a boost from the qualified support of the D. L.
Moody campaigns of 1873–5 and now again in his most recent
visit. C. H. Spurgeon, Dr. Barnardo, F. B. Meyer and other
evangelicals, though they too did not link temperance work directly
with evangelism, made special appeals to city missionaries to teach
temperance to those among whom they worked.

These Blue Ribbon temperance campaigns, much under the
influence of campaigners from America, for the first time closely
combined the preaching of the gospel and the advocacy of
temperance. Those who professed conversion were straightway
asked to sign the pledge and then presented with a blue ribbon
which they were expected to display at all times. Inevitably linking
temperance and evangelism was on occasion to mix objectives.
Sometimes, as we shall see, people signed the pledge first and

conversion did not come till later. But it became a serious distortion of what Christian commitment was all about when people signed the pledge and were not converted at all. It led to temperance becoming an end in itself. In a generation or two, not to drink became a ground of self righteousness in many chapel people who would advocate temperance while rejecting the gospel.

But for people like Pugh the whole point was that they saw the gospel as the only power that could really rescue. With the Victorian evangelical genius for combining gospel and social work, they saw the grace of God at work 'at the coal face' rather than just in chapel. The Pontypridd campaign of 1882 again showed how Pugh was in touch with trends among Christians outside Wales. Alongside Pugh as leader was Colonel Colwill of the United States and the evangelist Richard Booth, also from the States, who was invited over by bodies like the National Temperance League and the Good Templars (– an international temperance body – Pugh had been a pioneer of the Templars at Tredegar and had the satisfaction of seeing 1500 Templars in the town). Richard Booth's main appeal was to wealthier members of the community. He was frequently to be found at gatherings in Broadlands, Hampshire, the home of Lord Mount-Temple,[9] an evangelical aristocrat. But he was also a frequent speaker at rallies in industrial communities like Pontypridd. This rally ran for a month and more than 2,000 had signed the pledge in a fortnight. Excitement ran high and local public houses saw a massive dip in popularity. A sidelight on that was the complaint of the Llantrisant and Pen-tyrch small holders who had to return from Pontypridd market grumbling at the lack of 'soeg' for their pigs, that is, grain left over after the process of beer making.

But these times of rally evangelism in Pontypridd have an interest for us much deeper than the issue of temperance. Those meetings had a life changing impact on the two other men of our story, Frank and Seth Joshua, not Christians at that point, and Seth certainly prone to fist wielding and foul language. Unknown to Pugh they had recently moved to Pontypridd. We trace them first to their birthplace at Pontypool.

Seth and Frank Joshua – Conversion

It was a Monday morning. The young lad made sure no-one was watching. He quietly opened the vestry window of his local chapel, climbed in and made for the pulpit. Seth should have been in school. But he usually skipped and often on a Monday the memory of the preacher's message the previous day stayed with him. Despite his many boyish pranks he secretly desired to be a preacher. Before an imaginary congregation he preached a rousing sermon, imitating the 'hwyl' and the Bible thumping of his minister.

But then it was his heart that began to thump, for into the chapel came his grandmother, the church caretaker. Grandma was a terror to Seth. Catching him in the act of preaching she immediately concluded he was doing it in mockery. She made to chastize him with her broom, but Seth made good his escape and in her fury she flung it after him. 'Thank heaven that old broom missed the mark,' said Seth in later years. 'I have preached in many meetings, where if dear old granny could have been present to see the sight she would have shouted in her old Welsh way, *Gogoniant* (Glory).'[10]

The brothers Seth and Frank Joshua were born in Upper Trosnant, Pontypool, Seth in 1858, Frank in 1861. There were six children, five sons and a daughter; three of the sons later became ministers.

They were altogether different in temperament and this contributed to their attraction and effectiveness as a team in later evangelism. Seth was the more colourful and headstrong. If Seth skipped school Frank persevered hard with his lessons. His happy personality carried sunshine wherever he went and he even played the harp. He was to remain a bachelor all his days. In contrast, Seth's mischief became the despair of his grandmother who seemed to care more about his welfare than did his parents. She was a strong character, with an intelligent grasp of the Scripture, and preachers loved to discuss the faith with her. She was not averse to warning that the gallows awaited him if he did not mend his ways. The thought coloured the boy's dreams and robbed him of many a night's sleep. Seth later warned people not to frighten children in such a manner.

As often with impetuous and mischievous lads (grandma called him 'a broth of a boy'), Seth took much more secret notice of her and what he was being taught than anyone would have suspected at the time. It is still so with many a troublesome Sunday school lad. As we have seen, Seth was fascinated by his local Baptist minister, David Roberts, especially his mighty voice. Seth vowed that on a calm evening he could be heard on a hill a mile off. Seth too was endowed with a voice that was in itself a fortune. If Whitefield could sway an audience with 'Mesopotamia', the Joshuas could do the same with 'The gospel of our Lord and Saviour Jesus Christ'. To hear their reverent, throbbing, convincing, joyful rendering of that phrase was unforgettable. The secret of their great personal charm was the boundless grace of that full and free gospel. And they improved their gifts by entire consecration to the Lord.

But that was yet to come. How Seth was to rue his folly at missing school. Yet he learned from everything the school of life offered. His first job was driving a donkey. Without knowing it he took on the task of perhaps the most obscure character in scripture, Jehdeiah the Meronothite 'who was in charge of the donkeys' (1 Chron. 27:30). He stuck it for three and a half years and never regretted it. 'I had more out of that donkey than I could get out of any College in the land.... I bear many marks of his back kicks on my lower extremities. He was a great donkey to object. I maintain that if a man knows how to handle a donkey for three and a half years he is qualified to handle anything awkward.'[11]

Ambition eventually goaded him to become an engine driver on the Great Western, like his brother John. He got no further than a cleaner at the sheds. But he flung himself into sport. He was a natural sportsman. He became champion over 440 yards for Monmouthshire, played three-quarters for Pontypool for years, boxed in organized and unorganized matches, and was rapidly going downhill in the company be kept. 'Now when I look back on it, I think of the grace that stooped so low to pick me.... How glad I am that mam and dad lived long enough to see my return home.'[12]

Then the family moved from Pontypool to Treforest, Pontypridd, where Seth's father was a blast furnaceman at the iron works. Seth's splendid physique coped with carrying hundreds of tons of pug iron over the hot beds of the blast furnaces. Frank was engaged as a pupil teacher at a local school. Both joined a church choir and the solo parts were entrusted to them. Seth added to it the role of pianist and singer at the 'local' where he became a regular.

This was not long after John Pugh's arrival at nearby Pontypridd. In January 1882 Pugh combined with the Salvation Army and others in a month long gospel-temperance campaign. 'The Forward Movement,' said Pugh later, 'stands midway between the Salvation Army and the ordinary churches. We endeavour to combine the go ahead of the Army with the solidity of the older churches, avoiding the extravagance of the one and the stiffness of the other.'

The arrival of the Salvation Army in the valleys astonished religious and unreligious alike with their 'extravagance'. At Treforest they placarded the place: 'This town will be bombarded.' Such kinds of 'ads' were absolutely unheard of in connection with chapel. Seth was the chairman and the life and soul ringleader of the 'Free and Easy' at the Ricketts Arms. He anticipated a great time.

'Boys,' he said, 'we are going to have some fun. It's been pretty dead here for some time. Let's go down on Sunday to see this bombardment business.'[13] He didn't know what to make of his first sight of Salvation Army open-air meetings – girls with tambourines wearing scuttle bonnets praying for 'this wicked town'! Frank was the first to go to their meeting place, which they called 'the barracks'. The following morning at work a friend, Dai Caravan, told Seth he'd been to the barracks and seen Frank go up to the penitent form crying like a kid. 'What's he want at a penitent form? Doesn't he come from a respectable family?'[14] That evening he watched the Salvation Army procession go by in the street, surmising that if Frank had been converted he would be with it. There was Frank in the front rank, his powerful voice ringing out 'Fire away! Fire Away!' To Seth this seemed beneath the dignity of someone used to singing the Te Deum in the church choir. He felt ashamed of such conduct.

But then ... then the thought came to him, 'Frank is going up and I am going down.'[15] Determined to choke the feeling he went to the Ricketts Arms and banged the counter for a pint. But he says that the beer would not drown the thought because it kept on coming back up 'like a cork'.

A little later Seth was down at a hotel in Pontypridd where he won a billiards competition. As he came out his friend Dai Caravan invited him to a Gospel Temperance meeting in Gelligwastad Wesleyan Chapel. One of the main speakers was Colonel Colwill. Seth's favourite argument at the time was that 'drink is the good creature of God'. Colwill began by saying, 'I suppose there is someone here who says that drink is the good creature of God.'[16] His reasons for total abstinence carried conviction. Seth sat in the back and watched his brother Frank go up and sign and receive his blue ribbon. The strong competitor in him wouldn't allow him to be beaten by his brother. So he gave in and there was great applause as he went up and signed. When he went to see Mary, his girlfriend, the cook saw his blue ribbon and immediately poured out a drink for him. Mary sprang between him and the glass – 'Seth, play the man!' He called her 'Mary his good angel' and later married her.

But, he wasn't a Christian yet, and neither was his Mary. He was giving up things – drink, smoking, bad language – and his old pals started to give him up. All it did was make him miserable! Some three months later, in April he was wandering on his own one night, not knowing what to make of things, when Dai Caravan came out and said: 'Seth, your brother Frank is praying for you in there.'

'Praying for me in public? Let him pray for himself in public not me. I'm off down to the theatre.'

'Come on in here, Seth, there's a beautiful meeting on.'

'Look here, Dai, you got me to go into that place in Gelligwastad and I signed the pledge. I'll stick to it, but I'm miserable.'

'Well,' said Dai, nothing daunted, 'perhaps you will get happy in there, come on.'

Seth went in and he remembers the place all alive, some leaping, some shouting, 'Thank God I'm saved.' He knew them all, some old bruisers who he'd punched, and who'd punched him. Then he tells how a little girl got up and sang:

> I'm but a little pilgrim, my journey's just begun;
> They say I shall meet sorrow before my journey's done,
> The world is full of trouble and suffering they say,
> But I will follow Jesus all the way.

Seth dropped his head as if shot. 'I'm going to hell,' he thought.
He felt he was in it already. The Christian workers would often
ask people not saved to go to the penitent form. 'Don't you touch
me or you'll rue it,' said Seth. He was wild with temper. 'The
devil,' as he put it, 'was having his last kicks.' At length he went
of his own accord.[17]

He knelt by an old broken chair, on old broken bricks, with a
broken heart. When he rose he felt as if a great load had rolled
away. The following day felt like spring as he rejoiced in sins
forgiven. And he already felt a stir in him to tell others. He stood
outside the Ricketts Arms Hotel that night and they called him in.
'Boys, I've found another well; come and have a drink of it.' In
his own characteristic words he said, 'Thank God I took my stand
then; it was neck or nothing.'[18] He later exhorted young converts
to stand firmly where they were wont to fall, using the novel image
'although Herod might seek the young child's life they would
outlive him'. The convert to total abstinence in January became a
convert of Christ in April, surrendering himself completely to his
Saviour.

Pugh – pointer to the future

Meanwhile Pugh's labours as pastor and evangelist continued to
see much fruit under God. His ministry, as at Tredegar, gives
evidence of extraordinary divine aid. The small cause he began
met in a schoolroom but space became a problem again. Within
two years a new chapel – St. David's Presbyterian Church – was
erected. It was an impressive building and a monument to Pugh's
ministry. He continued to expand his range of contacts and the
church was full for the visit of H. M. Stanley, one of the late
Victorian folk heroes, who lectured there on 'Darkest Africa' soon
after his return from his successful search for Dr. Livingstone.[19]

Austin, the journalist, sketches his impression of Pugh's
preaching at Pontypridd. 'Though speaking English in the pulpit,
he is endowed with all the fire of his race, combined with the
polished diction imparted by careful preparation for the pulpit;
his fluency is increased by his earnestness; and his appeals cannot
help being effective, for they evidently come from a heart burning

with a desire to save souls, and a soul imbued with the faith that moves mountains.' Evangelistic Missions were frequently conducted at St. David's, some very successfully, notably those conducted by Rev. William Ross of Cowcaddens Free Church of Scotland, Glasgow. Ross too had vast experience and saw astounding gospel success amidst the poor and amidst the drinking crowds of Glasgow. What he told Pugh of his evangelistic initiatives there seeded the latter's mind with ideas that led to the Forward Movement as we shall see later.

Part of the power of the pub over people's free time was that there existed so little competition. Few amenities for cultural and leisure activities existed. Pugh's concerns to see a rise in the standards of general education came in his fight for a Free Library in the town. The licensed victuallers were opposed to the extra charge on the rates and feared the Library would prove too attractive an alternative and draw people from the public houses. A poll of the rate payers was organized on whether to establish the library. Pugh watched the polling station and as closing time approached went to the railway station – picked up eight travelling drapers off the platform – all Scots and members of St. David's Presbyterian Church, Pontypridd; the result next day saw a majority of eight for the Free Library.

By now we see Pugh to be a man who, once he set his hand to something, saw it through. His next project showed, once again, that he was more forward looking than many ministerial contemporaries and not prepared to wait when others tarried. He faced up to the urgent matter of the relevance of the church's witness in a quickly-changing age.

The English Question
'In the year 1884 two friends and neighbours, the Rev. John Pugh and another met in Mr. Pugh's parlour to talk about the welfare of the English churches. It was decided to get an English Conference of churches in South Wales.'[20] Who the 'other' was, the Calvinistic Methodist Historical Handbook 1735–1905, from which we quote, does not reveal. It gives something of a cloak and dagger atmosphere which reflects the sensitivity of the issue.

To Pugh the question of language had become a matter of life or death for the future of the gospel in South Wales. The denomination he loved and served was overwhelmingly Welsh-speaking. The church governing courts in North and South Wales were held in Welsh. That was entirely natural and appropriate in Welsh-speaking areas. But Pugh saw the pressing need of an English language dimension to its witness. Typically, and for the gospel's sake in his own land, he took the bull by the horns. After the private parley in the parlour he showed his willingness to take unofficial, innovative action if it would serve to break a mould of inertia.

At 2.30 on the 8 May, 1884 four ministers and nine laymen met at Pugh's church in Pontypridd. His motivation was exclusively that of a church reformer who is also a soul winner. Like the earlier translators of the Bible he wanted to get on line with the new vernacular. Patterns of worship also needed enlivening. He was not afraid to address 'the mode of conducting public services and how to meet the young people and win them for the Saviour'[21] – a familiar tension in times of cultural change. Finally, they needed to give publicity to the denomination in 'its *English garb*, that the English speaking world may know of its existence and feel we are a power in the land'.

As with all things that Pugh touched, matters soon got going. The First South Wales Conference met at Swansea in 1884, then at Pontypridd in 1885. The President was Edward Davies, J. P. of Llandinam and the High Sheriff of Montgomeryshire, with Pugh a speaker. The conference forged links between Pugh and Davies which proved hugely important later for the Forward Movement's evangelism of the English speaking communities. In 1889 the first national conference was chaired by T. Charles Edwards, who by then had gained wide academic respect for his magisterial English language commentary on the Greek text of 1 Corinthians. Pugh's voice was heard asserting that 'the masses were the easiest people in the world to get at if the gospel of Jesus Christ were only preached to them'. As we have seen he was backed by evidence of that in his own ministry.

This Conference proved to be a stimulating forum at which major issues of doctrine and life were debated. It showed that

Calvinistic Methodism in Wales still had some fine advocates of biblical thinking. It also had prestigious visiting speakers such as James Stalker (1893), F. B. Meyer (1895), James Denney (1897), P. T. Forsyth (1901) and Campbell Morgan (1908). It continued to meet up till the Second World War, though, by then, the theological tenor of the forum had become liberal. Its range of interests embraced worship and preaching, the doctrine of the church, evangelism and social duty, the church and politics, the church and its young people, and inter-church relations. John Pugh's drive in helping set up this conference in more orthodox days has tended to fall from view behind his Forward Movement achievements among the working classes.

Meanwhile, spontaneously, and without the aid of any church organisation, two younger men had launched into a venture of their own which was to show with a remarkable degree of apostolic assurance the truth of Pugh's confidence in the gospel. It arose simply from Frank and Seth Joshua's new-found love for Christ. Their pioneering, assertive and compassionate preaching in an English-language-dominated industrial area was a kind of pilot scheme for Pugh's emerging plan. Their credentials, renowned as these men were to become, came from no earthly authority, but direct from the God they served. There is no other explanation. It seems incredible that two brothers, without any previous academic training or experience, could have so gloriously succeeded. And succeed they did, not primarily amongst the privileged, but among the down and outs of the unemployed and the immigrant English labourers who had lost their own roots.

CHAPTER THREE

THE JOSHUAS AT NEATH

Vanity Fair

In 1882 Frank Joshua began his life's work in Neath. He was to be joined by Seth soon after. They started from scratch, aiming to win the complete outsider for Christ and thereby begin to build a church.

Frank's arrival coincided with the great annual Neath September Fair, an old institution dating back to the Middle Ages and the rendezvous of thousands of people from the surrounding districts. The fame of the evangelist who had the courage to sing and speak in the open air captivated the crowd and he became the talk of the town. Dr. Llewellyn Davies, a Neath GP who was present at the unveiling of a memorial plaque to Frank at the Gwyn Hall, Neath, in 1922, tells of his first memory of him.

I was in the surgery on a Sunday morning when I heard a lovely voice singing outside. I realized it was a hymn. I couldn't see anyone so I put on my hat and walked to the square. There on the corner where Lloyd's bank now is I saw a fine looking young man with about half a dozen others. He was playing an accordion and singing till the town rang. I watched the half dozen grow into a procession led by Frank Joshua. His faultless character and gentleness made him a mighty power for good. What wonders have been wrought since that first Sunday morning service which I had the pleasure of attending in the Square.[1]

Then Seth arrived. They had no clue how to preach, though they learned fast. 'I know now what a sermon is, but I did not know then any more than the man in the moon,'[2] said honest Seth. They applied to others the bold 'outreach', as we now call it, that had got them. They were plunged into it almost immediately without any college preparation. They began open-airs in the streets, using a table. Then local vestries were borrowed. The Quakers lent their meeting house for nightly meetings and many were the epics acted out there. Every night after the meeting the women would set to and scrub the floors clean. Then an anonymous friend gave a tent which was pitched in Alexandra Street. Even when rain percolated through the canvas the crowds remained steadfast. It was not unusual to see women with umbrellas open inside the tent. A Baptist chapel in Water Street was used, only to prove wholly inadequate for the growing crowds. T. Mardy Rees' boyhood recollections indicate that there was a touch of revival in what he calls apostolic times, with the brothers presenting as a Peter and John partnership. He was at the first meeting Seth and Frank held at Water Street. 'How well I remember that Saturday evening when I was separated from my father by the singing crowd in the street and how we found each other later in Water Street Chapel. The fervent prayers and hearty singing still resound in my ears. The bliss of that first meeting is ever an inspiration. Unfortunately neither Seth nor Frank kept records. They were too busy harvesting souls.'[3]

Fortunately *The South Wales Evening Post* in a full four column article in September 1945 gives a vivid picture of their early Fair Evangelism.

Sixty years ago [1880s], the Neath September Fair, with its romantic naphtha flairs which flickered on our fathers roundabouts and swings, was the occasion for coarse dissipation and excess. The miners of the valleys and the tinworkers of Briton Ferry came swarming into town, determined to make a night of it – such nights are never seen now [1945]. Brutalized by their work, they asked for bright lights and beer. [4]

The respectable kept out of the streets at Fair Week. It was left to two strangers, two brothers born in Pontypool, to begin the work of cleaning up the town. On Fair Day 1882, when the narrow streets were crowded with rollicking ironworkers, tinworkers and colliers, a heavily built young man with a pair of formidable moustaches placed a strong packing case on the pavement outside a public house and climbed on to it. The crowd swarmed, delighted to find free entertainment. To the left a Punch and Judy show competed for attention, to his right a drunken fiddler....

'Some listened quietly, some jeered and one, an ex-pugilist who looked as if he had taken more punishment than he had given, stepped forward, infuriated at the most forthright sermon he had ever heard and cursed the evangelist.

'The young preacher stopped, and noticed the pug nose and cauliflower ears. Slowly he took off his jacket, saying not a word. The ex-pugilist looked at his barrel chest and the knotted muscles of his arms and slunk away. He did not know that the evangelist was Seth Joshua, former tosspot, one who had been "unenlightened so recently that even now he could be tempted to use his muscles in the service of the Lord".[5]

'The ex-boxer slipped into the nearest pub to conceal his discomfiture. If he had wandered off into the crowd he would have encountered Seth's brother Frank, standing on his own soap box and fighting the same war as Seth – though in a different way.

'Frank, his lovely tenor voice exhorting the crowd to temperance and chastity was the lamb to Seth's lion, a man of peace and gentleness who was to earn the title of "The Saint Francis of Neath". Though so soft-hearted, Frank was no soft touch. The local police superintendent said Frank was better than three policemen at stopping a street brawl.'[6]

After several years selling Bibles at the Fair, the brothers were able to hold a proper service for the showmen. On the Sunday that the Fair closed down in 1888 they spoke among the shows from 3.30–5.00 pm when about 2,000 people attended.

As they continued to forge closer links with some of the edges of society they both gained uncommon respect from common folk.

For example, once, late at night, a woman came to see Frank. 'You know who I am,' she said, 'there ain't no good in me and let me tell you, Mr. Joshua, at once that I've not come to see you about my soul, but to give you a warning. Tomorrow night you will be called to a certain public house to see a sick woman. Don't go. It's only a trick to ruin you. Good night!'[7] He asked advice and when the invitation duly came he took with him three friends.

Gradually as the work went on, they built up a congregation. It grew all the time. They sang and preached, lived by faith in their early years, held open-air meetings, sold Bibles at fairgrounds, faced opposition and ridicule, and not a very helpful attitude to open-airs from some of the police. The town could not escape their impact.

The Rector of Neath

Now we come to one of the romance stories of evangelical cooperation across the Anglican-nonconformist divide in Wales. In later years Seth Joshua would sometimes be seen making his way to Llandaff Cathedral, not far from his home in Cardiff. He would go to a spot where hung a memorial tablet to the Rev John Griffiths, former rector of Neath and Archdeacon of the Cathedral.[8] There Seth would kneel down and pray. In the burdens of life he often found comfort and inspiration, seeking the Lord near that reminder of the friend of his youth. Griffiths had been a strong tower to him and Frank.

It was a sweet touch of providence that these two raw but brave recruits of Christ should have begun in a town where, most unusually for the times, the local rector was a man of such openness to evangelical nonconformity that he was hailed by the national nonconformist press as the perfect example of what a churchman should be. He maintained that position despite many strong attacks on him (including episcopal) for being too friendly to nonconformists. He soon thrilled to the good work of the Joshuas and, rather than being professionally 'embarrassed' by their earthy flamboyance, recognized that these untutored men were servants of Jesus. He invited the converts to Holy Communion at St. David's Church at 8 am on Sunday mornings, the new Christians marching in procession to the church from the tent. Who could not but rejoice in that especially in the light of the tensions between church and chapel in Wales. But some busybody, more interested in ecclesiastical niceties, wrote to the bishop stating that these people taking the sacrament were not confirmed, and the practice was discontinued. But the archdeacon's friendship was not affected and there were seasons of rich blessing in regular informal fellowship gatherings. He frequently preached in the tent. Frank commented, 'He never preached in St. David's Church like he did in the tent. In the tent he was a living force. And under his tent ministry many professed conversion.'

Griffiths' life and ministry (he died in 1897) was much wider than his work alongside the Joshuas. He was a senior figure in his church and in public life and the friend of leading national figures. But he was so close a friend, so supportive of the evangelism of tent and Mission Hall, so committed to temperance work (unusually so for an Anglican) and so much part of the public face of the Forward Movement when launched, that a brief picture of his ministry fits well into our story. His concern to see the Mission Hall prosper was an outworking of his clearly stated view about his Church: 'she must remain a Protestant Church ... a Church of deep doctrines and of wide sympathy, with a very large heart, and with very long arms to embrace not a few, but a nation.'[9]

He had been appointed to the parish of Neath in 1855 by the trustees of the late second Marquess of Bute, an evangelical. In 1891 Griffiths claimed that when he came to the parish there were only three English services each Sunday, and a congregation of about 150, but by that date he had five churches, with 1300 in his congregations, over a thousand in his Sunday Schools, of which one third were adults. He attributed a great deal of credit for this to the support of the Church Pastoral Aid Society. But the power house of growth lay in his exceptional preaching ministry in which he expounded eloquently the Reformed faith of the Anglican communion. Throughout his ministry he was an evangelical. He would have described himself as a Christian rather than a churchman. Frequently he expressed the view that too often the church of his day was elevating the altar at the expense of the

pulpit. He had an intense dislike for Anglo Catholic high ritual.
Preaching was his forte: 'The simple, warm, energetic preaching
of the pure gospel of Jesus Christ which will carry that gospel to
the homes of the people.'[10] It became sufficient to announce the
archdeacon's name to draw a large congregation from among
dissenters and churchmen. Maybe he learned something himself
from Frank and Seth! 'He felt the sympathy of a crowd and as he
warmed with his subject, his eye would kindle, his fine and
expressive face would be lighted up, and he would pour forth a
torrent of eloquence which held the listeners spell bound.'[11] His
favourite subject was justification. When acknowledging the help
of the Church Pastoral Aid society he wrote: 'The grand old
historical Church appeared to be animated with a new life. Her
voice was heard proclaiming the clear Evangelical doctrines of
her creeds and Articles. Christ dying for man's sins and rising for
man's justification was the theme of her pulpits. The supremacy
of God's word, and the testimony of Jesus, for which her martyrs
died, was her constant utterance.'

O happy Neath that heard with one voice from St. David's parish
church and independent Mission Hall such gospel power!

It can not have been lost on the quick-witted Joshuas that the
rector's reading and awareness of evangelical roots was much
deeper than their own. In the midst of all their eager outreach,
aware of their lack of training, and determined to feed the minds
of their hearers as well as their own, they found time to read more
widely. They discovered and relished the Puritans whom they
distilled to their people in appetising form. They picked them up
at second-hand bookstalls in Neath and Swansea markets. Seth's
joy was unbounded when he brought home such writers as Richard
Sibbes, Richard Baxter, (who had himself learned faith in Christ
from Sibbes' *Bruised Reed* sold to his father over the doorstep by
a pedlar), Thomas Manton, John Owen, John Howe, John Wesley,
R. W. Dale. 'Bought a history of the Puritans,' he noted. They
were not just shelf fillers either.[12] 'Rose at six this morning and
enjoyed reading Dr. Sibbes *Bruised Reed*.' 'Much blessed in
reading Owen on *Communion with Christ*.' What an example this
is from an entirely untutored man preaching generally to others

with like background. And what light it casts on his future maturity of judgement in pastoral and spiritual matters. The converts of the tent meetings had a substantial diet of theology as well as good singing!

It could be said of Seth, as has been well said of C. H. Spurgeon, that 'he related Puritan theology to his own ministry among the common people who had to work in the grind and fog of a commercial city ... distilled old thoughts into plain English ... [and] used the solid doctrines of a bygone age to evangelize in a different historical context'.[13] Consequently the Joshuas' evangelism, though wonderfully popular in appeal, was far from superficial in content or temporary in results. The reading of old divines did not take the edge off their preaching to their own world.

It is not unusual for adults, deprived of an early breadth of education, to make valiant efforts to catch up by reading, and yet still to betray their lack of early foundations. 'Though not a cultured man in the ordinary acceptance of the term, he has assimilated much solid intellectual food and knows a great deal more than some of his critics give him credit for,' a friend of Seth wrote many years later. 'It is not too much to affirm that he is one of nature's orators,' wrote another. He added, rather pompously, knowing little of Seth's background: 'though the cultivated taste may at times detect evidences of a scholastic education commenced perhaps rather late in life.'

Neath Mission Hall
Because the conversions were many and the numbers of hearers so great, temporary arrangements in different buildings were totally inadequate for the crowds. In 1884 the foundation stone of the first Mission Hall, seating 1000, was laid by Sir Hussey Vivian, M.P. for Neath. Leading local residents, including the archdeacon, who organized a bazaar to help raise funds and who was a trustee of the new building, took profound interest in the venture.

The brothers endeared themselves to a cross section of the community. They were a perfect team, 'Happy' Frank and 'Hallelujah' Seth. Frank used to say that Seth knocked sinners down and he picked them up. After the fearless fighter came the peerless comforter. Mind you, Mary his wife, who had been an Anglican, would never let it be said that Seth was ever a ruffian. They were married at Neath by Archdeacon Griffiths – though a day late. The wedding had been fixed for a Saturday but the Archdeacon returned from a pressing duty in London a day late and the ceremony had to take place on the Sunday.

Mary Joshua had known Seth well before either of them was converted. 'I heard a lot about his running, wrestling, boxing and billiards, but Seth was always a gentleman. He could not do a mean thing. However, I told him one night that I could never be his wife unless he gave up the drink. And he did.'[14] But it was Seth who led her to the Lord. She called him her spiritual father. 'One day he turned to me and asked, "Mary, are you saved?" Surprised I said, "Well, you know Seth that I have been confirmed." "Yes, my dear," he added, "and vaccinated; but are you saved?"' That was the means of her real turning to Christ.

'When I look back I am filled with wonder and praise. It was a most amazing time, living by faith and yet wanting for nothing. I never handled a salary till we went to Cardiff. Whenever I wanted anything Seth would say, "Pray first, Mary, and when you receive, never forget to say thanks." His faith was endless.'[15]

God honoured it in different ways. One morning a man in poor circumstances came to the door for assistance. 'Mary,' said Seth, 'I am giving away the last groat. The Lord will provide.' Walking down the street a little later Seth met a gentleman who shook him by the hand and left a sovereign in it. 'Here, Mary, paid sixty fold already.' When they once ran out of coal Seth said they would pray for some. During family worship they heard the tipping of coal outside the house. It had been sent by a lady who had got up out of bed to order it for them.

Seth and Mary had six children – 'six living volumes on original sin', as Seth put it.

Cutting new ground

The eventual impact of their ministry among ordinary people is incredible in today's terms. They started with no congregation and so had to go to the streets to find one. When Seth was asked to comment some months before his death on the need for practical experience for men training for the ministry he wrote: 'By all means have your Arts and Theological training.... But to take over an old established country business with old established customers is one thing. To cut new ground and get new customers in the face of strong competition is another matter.... In my judgement there is no better way than that of being a man amongst men. Move among them. Mix with them and disarm them as to their conception that you are standoffish.'

There are few more masterly examples of 'cutting new ground' than their joint ministry. The brothers laid great emphasis on engagement with people through open-air work. In the open they found scores of their most remarkable conversions.

Before each morning and evening service there was an open-air meeting. On Sundays they would often gather near one or other of the lodging houses for immigrant employees of the expanding works. Often people would follow the meeting back to the hall and attend for the first time.

In his diaries of 1887–90 there is ample evidence of their diligence and courage and the prayer that lay behind it. The brothers and their co-workers desired intensely to possess God and their desire was granted. Work of real social transformation was carried on in the face of overwhelming odds. The abundant harvest that was the Mission Hall, Neath, was the result of seed sown in tears.

'Held an open-air service near the lodging house. While singing the hymn, "Just as I am", a man came into the ring and gave himself to the Lord. He knelt down on both knees. I feel sure this was sincere.'[16]

During the week they were more likely to lift their voices near the public houses. In the early years especially this produced a fierce reaction from publicans who saw it solely as a kill-joy attempt to deprive them of cash and customers. Many changed their attitude when they realized what good work the brothers were doing for families who were wrecks of humanity – the consequence of drink problems that the Mission Hall saw a great deal of. The first Sunday after Frank died many noticed the wife of a publican laying an expensive wreath on his grave and 'shedding tears like rain'.

Nevertheless the battle waged in no uncertain terms:

Monday 3rd February, 1890: 'Visited a great number of sick ones today. Held an open-air service near the Falcon public house. When I began to speak the landlady commenced to mock and jeer. I got warm and my voice became loud like a trumpet. She raised hers. This drew a large crowd, and I had much liberty. In the Hall later two souls sought mercy – a man and a woman. The man came from the public house, so the Devil kicked, knowing what was going on.'[17]

Good Friday, 4th April, 1890: 'Was helped today to enter into the worship of my Lord. In the open air we were much opposed by a publican. While I was speaking he was very wrathful, but the truth triumphed. We afterwards had a very blessed meeting with God when *many* (my italics) spoke with power.'[18]

Monday, 7th July: 'This night we had a most fierce opposition while in the open-air. Two publicans got enraged. One danced in our ring and sang a comic song, while the other blasphemed fearfully and called us fearful names. He caught hold of me and pulled me about. The crowd, taking our part, broke in and pushed them. The meeting was broken up. We marched to the Hall and were used in bringing one soul to Christ.'[19]

But he saw tragedy too among those who mocked. One Friday evening he saw 'the young woman who jeered at us the last two Saturday evenings carried home dead. She had drowned herself in the canal. I conducted a prayer meeting.'[20]

When hostility was fiercest Seth wrote: 'We need special grace to enable us to keep pegging at it.'[21] They pegged at it till the opposition pegged out, says Mardy Rees. But not yet. 'The next time he holds a meeting outside our pub,' said the landlord of the G ... public house, 'I'll shoot him.' Frank was informed. The meeting was held as usual and there was no shooting. A short time before Frank's death a request came from the Neath workhouse to visit a dying man. 'You do not remember me, Mr. Joshua,' said the sick man. 'I am dying and I want to ask your forgiveness. I threatened to shoot you many years ago if you held another service in front of the G ...'

'The Lord forgive you, my friend. I had forgotten the incident and forgive you freely.'[22]

What disturbed the brothers most were police restrictions on their open air gatherings. As there were some 'incidents' this was partly understandable, though not all police were prepared to restrict them, as we shall see. Seth was convinced at one stage that the Mayor was responsible for police interference and was determined to stop their testimony.

One official train of events had a sensational outcome. Frank and Seth were brought before the magistrates for street obstruction and were fined. There was a great stir in the court when a woman convert cried out: 'Those men on the bench are men of sin. I know them and they know me. These men of God have saved me, and you on the bench would stop their good work. But you cannot.'[23] The brothers refused to pay the fine (could they have paid it?). The alternative was imprisonment. At the time they were living in Alfred Street, and Seth and Mary had just married.[24] 'Well, this is a good beginning,' said Seth. His wife prepared a good dinner and the irrepressible brothers talked about the service they intended holding in prison. If Paul and Silas sang praises at midnight in the Philippian gaol, Seth and Frank would follow their example (and probably with more volume!).

But the police were a long time coming. A messenger then brought the news that the police had been instructed to seize some of the furniture for the fine, but a crowd had taken the horse out of its shafts, and the matter had ended in fiasco. Then someone else came to inform them that they were not to go to prison after all because someone had paid their fine.

Some police were prepared to risk their jobs in support of the evangelists. When the Borough Police were ordered to prevent them meeting in the street a table was lent them by a County policeman, and in front of the County Police Station a huge congregation was addressed. That policeman afterwards received rapid promotion and Frank smilingly used to tell him, 'You were well paid for lending that table for the Lord.'[25]

When a constable was ordered by his Superintendent to prevent the brothers holding a street meeting and 'move them on', the constable answered, 'Sir, here's my coat, but I am not going to order those men away.'[26] Afterwards the Superintendent admitted that it would have been on his conscience if they were moved away.

They retained unfailing good humour even in tense situations. They were quick off the mark to make a point. On one occasion an educated young man took issue with Seth's theology. 'Do you really expect me to believe in original sin in the late nineteenth century, Mr. Joshua? You can't expect me to swallow that.' 'No need to swallow it, my boy,' said Seth quickly, a big finger pointing to the man's stomach – 'it's there already.' They took competition patiently. One Wednesday evening open-air service was joined alongside by a man with a performing monkey – Seth had to admit to be second attraction. Only a few stood around the open-air till the man took his monkey away. 'It reminded me of the lunatic who exchanged a sovereign for a brass button.'[27]

Their initiative in new ideas knew no bounds. One Tuesday night in 1890 they borrowed a coal wagon, loaded it with some chairs and a table and went out to neighbouring Cadoxton to preach. 'A large number of young men had agreed to oppose us, but when we commenced they lost power to act. We marched back to Neath behind the wagon.'[28]

This trip led to a crucial development. Why not buy a proper tent and set it up at Cadoxton and Skewen and other sites? They did. It cost a massive £50 but was a great acquisition to the work of the Hall. A year later found Seth on his way with it to Cardiff and the famous tent meetings at Splott where he took on Beelzebub.

The Mission Hall had a brass band for open-air services and Seth was the conductor. For some time he used a crier's bell to announce open-air meetings. The novelty of it attracted the crowds (it still attracts the curiosity of visitors to the Mission today!). Although Seth never became 'formal' even in his most mature years, even he might have looked back with some reservations on the time when he roused a whole street one Sunday morning by ringing the bell and shouting, 'Fire! Fire!' People ran out of their houses asking, 'Where, where, Mr. Joshua?' They were met head-on with the reply, 'In hell, and there you will all be if you don't attend the Sunday morning prayer meeting.'[29]

As they got more widely known the brothers made visits further afield. Four trips to Cornwall between 1888 and 1890 saw another open air initiative – though with some New Testament precedent! Frank took his harp on a boat and as it sailed up one of the rivers many people thronged the banks to hear the gospel sung and preached. Behind all this visible endeavour for the Lord lay hearts aware that without the Lord's blessing it would avail them nothing. Seth's picture of the need of prayer is memorable – 'Make the valley full of ditches. There are plenty of surface workers in the religious world; what we want are diggers, those who prepare reservoirs for the living waters.'

14th February, 1887 (Monday): 'We spent a precious time in prayer at two o'clock today. We are praying for a general revival of religion in Neath.'[30]

As believers were added to the church, so cottage prayer meetings were held to back those who took their stand in the open air.

2nd February, 1889 (Saturday): 'We all agreed to lay hold on God for blessing upon Neath. My soul is much exercised. I could not eat my dinner today on account of it.'[31]

15th February, 1889 (Friday): 'There is a growing desire to see God's work revive. I feel sure God is not going to leave us much longer without His divine blessing upon Neath.'[32]

6th August 1889: 'The deadness of things weighed me down. I was not better until I had wept away the heaviness and had much prayer.' 'My heart is heavy while I think of the money hunger shown by so many professors of Christ in the town.'[33] His self-criticism was impartial. 'Have been led into close communion today. I find I am far too leaky. I get and lose too soon.'[34]

Both brothers carefully observed their seasons of private prayer. Rees, who knew the family habits well, says that the family altar was kept in good repair and church members followed their example. In an image aptly adapted from the Old Testament he says, 'The ashes of indifference, worldliness, unbelief, tradition, were not allowed to choke the fire of this altar for they were taken outside the camp morning and night.'

But by the close of 1889, after seven years of bold preaching of the cross, there was evidence enough that God was at work with power. 'God has permitted me this year to see 455 souls seeking Christ.' The previous year the total had been 348, of whom 219 came forward at the weeknight services. People were saved at the 7.30 am Sunday morning prayer meetings. Where can one find more interesting 'human documents' than are to be found among these figures? Fortunately many of the figures have faces, faces that were often first glimpsed in previously unreached parts of the town and who by grace sooner or later became the backbone of the work.

'Their message,' says the *Swansea Evening Post*, 'like that of most *good preachers* [our italics] was not for the respectable. Their finest work was done in redeeming those wretches who would have been called scum.'[35] It's typical that whilst conducting a tent mission in Porthcawl Seth allowed a tramp to sleep in the tent – to make his home there virtually. When the gospel meetings began the tramp at first would slink away, then hang about the door and finally he stood up and confessed faith in Christ. In his new life he found employment with a Christian.

Whatever the Evening Post meant by 'wretches', the vast majority of those to whom the brothers preached were ordinary folk who certainly lived in wretched housing conditions and often crippling poverty. Their preaching was often unsparing in its indictment of rapacious landlords. An extract from a sermon of Seth preached in July 1988 shows one of the ways he approached this. As often he sets up a dramatic contrast between two differing people. His theme is 'Thanks be to God for his unspeakable gift' (2 Cor. 9:15).

'This gift is unspeakable because of its unspeakable worth. How often have you heard it said about some rich person – "He does not know what he is worth" – he could not tell you. This is the sense in which the believer can speak. He is unspeakably rich and does not know what he is worth. A man can take stock of his earthly wealth and tell you to the shilling what he is worth. But who can take stock of the unsearchable riches of Christ? And he who has Christ as God's gift has the riches of Christ also. He knows not what he is worth. Take an illustration:

There is a man who, by wading through the blood of widows and orphans, by stifling his conscience, has made a vast fortune. Count it up –

£100,000 in landed property
£50,000 in stocks and shares
£20,000 in goods and chattels
£30,000 in hard cash
Total £200,000.

There is a man who has laboured all his life. His home is a cottage for which he pays a rent to a man who says that, if he doesn't pay, he will turn him out. Reckon up his possessions –

Landed property	£ none
Stocks and shares	£ none
Goods and chattels	£10
Hard cash	£ none
Total	£10

Now count up the spiritual ledgers. Count up the rich man's first. Here it is:

A blighted character. A miserable retrospect. Bring both on to a death bed and what have you? The one has been a humble labourer serving God, the other a rich rogue serving his own lusts. On these two death beds how do they stand in the light of eternity? The one has an awful hell. The other – how much is he worth as he lies with his death sweat on his brow and a haze in his eyes – how much is he worth?

Listen. He whispers something. What is it? Did he not say "Jesus is mine?' Then write it down. Unspeakable riches. His riches can never be told ...."[36]

More Mended Crocks

Seth's lecture called 'Wonderful Conversions I have Seen' 'might have been added to the Acts of the Apostles without breaking upon the loftiness of the inspired record', said a fellow minister. They provide rich stories of brands plucked from the burning, once broken earthenware. People like Dai Rees the Beer Barrel of Marl Pit Hotel, Sergeant of the Marines, Dowling the Swearer, Gough the Coal Trimmer, Mrs. Lacey, Dipsomaniac, Tom Clomen.

Tom Thomas, locally known as Tom Pigeon (Clomen), was one of the earliest and remained a gem of grace. 'Forty years ago,' he said, interviewed by T. Mardy Rees in 1922, sitting like a gentleman in his front room parlour, 'I had no furniture but a few boxes. I was the biggest sinner in Neath. This is not bounce, but the naked truth. I had paid enough fines to cover the cost of the old Town Hall. I thank God that the Joshuas ever came to Neath. Unto God be the glory for changing me and keeping me through a thousand temptations. One Saturday night during the Fair week Frank was singing in the Square, "Where is my wandering boy tonight?" Although at the time I was under the influence of drink he got me. I had a godly father whose Welsh Bible was always on the table beside the loaf of bread. I felt guilty because I had caused the old people so much trouble, but I refused to be conquered by a hymn like that. I had more beer, then took my Sunday allowance in a jar and went home, I fell asleep on the hearth but sometime in the night heard a voice: "Tom, Tom, thou art gone far enough."

'Thinking it was the voice of my poor wife upstairs I turned on my side and went to sleep again. Then I heard the words again and it sobered me. I cried, "Lord, is it thou? Have mercy upon me I'll never touch the beer again." I got up, opened the back door and hurled the jar of Sunday's beer against the wall outside. "There Satan, take that as the first clout from me, I've received enough of them from you." Praise God I've never looked back since. The boys made fun of me and gave me a fortnight. They poured beer on my head from a window, my wife and baby in arms were drenched too. But I controlled myself and said, "Thank God, it's outside me, boys, and not inside!"'[37]

The following summer he had to go to a camp of volunteer soldiers. They gave him charge of the beer. 'I prayed earnestly for help to resist, for I would smell it every day, and thanks be to Him, He kept me.' The raw kind of life he had been saved from comes out in this reaction to a bully: 'He would have hit me had I not been cautious. "Forgive me this once, Lord," I said, and I landed him one which sent him sprawling. Then I was sorry, but he got up a better man. I knocked religion into him, for he joined the Salvation Army and became an officer.'[38]

Men who were illiterate found a quick appetite to learn to read after conversion. David Thomas, a collier, could neither read nor write when he came to Christ. His first prayer in public lives in the memory of some of his old comrades. 'Lord, thou hast a big job on hand now that Thou hast brought me to religion; I can't read or write. Thou must teach me.'[39] The prayer was answered speedily, for several members, as well as the Joshuas, taught the new recruit and in six months Dai could read very well and write a little. His continued application was impressive and he became one of the brightest spirits at the Mission. In the open air he was most effective, for he had been redeemed from the low depths of sin. He brought a fresh turn of phrase to prayer, 'Lord, make us shining Christians: we have been shining long in the service of Satan. Yes, Lord, shining like (what shall we say) ... shining like BLACKING' (used to blacken working boots).[40]

The most thrilling conversion in Frank's memory was that of a strange character, Maggie, who sold nuts and other things which she used to hawk about in a basket. She was, of course, called Maggie the Nuts. Frank tells the story: 'She lived in a lodging house and was addicted to drink. Late one night she returned in a drunken stupor and found the lodging house door locked. Knowing of an old outhouse in the back yard she crept into it through the window. As soon as she reached the floor she felt herself instinctively in the presence of a strange animal. Poor Maggie felt the nose of the beast and its warm breath. In terror she dropped on her knees and prayed, "O Lord, save me and I'll never touch the drink again."

'The animal withdrew from her and Maggie huddled up in the corner and began to sing one of our Mission hymns. The singing woke the owner of the animal. He got out of bed and listened. To his horror the hymn came from the outhouse where he had placed his performing bear. Alarmed, he opened his window and spoke soothing words to Bruin. He then rushed to unlock the door of the outhouse. To his utter amazement he found in the far corner the hapless singer and the bear lying down quietly. "You can thank God, my woman, that you are alive," said the man. "I have," answered Maggie, "I know he has saved me from the bear and he has saved my soul at the same time."'

'Maggie kept her vow except once,' said Frank. She slipped on one occasion through strong drink, but afterward was a beautiful

Christian. Her fall was atoned for, and her restoration was complete and touching. She had great faith and in her way rendered remarkable witness.'[41] Frank preached a funeral sermon in memory of Maggie, and another well-known character Caroline Lloyd, who passed away at the same time.

The story of Mrs. Lacey comes from a mission in Hoylake which Seth led. She entered the service with a blackened face and arms and her sleeves tucked up. She sat in the back but he noticed her and said, 'Jesus Christ can wash you clean.' He felt as if the devil looked back at him.... He asked a lady worker to take the strange visitor, help her wash and give her food and then bring her back. As they talked she despaired of her own salvation, being addicted to strong drink. But he succeeded in leading her to salvation. She became a missioner among women, especially prostitutes. She showed a strong compassion for unfortunates. She led a mission for Seth at the Central Hall Forward Movement in Swansea. After her funeral her husband and son thanked him for restoring her to them.[42]

Evan Rees, who had known the brothers in their unconverted days at Treforest, became a Christian at the beginning of the tent meetings in Alexander Street, Neath. He was one of the first few to get the Sunday School going and his own class of girls was gathered from the poorest streets in the town. Evan became a highly respected leader at the Mission and could hardly mention Seth and Frank without tears coming to his eyes.

It is hardly surprising that Seth's evidence to the Commission on Sunday Closing in Wales, June 14th, 1889, was based upon his experience of the drink problem at Neath. The brothers witnessed distressing disasters. One especially grieved Seth. 'Dr. ----- visited. Gifted man. Lost sight of Christ by reading philosophical works. Drinks heavily. Fell downstairs. Once a preacher of the gospel in Scotland. 'I hope,' he said to me, 'that God has not given me up.'[43] From early days total abstainers alone could be members at the mission.

The Mission Hall, of course, would have shared its strong temperance stand with other nonconformist churches in the neighbourhood. What about the archdeacon's attitude to the drink problem? One would assume there would have been 'cultural' differences and he would have had a much more liberal stance. But no! As he began his ministry at Neath he began to realize the need for temperance work. The results of heavy drinking were all too obvious. At first he endeavoured to counteract Saturday night drinking by holding popular entertainments in the town, but when he complained to an old Quaker that he was not making as many temperance converts as he wished, he was told, 'Thou hast tried what speaking will do; try now what thy example will do.'[44] As a result he became a total abstainer and toured up and down Wales advocating this cause with all the energy he possessed. He found it a hard battle to hold his position for many whom he respected were opposed to the principles of total abstinence. And he felt his stand would be misunderstood within the parish. But for Griffiths it was not simply a social campaign, although he recognized and made clear its domestic and national implications. Rather it was a spiritual campaign, for alcohol abuse 'hindered ... the progress of all good, tied the wheels of the gospel chariot ... and produced in fact a physical incapacity for the reception of religious truth...'[45] It was all part of that 'most important work under heaven' in which he was engaged, of 'winning souls to Christ and to prepare them for another world'.[46] The temperance cause was also for Griffiths another way in which the various Christians traditions could cooperate together.

Seth identified. But he did become unhappy with a growing tendency in temperance rallies he attended in different parts of the country. Having heard a London orator on temperance 'who spoke much but said little', he wrote in March 1889: 'I lean more and more to the solid and the serious side of the temperance question. I rather think we defeat our ends when we make a meeting the occasion for jokes and mimicry. The subject for me is too solemn. However, it takes. This is an age of froth.'(!) Was this a sign that the movement was beginning to take leave of serious gospel concerns?

Some of the early converts at the Mission were men of high intelligence. Two – H. G. Howell and C. L. Perry – became evangelists of outstanding calibre. Perry was a native of Cornwall whose family moved to Neath for work. He dated his new birth to February 18, 1887, under Seth's ministry at the Mission. He first joined the Church Army as an evangelist and then the Forward Movement in 1896. He preached widely, including New Zealand and Australia, and was considered the most eloquent of the early evangelists. Another among the first batch of converts who were from a more middle class background, was Grice Lloyd, a leading colliery official, who initially went to hear the Joshuas out of curiosity. His extensive commercial and church commitments put him under strain, such was his eagerness to support the church. Being chief official of the Main Colliery Company, he would spend the week in Ireland or France or London, but was invariably back at his post on a Sunday. He was secretary of the church for twenty-five years and Superintendent of the Sunday School. He was much beloved for his Christ-like life and character.

The work went from strength to strength as God increased the numbers through conversions. But money was scarce for most of the people among whom the Joshuas chose to work. The collections were taken away on Sunday night and not counted till Monday, when the bills for the week were paid. When all the obligations were discharged there were often only a few coppers left. One week the surplus was four pence and one half penny. 'Frank, you take two and a half pence this week and perhaps it will be the other way round next week.'[47] Thus they toiled for God without a salary, but he provided their needs. Seth said to the congregation after Frank's death: 'I will say this to his memory, I never heard a word of complaint from him all my life.' Seth described their home in Alfred Street as 'not a very flash place. There was no swank at all. All that I could do at that time was to rig up a room for Frank, and then another bedroom and the kitchen – which was more like a scullery. The front room had the blinds down. We started our marriage like that.'

For the first five years the brothers struggled to run the finances of the church themselves. But then a secretary and treasurer were appointed and this relieved them of what had become by then a burden. The financial report was presented on 10th October, 1889 and showed that the expenditure for the previous fifteen months had been £379 3s. 10p. and the income £379 3s 11p. 'May my faith in days to come look back on this and be encouraged,' wrote Seth.[48] Direct answers to prayer were numerous every year. On one occasion ten painters came and decorated the Hall for nothing.

If there was lack of money there was no lack of musical talent among the people. Frank's marvellous gifts brought the Mission Choir together. This refined the musical taste of many and became a formidable factor in the life of the church. God trained them to perform sacred cantatas which were heard in the Mission and surrounding districts. These midweek events added welcome colour, uplift and a sense of communal achievement to many who before their conversion had found little else to do but hang about the streets and pubs. The church was constantly equipped with gifted people from among its own converts. Bob Jones followed Frank as choir leader. At the age of fifteen Bob and seven other young men had gone into the inquiry room in response to the call to turn to Christ. 'God wants you, Bob,' said Frank. 'Will you do what he wants?' 'Yes,' was the answer.[49] Frank took great pains with him, recognizing that he had been given conspicuous musical gifts and had a calling to use them for the Lord. At the age of eighteen he was asked to sing his first solo in the open air. He broke down attempting it. But Frank persevered with him. When, years later, Frank declined in health he took up the baton in his place.

Seth and Singing
There was a lot of music in the brothers. 'Seth can sing well and play the cornet and the piano to distraction' was the comment of one grudging soul. He also had a high view of congregational singing as worship and derived a lot of inspiration from it as a preacher. He strove to find a balance between choirs and congregation. He wrote an article 'On Our Congregational Singing' and based it on the text 'And they ministered ... with singing' (1 Chron. 6:32). 'Thus the families of the Levites served. They ministered with singing. We must needs go back to Old Testament times to find a true conception of congregational singing. The preacher ministers to the congregation in his preaching, and is often

dismissed for careless preparation, but the congregation ministers in singing to the Lord and often deserves dismissal for the same reason. Here is the root weakness of much of our congregational singing. It is so thin and heartless just in proportion as it lacks the Old Testament conception. Let this truth grip the people and then the best will be placed upon the altar. Singing will be transformed from a mere item in the programme of a service into a sacrifice of praise and into ministry to the Lord and to each other.'

This did not happen if a choir took precedence. Choirs and their conductor could rule the roost then as music groups and their worship leaders can do today. 'There is a possibility of a trained choir being more of a curse than a blessing. Preparation, choice, selection is made out of a regard to the capabilities and tastes of the choir, rather than the ability of the congregation. There may be wretched singing by the congregation when there is good choral singing, and the abler the choir may be the greater is its curse. This is a great danger in a working class population. The singing may be done professionally for the upper classes, but the Protestant working class must sing. It is to them an escape valve and it is a sin for any choir to shut it down. The penalty comes sooner or later in one of two ways. Either the congregation thins off, or the choir becomes too conceited to live with. Where congregational singing is attended to, the choir is taught to regard itself as a mere help. The whole church is a royal priesthood and every priest may minister with singing.' So he argued for wise choice of tunes, appropriate to the size of congregation. 'It is perfect cruelty to ask a small congregation to sing some tunes. They are written for the crowd and the author would have done well if he said, "This tune must not be sung unless there is a congregation of 500 or a 1000 present." When there is no wind to fill the sails do not blame the ship for not making headway. Good congregational singing is the great antidote, or safeguard against sacerdotalism. As a rule there is a better theology in the hymn than in the sermon. At any rate our Welsh hymnology is the theological backbone of the nation. It is to the church what colour is to the cheek. It indicates health or weakness. Our Lord is worthy of the best. Let us all minister to the Lord in singing.'[50]

CHAPTER FOUR

GLASGOW, CARDIFF AND THE FORWARD MOVEMENT

Clifton Street, Cardiff 1889

At the age of forty-three Pugh received two calls – one to a church in Glasgow, the other to Clifton St. Presbyterian Church, Newport Road, Cardiff, (now the Inkspot Arts Centre). He was drawn by the Scots call to be near his great friend, William Ross, for whom he had preached as early as 1877. But Cardiff it was to be and he joined Clifton Street a few years after its launch as an English branch of Bethania Welsh church, the Docks. His major life's work now lay ahead of him and the Word of God was soon to encourage him to proceed.

At the time of his call to Clifton Street the pulpit there was filled on one Sunday of each month by no less than Dr. Cynddylan Jones,[1] who was accustomed to preaching to many hundreds in both Welsh and English speaking chapels. But only a small congregation turned out to hear him at this new English church which had cushioned pews and many of whose members turned up in hansom cabs. Pugh took in the situation quickly. As usual his gaze looked beyond his own walls. He saw the immediate neighbourhood Splott, and its teeming population with scarcely any spiritual provision. When the ability to reach the lost declined in the church, it ceased to be a church. According to his daughter Pugh suggested to Cynddylan that he should continue to build up the saints, 'I will go after the sinners.'[2] An elder shared his sadness that they lacked signs of God's power in the services.

On Pugh's first Sunday a new breeze blew among the church members themselves. 'When those who had been present that night spoke of it, they lowered their voices. God had spoken to them. My father had not expected to see what happened. The words flowed, they were his words yet not his words. At the end he asked the congregation to follow him to the school room below to hold a short prayer meeting. That unforgettable prayer meeting! The thing was so new, so striking, so strange! It all comes back so vividly – the old fashioned school room beneath the chapel, the solemn minister; no noisy excitement, only a quiet gravity which couldn't be described coming over the people. Then, as the meeting went on, first one and then another going forward until twenty two souls knelt in repentance before God.' A quiet revolution had begun within the church and it was to tip over into the community. Calvinistic Methodism in Cardiff was being true to its birthright and was seeing the power of the gospel to save.

Cardiff Prison

Passing the gate of Cardiff prison one morning in June 1890, Pugh's observant eye noticed a crowd of suspicious looking characters waiting outside for the release of some of the prisoners. He watched their movements carefully, his curiosity aroused. He saw what was happening. They were waiting to recruit the ex-prisoners back among them to aid their own criminal designs. It shocked Pugh to realize that there was no Christian there with a view to showing care and concern for their spiritual welfare, their future and families. He got no peace until he had written to the press inviting friends to undertake a ministry for ex-prisoners. Within a day or so he managed to arrange a meeting with John and Richard Cory. They undertook to be president and treasurer. Together they visited Major Howard, the overseer of the prison to discuss their plans. From then on, at 8.00 am each morning, volunteers would be outside the prison with an invitation card for each released prisoner, both men and women. A free breakfast was provided then and there at the Heathfield Coffee Tavern in South Luton Place. After breakfast, hymns were sung and a Bible message shared. It was usually a call to Christ, an invitation to the gift of new life in Him, based on the confidence that that was the surest foundation for a new start. By mid-1891 over 2000 had breakfasted and some instances of marvellous conversions had occurred. The 'Society for the Aid of Released Prisoners' had got under way.[3]

Moody and Sankey in Cardiff

Pugh's yearnings to reach out to people were fired again in 1891 when Moody and Sankey visited Cardiff for a mission. Wood Street Congregational Church, the largest building in Cardiff, had a 2000 capacity. Long before 7.00 in the morning queues formed, including many non-churchgoers and the church filled up for a time of singing the spirited tunes of Sankey hymns. It is interesting that Pugh, who had used Sankey hymns since his Tredegar days, saw in the criticism of many to the Sankey kind of hymn, less a sign of theological perspective than one of conceit in the church – by which she was destroying herself by showing a superior attitude and making a barrier to ordinary people.[4]

Pugh was keen that his daughter hear and remember Moody. He took her to hear him preach several times. Excited and a trifle awed the young girl went with him to Richard Cory's home, where Moody was staying. 'Before leaving,' she wrote, 'my father asked Moody to pray. He later said to me – "this is a good man and one day you'll be glad to know that you've met him. I didn't want him to leave Cardiff without you two knowing each other." Mr. Moody invited my father to join them in their work in Chicago. His answer was "Cardiff is Wales' Chicago, and just like Chicago, the sudden increase in our populations and trade becomes insignificant in comparison with the increase in immorality and godlessness."'[5]

A Vision Fulfilled

By now Pugh had seen where his great work lay and there was no way he could be diverted from it. Ever since coming to Cardiff there had dawned upon him a vision of much larger scope than his own flock in Clifton St. – the whole city of Cardiff. The passage of Scripture that riveted him was Revelation 21:2, 'And I saw the holy city, new Jerusalem, coming down from God out of heaven', wrote John the Divine. This John looked for a new Cardiff. He proceeded prudently, having learned something about reining in his personal drives to go ahead regardless and involving the support of others. For two years he had been giving himself to a close study of the local situation, determined to know Cardiff from end to end. It had 128,000 inhabitants and was a seething melting pot into which ever more people were pouring. After careful research he found it had seating for 49,178 churchgoers. If every church was full to the doors, they could not hold nearly half the inhabitants. This discovery was to galvanize Pugh into the Forward Movement church building programme which became almost obsessive and remained throughout his life.

He began to show gifts of organisation unsurpassed in the history of the Welsh Presbyterian churches. He asked local authorities about their building developments. He visited new sites, marking suitable spots for churches, secured them and met the ground rents by getting bill posters to erect hoardings and pay him rent. He got prominent situations. He consulted Christian employers like the Cory brothers and church leaders like T. C. Edwards. He also made contact with the Davies of Llandinam family, the coal and dock owners, many of whose employees Pugh had pastored in Pontypridd. They were Welsh Calvinist Methodists. But he specially sought the help of the son Edward Davies.

'When the deplorable spiritual conditions of tens of thousands in Cardiff were almost crushing me ... I poured out my soul in a letter to Mr. Edward Davies of Llandinam in 1891, asking him to be treasurer to the enterprize before there was a church or a committee at my back.'[6] To his delight Davies agreed. He had won a powerful and godly advocate who stood by him through thick and thin. Though the denomination was now seriously examining the English language needs on committee Pugh feared that resolutions would only end in a talking shop and not transfer to action. Getting Davies on board meant more to him than anything.

The start of the campaign – Splott

So, after a great deal of planning and prayer, casting himself and his family on God and His promises he had his third 'big pew' conference this time at Clifton Street. Again for a while there was inertia – neither encouragement or opposition! He tried to convey the needs of the nearby area of Splott and went ahead to procure a plot of land near the centre of the area on which he hoped to erect a tent. 'You might as well try to demolish the Fort of Gibraltar with boiled peas as to convert the people of Splott in a tent' was one helpful comment. But 'Pugh believed that the gospel, as the dynamite of God, was capable of blowing up the firmest of Satan's strongholds.'

The Scottish Connection – The Influence of William Ross

There was one man whose powerful influence on Pugh outweighed all detractors and strengthened his hand in God. Encouragement came from his acquaintance with the way the work of his friend William Ross in Scotland had been transformed by bold planning and trust in God. If the Joshua brothers had John Griffiths, Pugh had William Ross, a Free Church of Scotland minister. They had known each other since 1877 when Ross was minister at Rothesay, Isle of Bute, and Pugh had cooperated in a mission there. In October, 1883, Ross had moved to a church of 100 in Cowcaddens, Glasgow with £5,000 debt. He instituted a mobilization of every church member, a training scheme for Christian workers, had the church open every night, organised open airs on a large scale. In five years the membership was 1,249, the Sunday School 1,192, the men's Bible class 470. There were two assistant ministers, two male missionaries, four women missionaries and all this was to develop even further. The women's work grew into a Pioneer Mission which consisted of teams of two young women each, living right in the heart of the slums. 'They visit, teach, nurse, counsel and encourage as opportunity offers and have won the hearts of the most diverse kinds of people, Catholic and Protestant, thieves, prostitutes and drunkards as well as the honest poor. No one now molests these missionaries. No one dare,' reported the Forward Movement *Herald* (later *Torch*). In one of the toughest arenas for the church in the United Kingdom Ross saw the love of Christ prevail and that in abundance. 'There are churches with larger membership in this country, but few which vindicate their existence so emphatically.'[7]

It was later said by Principal Prys: 'If John Pugh was the father of the Forward Movement, Ross was its grandfather.'[8] This Celtic cooperation spanned many hundreds of miles and many journeys in each direction. A brief introduction to Ross will show us something of the mutual stimulus each man gave the other.

In Ross's biography, written by his son in 1905, the keynote of his ministry is captured by this quotation from George Whitefield. It could be said too, of The Three. 'Everything I meet with seems to carry this voice with it: "Go thou and preach the gospel; be a pilgrim on earth; have no certain dwelling place." My heart echoes back: "Lord Jesus, help me to do or suffer Thy will. When Thou seest me in danger of nestling, – in pity, tender pity, put a thorn in my nest to prevent me from it."' Ross gave his life in ministry to the unevangelised. His work in Cowcaddens is a striking example of how the church can have effective outreach to the socially deprived and religiously antagonistic.

Out and out though he was, his temperament, like that of Pugh and of the Joshua brothers, was engaging and outgoing. He had an enormous capacity for friendship. 'He lived in the perpetual atmosphere of thankfulness and he was constantly trying to create in others the same hopeful spirit as he manifested in himself,' wrote his son. When he was asked once for his favourite heroine in fiction he replied 'Christiana' (from Bunyan's *Pilgrim's Progress*). Why? 'Because she did not get into the Slough of Despond like poor Christian.' 'Keep your face to the sun, he said to a group of friends on saying farewell, 'and you will see no shadow.'[9] However Pugh and he came into contact, they obviously hit it off immediately.

However, a man is not built in a day, as his son commented, and Ross went through a change, for example, in his view of music and worship. As a young man he had been an opponent of the use of hymns in public worship. As a student he had been delighted at the passing of an anti-hymns motion and as minister in Rothesay, his first parish, had moved for a delay in their introduction. Yet when plunged among the unchurched masses in Glasgow he became an enthusiastic and practising advocate, so supportive of their use that at times he had four or five different hymn books in use by his congregation at the same time. He was, says the *Dictionary of Scottish Church History*, conservative in doctrine and progressive in worship. He had met Moody in 1874 and the 'Sankeys' were to become his constant companion in his regular seasons of evangelism at Cowcaddens.

One of the most regular preachers at those events was Pugh as his biographer records: 'Two Welshmen came almost annually. They were among Ross' most intimate friends and the people welcomed them both for his sake and for their own. One was Thomas Evans of Victoria Park Congregational in London and the other John Pugh, still alive, [written in 1905], and at the head of the great Forward Movement of the Calvinistic Methodist Church of Wales.'[10] This was one of the 'other fires ... kindled at the Cowcaddens work. Dr. Pugh has often told how the first suggestion of the Welsh Forward Movement which has now attained such great proportions, came to him from what he saw on some of his repeated visits to Cowcaddens.' Ross was almost as frequently in Wales, 'seeing his loved Welsh friends and helping them in their work.'[11] In 1899, he addressed several sessions of the General Assembly of the Welsh Church. The striking photograph of Ross in his biography was taken in the Cardiff studios of E. G. Sadler.

Pugh certainly learned from him. But he was not a mere imitator. It is instructive to compare their strategies. Ross had four central principles.

1. The church must aim at the spiritual, not the temporal well-being of the unevangelized.

2. The local congregation must be the agent of evangelism, not a para-church body.

3. The congregation must have a clearly defined target area for its activities. 'It's better to plough a small field than scratch a whole acre,' he would say.

4. The church building must be in constant use as a centre of outreach with daily evangelistic meetings.

Pugh's Plan of campaign

It is evident that Ross' plan was intensive and Pugh agreed with the local church principles. But what if the buildings did not exist? Pugh was beginning to think more boldly. The plan clarifying in Pugh's mind was extensive. His plan read like this:

1. To 'open fire' by preaching in open air and Mission tents all the year round, for the enemy has his temples open every day.

2. If successful a wooden structure to go up next.

3. In due course bright large halls with wide doors and no steps so that invalid chairs may be wheeled in easily.

4. To secure men with GRACE, GRIT AND GUMPTION for methods without men would be worse than useless.

Here was a clarion call. Where were such men to be found and available?

Seth Joshua

It was during 1891 that he thought of Seth Joshua. After Seth and his brother had been converted ten years previously at Pontypridd we have seen how they had taken the town of Neath by storm – a storm of love and labour for Christ. If ever God had granted grace, grit and gumption to men, these were they. Pugh arranged to meet Joshua when down at Aberavon. It was a meeting pregnant with spiritual life for the Principality.

For years Frank and Seth Joshua had toiled as a team. They had ploughed and sowed and reaped in happy and hectic harmony and God gave the increase. Then in 1891 this fruitful partnership changed, but only to be replaced by a partnership that had much wider consequences for the work of God in Wales.

In the spring of that year John Pugh and Seth Joshua walked across the mountain behind Port Talbot. They had just had tea together in the home of the Rev. Moses Williams which had allowed them to get to know each other better. Now they were deep in conversation. Pugh had had a great idea. He was sure it was God-given. He was also sure it was the right moment to share it with Seth, who he had heard was intending to launch out into another work.

'Are you going with that tent away from Neath?'

'Yes, Mr. Pugh,' said the younger man, 'I am going to Rhondda.'

Pugh pressed his invitation: 'Do come to Cardiff. It is an awful place. Come and join me there.'

Seth met the request straight on. 'Well, give me a week to pray about it, and then perhaps I will come.'

A week later Seth sent word that he was coming.

But why leave Neath when he was so successful and happy? Why break up such a good team when the work was bigger than either could really cope with? He tells us:

'One day I said to Frank: dear old mam and dad are old. The church is going strong here now, so you get mam and dad to Neath and make a home for them and I will go away and take the tent up to the Rhondda Valley. I did it for mam and dad. I don't want any praise. I simply cleared off.'

Frank stayed to minister to an ever-growing church, and as for Seth, John Pugh arrived at just the right moment.

Seth's Move with the Big Top

So Seth moved to Cardiff with tent, Mary and six children, with no salary ensured. It was a venture. Seth was a crusader and he and Mary entered upon the task with abandon, zeal, faith and the assurance that God would provide. 'If we had waited for a big fund to be collected,' said Pugh, 'we would never have started.' But start they did.

The tent was put up in East Moors, Splott, and, as we have seen at the start of the book, with Pugh and Joshua in shirt sleeves and swinging a sledgehammer, the battle with Beelzebub began. During the week before the tent was erected the young people of Clifton Street visited the houses of the area handing out invitations. When Pugh's young daughter gave a card to a young woman 'whose appearance had been made ugly by sin' she just spat in her face. 'But on the Sunday evening she was seen in the tent and she became the first in the history of the Forward Movement to be converted. Not only so, she became a great supporter and for twenty years served her Lord in the first headquarters of the movement till He called her home.'

So the Forward Movement was born on a piece of waste ground on 5 May, 1891. Seth preached am and pm; Pugh, who had to occupy his own pulpit at Clifton Street, preached in the afternoon. The tent was 120 ft. long and 33 ft. wide, with sawdust floor, and un-planed benches. It drew so many, and so silenced the critics that within a month another costing £50 was put up in Canton, a nearby district of Cardiff. Seth, ever the pioneer, and not one to build on another's foundations, moved there in June.

Who was to succeed him? Ultimately a weakness of the Forward Movement that never went away, and was one reason for its later decline, was the lack of enough men gifted at getting close to and through to the uneducated poor. It was now that Pugh's doubts about the suitability for this pioneering evangelism of men trained for the ministry of the Presbyterian church led him again outside the denomination. A man lay to hand who had not only intellectual equipment, but also ready experience of the peculiar demands of tent and outdoor evangelism. H. G. Howell, well educated and a former engineer, had come to know Christ in Neath and had become immersed in evangelism along with the Joshuas'. He then gave himself to full time mission work in London and later in North Wales. His labours were so blessed of God that Pugh invited him to take sole charge of East Moors in July 1891. Under his ministries there, and at Monthemer Road Hall, Cardiff and elsewhere, many hundreds were brought to the Saviour. 'Mr. Howell,' wrote Pugh, 'began his glorious ministry in July 1891. I found in him a veritable "Stonewall Jackson" (a famed southern general in the American Civil war) who stuck to his post day and night and who never gave up a position once he had his foot down.'

The East Moors tent remained open till October 13 when a great gale, which caused havoc on land and sea, destroyed it. But by November a large temporary wooden building seating 500 people, humorously called 'Noah's Ark' replaced it. 'It was an excellent name,' says Ann Pugh, 'and many were saved in it from the flood of sin.'[12] On Sunday July 17, 1892 the First Hall erected by the Movement was opened in East Moors – seating 1000 and costing £2000.[13] The regulars had mixed feelings, as captured in the delightful prayer of an elderly woman on opening day, echoing the joy of the angels in Luke 15. 'Lord, thank you for this fine building, but we have a "hiraeth" for Noah's Ark. That's where we saw your glory and where we first proved the joy of your salvation. The angels were flying every night around Noah's Ark and every night their wings took them to the land of glory with news that souls were coming into the kingdom.'[14]

The new hall was designed by Fawckner of Habershon and Fawckner, Architects, Cardiff. Pugh paid tribute to Fawckner's vision and sacrifice. 'When I first suggested to him the idea of cheap and bright Halls instead of costly and heavy chapels as best suited for the work we had in mind he jumped for joy. "Thank God for putting that thought into your mind, it has been in mine for thirty years and I am sure it is of the Lord.'[15] At the completion of East Moors – the Alpha of the Movement – Fawckner said with deep emotion from the platform, 'I believe I have been as much inspired by God to design this hall as John Pugh has been to start the Movement.' He became the Forward Movement's architect and Pugh reminds us that in carrying out these plans he was going against his own profession and his own pocket, 'but he counted nothing a sacrifice that would bring Christ glory in the salvation of others.'

Meanwhile Seth's great personality was working wonders in Canton. But the tent at Canton also proved too frail to stand winter storms and the worshippers moved into the loft of a workshop owned by an undertaker called Marsh. 'Mr. Marsh', Seth was wont to say, 'is in one room making coffins for the dead, and I'm in the another trying to raise men from the dead.' The loft was affectionately called the 'Upper Room'.

The Rays in Canton
The social conditions in the Canton area were appalling. A few months after Seth began to work there, Pugh took over a building in Clive Road, about a mile to the west of Canton centre. 'There

were two notorious streets on both sides of the mission hall, and the whole vicinity seemed left without let or hindrance as the happy hunting ground of the Enemy,' wrote Pugh.[16] In September, 1892, he secured the help of full time evangelist Mr. J. E. Ray who had been instrumental in Seth Joshua's conversion at Treforest.

J. E. Ray became a leading force among the Thirty. We are familiar with stories of the sacrifice of many middle and upper class young people in Victorian Britain to serve Christ in fever ridden foreign mission fields. Ray and others like him in the Forward Movement remind us also of the total commitment of young men, some little more than lads, who, when converted, became totally committed to evangelize among their rough local industrial communities. There were many untutored men of this generation who said, 'Lord, here am I. Send me', to the Lord of the harvest and he sent them to be a light to their immediate neighbours. Ray was born in Merthyr Tydfil and moved to the Rhondda for work where he was converted at sixteen. It was not long before he began to give himself to preaching from the old Company shop in his Treforest works in 1882. He was no stranger to threats and unpleasant reactions on account of his message. His ministry was noteworthy for the number saved who themselves became evangelists. When Pugh secured him for the Forward Movement he wrote: 'The Joshua brothers (Frank and Seth) were brought to decide for Christ through the instrumentality of this humble lad from the Rhondda Valley. If they were the only fruit of his earnest effort it would have been well worth living for; but Johnny Ray, as he is familiarly called by his friends, has been blessed to hundreds all over the land and we are glad to have him join heart and hand with our efforts to win Cardiff.'[17] One of those converted through his ministry was a Miss Jones, who soon gave herself to work among women. They later married. Johnny used to claim her as his wife, sister and daughter. They worked hand in glove for the Forward Movement in Cardiff.

It was immediately obvious that any evangelistic work in Canton had to be done alongside basic social care. So within months of the Forward Movement being launched it saw the beginning of extensive social help rendered to the area without having or expecting any sort of monetary recompense. Harrowing poverty prevailed in the Clive Road district, and under the supervision of Mr. and Mrs. Ray, strenuous efforts, generously supported by some friends in the city, were made to feed and clothe children at risk. Between two and three hundred were fed daily in the Hall.

Feeding the Mind

Pugh also saw the priority of feeding the minds and getting people to read. In July 1891, within two months of the start of the movement, a monthly magazine appeared, initially called The Christian Standard, which later settled on the name *The Torch*. Pugh did not believe in hiding either himself or his crusade under a bushel. He would have no hole in a corner campaign. He believed in aggressive Christianity not only by word of mouth but also by the pen.

The magazine had four aims:

1. To advocate initiatives in evangelistic methods among mass population centres which ordinary methods barely touch. One of the early articles was by William Ross. It was entitled 'On the Night Shift these Nine Years' and was a stirring account of the way Ross had seen his dream of 'round the clock' availability of their church premises fulfilled. For the past nine years the Cowcaddens church had been open for 3,200 nightly meetings 'with the purpose of evangelizing the district'. Over that time 2,160 new communicants had been added to the fellowship of the one congregation.

2. To teach converts the great truths of the gospel.

3. To warn of the dangers of advancing ritualism and romanism.

4. To make the people conscious of the thrilling heritage of its Calvinistic Methodist background. To this end Pugh included biographies of great Welsh preachers of the past and present. The most popular monthly feature of the magazine became Seth Joshua's racy account of his missions.

So, there had been a whirlwind start. Within a year the new movement had become a 'fait accompli' even before the denomination it served had given its official backing. The first years balance sheet was, however, examined by official auditors. It was a going concern. There were now six Mission centres, 2,680 hearers, 433 believers in membership and a Sunday school of 1,161.

Through the daring of one minister, who was overwhelmed by a deep sense of the spiritual destitution of large areas of Cardiff and who felt that something out of the ordinary was needed to reach them, the church sat up and took notice of what had been launched. Suddenly things began to move. Under the spell of Pugh's appeal to the General Assembly a special committee was set up under Principal T. Charles Edwards, one of the young students who had helped Pugh turn to Christ all those years ago. It reported 'we greatly rejoice at the success of the new and strange enterprize commenced in Cardiff by the Rev. John Pugh and his helpers Rev. John Griffiths (Archdeacon of Llandaff) and Mr. Seth Joshua' .[18] In 1892, the Forward Movement was formally taken over by the church and Pugh recognized as a 'special missioner to give his whole time to the work of the society'.

It was not what Pugh had expected for his 'new and strange enterprize'! The chemist in whose home he had stayed for the Assembly had noticed how surprizingly taciturn he had been and it was easy to see how troubled he was as to the outcome. But after such a response 'a change came over him and he was as cheerful as a bird on top of a tree'. He now had a committee of godly and forward looking men to back him. News of the launch was read from every pulpit of the denomination on the first Sunday of 1893 – and the first collection to support the Forward Movement amounted to £1,078 8s. 10d. Pugh had great hopes for this as a source for future expenditure. Sadly, the church at large, partly because of limited resources anyway, but also from a lack of any urgent and sacrificial motivation, was never to be a provider of adequate support.

But at least Pugh himself was now provided for and free of pastoral charge.

His vision widened.

Soon 'Cardiff for Christ' was to become 'Wales for Christ'. A hymn from those years burns with the flame of the small band of evangelists:

> Sound the wondrous proclamation
>   Wales for Christ
> Spread the news of free salvation
>   Wales for Christ
> For a work of grace we pray
> For the Spirit's power each day
> Turning souls from sin's dark way
>   Wales for Christ.

The need for 'the Spirit's power each day' for their ministry and for financial backing to keep body and soul together from the better off churches will strike us again as we return now to the painfully deprived and sometimes dissolute areas in which these men were expanding the work.

The Canton district exhibited life in the raw. There the new open air drinking clubs called 'shebeens' flourished. (They were a wily way of bypassing the Sunday Closing Act by meeting in the open air!). They spawned some violent and tragic events.

'When I was in Canton there were clustering shebeens all over Cardiff,' Seth records. 'A woman was kicked to death in childbirth not fifty yards from our tent. (The only person sober enough to describe what happened, says Pugh's daughter, was a seven year old child.) Cardiff was an awful place in those days. I went down one Sunday to the biggest Club of the lot, nicknamed The Hotel de Marl. Just as I got there a fellow sitting on a barrel shouted: 'Look at that chap from Memorial Hall; there he is, he wants to talk to us.' I shouted back: 'Let me come and have a go.' I had been praying for an opening. My blood was up. The Irish section, bruisers and gaol birds, were there, sent by the brewers and the 'pubs' with money supplied, to smash the Sunday Closing. So I started. When they saw what I was doing one of them shouted: 'Begorra, he is preaching. Chuck him out. Let's get on with the blooming booze.'

'They had me out; I can see myself going. They would have

had you out too. But they did not get me far. Up went the old hymn again, "All hail the power of Jesus' name." '[19]

Seth's solo excursion into such territory was followed by something more concerted. The *Grangetown News* reported in the summer of 1893 that a group of six men, including Pugh, Joshua and H. G. Howell returned to the Hotel de Marl on a Sunday. Extracts from the article fill in Seth's story:

'The marl pit is a depression in an extensive tipping of red marl (clay). Men from the Docks met there Sunday after Sunday to carouse. The police were powerless to act and the public were incited by curiosity and visited the place in hundreds. Workmen could be seen sitting in bands from a dozen to forty in number, often those of a similar trade gathering in each group. There was the "Hotel de Boilermaker" in one place, the "Hotel de Labourer" in another and so on.

'In the centre of each group, generally on a heap of bricks or loose stones, stood a cask. One man was continually kept busy filling the mugs, cups and tins with beer, while others saw to the circulation of these among the noisy crowd. There was a small, hollow for the money in the middle.

'When the six Forward Movement men arrived that Sunday they saw hundreds drinking – each group having a cask to itself. The little band closed in, about a dozen paces from the largest group.

'"We don't want any preaching here."

'"Let me play you a few tunes on my cornet," replied Seth Joshua.

'Then H. G. Howell stepped forward and said he would sing a solo, asking them to join in the chorus. Some of them did. This was followed by a few earnest words by Seth and more hymns. By this time the crowd became larger, many other groups dropping their glasses and gathering round. How these evangelists valued and strengthened each other: "Seth," said Pugh, "was most tender in dealing out the truth as it is in Jesus to those so deeply steeped in sin. The preaching of Christ crucified from a heart of love and by a tongue of fire seemed to melt all." Pugh himself delivered a stirring soul-disturbing address, saying they would be there the following Sunday. But before that the owner of the land put a stop to it and sent a letter of thanks to Pugh.'

The purpose of the preaching, of course, was not 'kill joy' but to turn people to Christ as the source of true joy. We have an example of that change in one of the marl pit drinkers. After that first foray by Seth, one of the men, a Welsh speaker, was so greatly challenged by the gospel that he had no rest until he surrendered himself to Christ. The way the conversion came to light was yet another encouragement to Seth to further courageous initiatives.

It surfaced two years later. Seth was preaching from the YMCA lorry at the Hayes, Cardiff. The Hayes was then an open triangular space in the heart of the city, where the Forward Movement held weekly Saturday night open airs alongside the flourishing open markets. Seth was the star amidst the roll of the traffic, the squeaking barrel organ and the shouts of the tradesmen. His straight from the shoulder preaching, his musical voice, his wit and ready retort to the interrupters would win the attention of the multitudes which sometimes packed out the space available. Seth recalled a Saturday night when a man came up to the platform.

'I shall be glad if you will let me have a word, sir.'

'Well, I don't know. Are you a Christian?'

'Well, thank God, I'm a bit of a one.'

'All right then.'

I turned to the crowd and said: 'Here is a working man who wants to have a word.'

He got up to the platform and said: 'Mates, I'm no public speaker, a working man I am like yourselves, but I want to say something. Sometime ago this man here came down to the Hotel de Marl on a Sunday, and I was the chairman that day, sitting on a beer barrel I was. I knew him 'cause I lived in Canton, and he was the minister of a Canton church. The Irish section chucked him out, but he was not long out before he chucked something out of me. Now I am on the Lord's side. I was brought to him at Cilfynydd chapel, Pontypridd. That's all I have to say.' Seth used to call this convert 'Old Dan Rees the beer cask.'[20]

Those open airs at the Hayes, in the hub of the city, went on for two and a half years until the spot was closed in 1893 to provide for the enlargement of the Town Library. Meanwhile Dan the 'beer cask' became an elder in Cilfynydd and a mighty influence for good until his death at the age of 80. In a publication to mark the fortieth Anniversary of the Forward Movement in 1931 there are two photographs of the 'Hotel de Marl' site under the title 'A Miracle of grace'. One shows a Sunday gathering of over seventy men around their beer casks before the evangelists went to them. In the other, taken forty years after, Dan Rees stands on the waste ground with the Rev. John Thomas, the general secretary of the movement.

By 1894, such was the blessing of God upon the work in the difficult Canton area, one of the most famous Forward Movement Halls, the Davies Memorial Hall, seating 1,250 people, and with shops adjoining was opened at a cost of £4,900. Seth, well accustomed to preaching under open skies and in adapted premises, now had a magnificent auditorium and a packed congregation.

Fears and Fanfares

Like most pioneers, Pugh had to overcome obstacles. Vested interests like the drink trade and owners of slum property he expected to have to fight. But a negative attitude against the English language from ministerial colleagues hurt his sensitive spirit. He was himself a Welsh speaker and was in no way resisting its primacy where it was part of historic Welsh culture and church life. But he yearned to get the gospel to people in the language they understood – and that was now English to hordes in the industrial towns. There were, of course, very legitimate grounds for alarm for those who feared for the future of the language. There was also a depth of psychological struggle in people which only the most acute observers appreciated. We owe much to Archdeacon Griffiths for illuminating the issue. He comes at the problem from a different angle. Speaking on the subject of the linguistic condition of Wales at the Cardiff Church Conference in 1889, he revealed that he was all too aware of the tensions in his own position (he had faithfully continued to preach in Welsh as well as English at Neath) and in that of society. 'He saw two languages struggling for mastery, each claiming for itself superior dignity and usefulness.

The new language brings with it influence and power as well as prestige, and bids the old depart. This it refused to do, asserting its superiority, not in ordinary matters of every day life, but in matters relating to a cultural and spiritual appreciation of life. The language of one people can never be effectively adopted by that of another until they can assimilate its inner life, and this would take generations to complete. The grand mission of the gospel is to reach the heart, but "the heart has its language as well as its lips" and so the language of the heart must be used.' Griffiths was, of course, expressing his sympathy with the Welsh worshippers needs.

For Pugh, the fact that the lip and heart language of so many was now English meant they needed to hear the gospel in English.

Many in the denomination also opposed him on grounds of financial extravagance. 'Was he not travelling too fast? – engaging evangelists and opening so many new centres, overlooking the limited resources of the denomination.' Time would tell how limited these resources were and to that extent the objectors were right. Pugh was certainly mortgaging the future. With massive financial implications inherent in his drive to provide large halls and no clear financial policy of support from the denomination, it is understandable that some accused him of recklessness.

But most of his battles he won – many by his tears. To see him standing in front of church bodies with his broken voice pleading as if his heart would break often turned the tide. If men did not share his burden they were won round to recognize his. Many a battle he won by firmly marshalling his arguments – that exceptional work demands exceptional methods and that time must be taken by the forelock and opportunities must be taken up or lost for ever. He had done his homework on the spiritual needs of Cardiff and beyond and the possible means of meeting them. As he had pulled his own church elders after him in earlier years so now he did with the denomination, though the undercurrent of opposition surfaced as soon as he died.

Monied Men
One of the strong factors that goaded him on was his success in gaining the wholehearted support of two or three of the captains of industry in South Wales.

John Cory of Duffryn House and his brother Richard became friends and supporters of Pugh in 1891. Cory was a name to conjure with. The central siting of his statue in Cardiff reflects the national and international respect he gained. Pugh recalled their first meeting:

> 'John Cory invited us to spend the last evening of 1891 in his beautiful home. He invited us to place our scheme to evangelize the masses before him. Our simple but practical scheme so commended itself to his clear head and warm heart, that he there and then promised us his generous support.'[21]

At the opening of a new Forward Movement hall in 1898 his words must have stirred Pugh. 'I would remind you, my fellow believers, that the church of God exists not only for your own spiritual benefit, but also for the salvation of souls. It is the purpose of the Head of the church that you men and women, even the very humblest believer worshipping here, should have a hand, a share in the blessed work of the salvation of others. It is God's divine purpose that in saving you, you should become the saviour of others... I want to impress upon you that, next to the joy of realizing one's own salvation is that of being the instrument in God's hands of leading others to the knowledge of the Saviour. There is no worldly happiness that a man has ever experienced that is equal to this.'

With modern government now having to look once more to 'the private sector' for funding of many amenities, it is salutary to recall the personal integrity, evangelical faith and vast generosity of some of these Victorian masters of industry. The sleaze-free factor is notable. An anonymous tribute to John Cory, written in the autumn of his life, explained the motive behind his giving as well as highlighting some examples. 'He is saturated with the Spirit of Christ, who went about doing good ... he is thoroughly evangelical, and holds fast the truth as it is in Jesus, and holds forth the Word of life by aiding mission work in his own parish and in the uttermost parts of the earth. When he hears of good being done in connection with temperance, when he learns of the success of the Lord's work on local church lines, or in outburst by means of missions, or by workers among the rising generations, especially the YMCA and YWCA, or by the bold enterprise of General Booth, or by the Rev. Hugh Price Hughes or the Rev. John Pugh, or by anyone of pure character that upholds the Protestant faith, an open Bible and the One all sufficient Mediator between God and man, or by those who labour among the Jews or among the lost in Africa – the gladness of Mr. Cory's soul beams in his face; nothing rejoices his heart more than to hear of the extension of the kingdom which is righteousness, peace and joy in the Holy Ghost.'

He was the first president of the Free Church Council in Cardiff and a leader in local education. He donated the police with an Institute in Westgate Street where they could go to read and have recreation facilities. He presented the YWCA with a fully furnished block of buildings. He contributed substantially towards the new hospital for sailors in Cardiff. To aid the temperance cause he erected the Cory Memorial Hall, which was, for two generations, one of the main centres for cultural and Christian events in South Wales. In much of this his brother, Alderman Richard Cory, joined him. Thousands of pounds were given to the Salvation Army. They encouraged the London West End Mission. Similarly they cheered the heart of John Pugh when perplexed with difficulties in finding finance for providing Halls. 'The Cory brothers are not sectarians – they hold to New Testament principles and are ready to extend the kingdom of Christ.' John Cory persistently turned down requests to stand for parliament, preferring his close links with the locality through the District council.

At the close of 1899 D L Moody died. In July 1900 Seth received a parcel through the post.

Duffryn House
St Nicholas

My dear Sir

Feeling anxious to bring before the ministers of Cardiff a copy of the official authorized life of the late D. L. Moody, believing that it is calculated to promote the revival of spiritual life and of gospel endeavours which we all feel to be so essential, I send for your acceptance a copy of this work, trusting the perusal of same will be very much blest. With every good wish.

John Cory.

Edward Davies, Llandinam

Edward Davies of Llandinam was undoubtedly the Forward Movement's greatest supporter. He studied at Holt Grammar School and University College, London. He married in 1876 and had one son, David, and two daughters, Gwendoline and Daisy, who were to take on their father's mantle as supporters of the Forward Movement. Though he was a complete master of the Welsh language and worshipped in a Welsh chapel, he faced up to the 'English question' very quickly.[22] His was an active, missionary spirit. His unambiguous backing of Pugh's assertive evangelism meant that he received shoals of letters asking him to sever his connection with the Forward Movement. In 1892 he told some of his critics who he well knew had no acquaintance with mission work among the masses: 'You need not be severe upon the Movement, for you need not have anything to do with it. I know that Mr. Pugh is pressed by generous men to run it. But whatever you may do, I shall stick to it.' In 1895 he referred to a recent Home Office report which showed the heavy incidence of drunkenness, violence and sexual crime in Glamorgan. He regarded the Forward Movement's seventeen centres, 1,200 members and 6,000 adult adherents as 'a star of hope.' His heart beat along with Pugh's and no news stirred him more profoundly as that of men and women whose lives were reclaimed for the Saviour and from the power of sin. Though a munificent supporter of philanthropic institutions of every kind, he always acted on the conviction that the great regenerating power was the gospel of Jesus Christ and other agencies were regarded as subsidiary. Hence his great abiding interest in the Forward Movement. 'Mr. Pugh might be a fanatic – he would not be a Forward Movement leader if he were not' wrote a contemporary, '– but Mr. Davies was known to be a cool, calculating man of affairs, the controlling head of the largest and most successful business enterprize in the land, a man who could always be relied on never to identify himself with rash proposals

... it was thus largely due to this gentleman that the Forward Movement, when launched, received so considerable a measure of public support.' Pugh and the work missed him sorely after his early death at the age of 45 in 1898. (See Appendix 1 for Pugh's tribute)

The Three Principals

Most interesting of all was the backing Pugh received from church academics like the three college Principals – D. Charles Davies, T. Charles Edwards and Owen Prys.[23] Edwards was by far the most able of the three but died in 1900 at the age of 53. Prys however remained president of the Forward Movement for forty years. Their support of Pugh's methods and men shows a certain realism among the learned that the college courses they ran were not producing men prepared to take on the edges of society.

'We are surrounded,' said Prys, 'by a mass of dying humanity and to a large extent we are responsible for their well being.' He lamented, as early as 1897 that 'churches had become so abominably respectable that ministers had almost got to believe that anything but the Gospel of Christ was what was required.' The church seemed to be fated to become fossilized as a middle class institution. That would mean 'much preaching without the atoning blood of the Lamb, the cross itself would be hidden, and the churches, despite their respectability, would die in their sins. The Forward Movement had taught them, to some extent at any rate, that only by preaching the great fundamental truths of Christianity could they ever hope to save men to eternal life.' He saw the Forward Movement evangelists well placed to see the great work which had to be accomplished amid scenes of squalor. When complaints arose that Pugh went outside the denomination for evangelists Prys replied: 'That was at first unavoidable because the students were afraid that they would be expected to adapt themselves to some strange kind of work. But had they suffered from these evangelists? He was prepared to think they added to the Connexion.'[24] Prys' support went beyond the verbal. After a mission where he had been helped by three Trevecka students on vacation Pugh was asked to send a statement of the cost of their lodgings and board to Principal Prys, Trevecka College. He was surprized to receive a personal cheque from the Principal covering the costs.

The news spreads

Other religious bodies outside Wales sat up and took notice. The work was girded with praise. The Presbyterian Church of England, never strong and slowly declining, contributed £160 per annum from 1893–1900 to help support two Forward Movement evangelists in Glamorgan and Monmouthshire – a recognition that these were seen to be English speaking areas. Dr. Monro Gibson, an influential evangelical leader of the Presbyterian Church of England, called attention to the Forward Movement at Newcastle in 1895. 'The Welsh church caught fire in 1891, and the Forward Movement commenced. They did more in Cardiff alone in providing new buildings than we did as a connexion in the same time throughout the whole of England from Berwick to Torquay.'

The 'Christian' of November 1898 wrote, 'The history of the Forward Movement from its inception reads more like a romance than reality, in the remarkable cases of conversion it has recorded and in its general success.'

Across the Atlantic came similar words of wonder from the Principal of Central College (later University) of Kentucky. 'The account of the Forward Movement reads almost like a fairy tale. The reality surpasses any religious fiction.'[25] By the close of the century the success of the work was evident. The Halls were crowded out in areas where church life had been non-existent a decade before. Hundreds professed conversion, many of whom were drawn from the neediest ranks of life.

Whatever men's applause, and Pugh had shown he was not driven by that, his marching orders were his unshakeable conviction that he was called of God for this work. Necessity was laid upon him. This conviction upheld him even in days of conscious blunder and mistakes. 'Go your way and tell John how the blind see, the deaf hear, the dead are raised and to the poor the gospel is preached.'

CHAPTER FIVE

GRACE, GRIT AND GUMPTION

Pugh's plan was to awaken all the churches to their duties to evangelize their own areas. He never intended to found and perpetuate a separate organization within the church, but to infuse a spirit of life into the churches and rekindle evangelizing passion for the salvation of those outside. To do this he saw straight away that he must enlist the interest of ministerial students at Trevecka and Bala Colleges. In 1892 he lectured to both on Grace, Grit and Gumption.

'The men who would be leaders in this holy war must have these three things; first grit or moral stamina. A soft, flabby, goody-goody baby of a fellow in a man's clothes will never do much good for God, nor harm to the devil. Second, you must have a great grace: you must abound in the grace of faith and in mighty hope and love. Third, you must have gumption.' [1] He feared some were short on common sense and not street wise.

'There is a special wisdom needed for winning souls – "the wise winneth souls". This wisdom may be had through prayer, pondering and practice. Study the forms of dealing with anxious souls and careless sinners and the methods of soul winners of this generation such as Spurgeon and Moody. But you can never excel

85

in this glorious work by studying other people. You must come and practise in the work itself. We invite you to join us during the summer vacation.'[2]

To this end he urged the denomination to set up a training Mission Home for university students, similar to the Cambridge Settlement in South London, to supply the deficiency in the training of ministerial students for the actual work of evangelism. He proposed vacation initiatives where they would meet every morning for prayer, to hear a message from him or another evangelist, visit neglected families in the afternoon and preach in the streets at six and hold mission meetings in the halls in the evenings. He wanted men 'to drink of the spirit of mission'. Principal Charles Davies was so enamoured of the plan that he offered to give £30 a year towards the training, 'for I believe it will supply the missing link between the churches and the colleges, just as the hospital does between the medical student and his life work.'[3] This plan was active in his mind to the end of his life. The Mission Training centre was never realized though students did annually respond to vacation missions held in Forward Movement Halls.[4]

Seth Joshua looked with increasing unease at the failure to see such grass roots projects through, while two other developments in the ministry seemed to him to be removing them from vital touch with the man in the street. He was not enamoured with liturgical developments. In his eyes the wearing of gowns in pulpits was a strutting forth in petticoats. Neither was he much cheered by the growing number of graduates in the ministry. In his charmingly provocative way he said that they would soon be 'as plentiful as potatoes in Ireland – I beg their pardon – as numerous as stars in the firmament'. Though untrained Seth was not anti-intellectual. 'By all means have your Arts and Theological Training.' He put his high intelligence to the task of mastering theological niceties as well as centralities. But he went through a phase of heart searching over his own theological training. When he entered pastoral charge at Memorial Hall it was expected that he study for the denominational ordination exams. For years he had shown, both in Neath and in evangelistic work in Cardiff, that he had a wonderful command of the English language in its simplest terms. He was a master of basic English and there was something of a Spurgeon in his lucid, lively, and humorous style. This, of course, was a gift of the Creator. How much was it necessary to gild the rose with theological precision? He assiduously kept up with his reading of Puritan and other authors in the midst of his evangelism. But when it came for him to be ordained a problem arose. The incessant call on his time both in the Cardiff centres and much wider afield did not allow him to get his mind around the more subtle points of doctrine. At the 1893 examinations the Arian controversy of the early church regarding the divinity and humanity of Christ was one of the subjects set. He soon got into perplexity over the Greek terms 'homousios and 'homoiousios' which lay at the heart of the controversy over the person of Christ in the Godhead. He fretted over how necessary it was in equipping him for his present task. His own words sum up the dilemma for the man with the golden gift of the popular touch who was also expected to add more technical qualifications – 'those dry subjects were taking the sap out of him'. Never a man to avoid a challenge, he nevertheless decided to drop out of the exam. It was to the eternal credit of the denomination, where some were frankly unhappy with his evangelistic methods, that they saw Seth to be the man of God he was and he was ordained anyway. It would have been a cruel irony if the noblest example of the grace, grit and gumption which was so lacking in many of the more formally trained ministers had been disqualified by an examination detail. 'Seth Joshua is not rightly to be considered antipathetic to education,' says David Jenkins in his outstanding study *The Agricultural Community in South-West Wales*, 'but he was certainly convinced that it was inspiration and not education that fitted a man for the ministry and in this he was in accord with the Welsh Methodist revival leaders from the eighteenth century onwards.'

Initiatives in Scotland
Concern about the effectiveness of preaching was also exercising William Ross' denomination. It was especially a concern that it was failing to do its saving work. Having been such an outstanding

exemplar of the evangelistic gift Ross was, in 1901, invited to a special position, both to evangelise among the Highlands (he lectured in Gaelic in his church's Theological College) and as a counsellor on effectual preaching. The proposal appealed most powerfully to Ross and as he considered what to do he received this letter from a Welsh friend.

'Your short visits to Wales have done more to awaken our congregations and to inspire our ministers to aggressive work than that of any man I know. If that be the case in Wales, and from your short visits, what would be the effect if you were to devote your whole life to your beloved Scotland? I am sure this is the will of God concerning you. If you inspire Scots as you have inspired Welshmen, and especially my poor self, it will not be one Cowcaddens, but a thousand of them before your life is ended.'[5]

Ross accepted his new commission. 'The labourers are few. I do not mean that there is not earnest, evangelical gospel preaching, but there is too frequently a lack of personal application and a lack of the high responsibility of personal dealing and the direction of souls into the liberty of the gospel.' He laid stress on pointedness in preaching and the need to 'find out what is keeping the soul from Christ'.[6]

That seemed to expose what the need was in Wales too. Thirty years or so after the 1859 revival much orthodox preaching had appeared to become 'sleepy' and the fervent call to turn to God often muted or omitted. In a similar, though not so perceptive and theological a way as Ross, it was noted by Pugh's Welsh language biographer (not writing till the 1930s) that his evangelistic success at Tredegar had launched his career 'as an Evangelical preacher, because that is the title given to men who preach to the heart of the people and who are not satisfied until their preaching bears fruit in changing the nature of their hearers.... Calvinistic Methodists spoke much of "sowing time" and of how slowly God works, but it seems that they had forgotten that a period of sunshine was necessary for the grain to ripen. John Pugh possessed this gift of ripening. It was as if he forced the tender young growth into life and energy.'[7] This reinforces the impression that the warm, vigorous evangelism evidenced in earlier Calvinistic Methodist preaching was being lost and preaching was becoming too much of a display of the preacher's talent. 'The Welsh pulpit is in danger of being drowned in a sea of bombast' had been a warning of Dr. Lewis Edwards, father of Thomas Charles Edwards. When F. B. Meyer spoke at the Welsh Free Church Council meetings in Aberystwyth he said that 'he thought the Welsh were not so fond of exposition as the Scots were, for he judged Welsh preaching from what he heard at Bedford Chapel when Thomas Jones selected a verse and his discourse upon it developed into an exquisite poem, more or less related to the text, often less.' It was not fair to judge the many by the one, but that such a blight was on many a bud cannot be doubted.

Advance in the Seaport Towns
Where such preaching prevailed it could not hope to touch the new urban worker. Yet, thankfully, many of the Forward Movement evangelists shared what was said of Ross – 'the aim that filled his heart was one Lord, one faith, one baptism, and that baptism the baptism of fire.' We shall watch them in their task of founding new enterprises and cutting new ground. Those churches we shall trace are mostly those that still, a century later, retain their evangelical heritage.

We shall return to them in the closing chapter.

Pugh among the people
But first, let us follow Pugh as he got alongside the ordinary folk of these seaport and valley congregations. Nothing is clearer than that he won their love and allegiance. His daughter has given us a sample picture of him getting close to his people. It shows how he shared and applied Ross' principle of attempting to 'find out what is keeping a soul from Christ' and directing 'souls into the liberty of the gospel'. He saw the need of avoiding pulpit remoteness and some of his workers anticipated Evan Robert's later practice of moving among the congregation.

'It was my father's custom to preach in one of the mission halls every Sunday evening.... He would sit quietly in their midst and take note of those around him, watching them with friendly eyes as they sat listening to the orchestra or organ.'[8] He began a service therefore where they were, as part of the body. This would have been extremely unusual in late Victorian churches and chapels. It was an attempt, whether symbolic or not, to 'sit where they sat'. He would then take the platform with the Missioner in charge of the Hall and the Sister of the people. (See next chapter.) After the message there would be an after meeting. Then Pugh would invite people to stand who required further help in the counselling room. Without this opportunity to deal in specific ways with need, he felt the message was 'a writing on water'. The point of his message would centre around people's day to day problems, of which he was acutely aware, and their need of salvation for which he passionately longed. His messages were gripping. People listened 'with bated breath – and those words are not an exaggeration' says his daughter. There was a tone of command and a direct personal appeal which seemed to make personal response unavoidable. He was always preaching for a verdict. His overall stress of 'Submit to God's providence and offer yourselves to God in Christ'[9] was a call to obedience which he expected would help people further in how to respond. If the missioner and sister were so gifted, sometimes they would walk among those who had stood in the after meeting, courteously speaking with those who wished to share further. The Sister spoke to the women and the Missioner to the men. This rule was kept strictly when they then went into the counselling room along with Pugh. What happened there was Pugh's fulfilment of the 'high responsibility of personal dealing' arising from applied preaching. Counselling was an essential adjunct of preaching so that people could be personally built up and admonished. He therefore came face to face with so many of the Halls' people.

If the people loved him, his colleagues loved to work for him. 'The secret of success in work,' Pugh often said, 'is that you can place some of it on the shoulders of others.'[10] His complete trust in those who worked with him, especially his ministerial co-workers, encouraged them to give of their best. One missioner said, 'there was nothing so wonderful as the trust he had in us.' When someone showed a willingness to undertake some task, Pugh always took it for granted that it would be done and he no longer worried about it. This ability to delegate the work gave his colleagues space to develop their own gifts. In the atmosphere of equality and trust which emanated from him, each brought his own special gift for the good of everyone in general. It grieved him to see others unable to do the same thing. (The downside of this was that his generous spirit tended to go with a tendency to give the benefit of the doubt which sometimes meant he misjudged people and tended to think better of people than what they actually were. His daughter makes a pained reference to the consequences of this. 'He often suffered personally because he was too endearingly honest to find in other people the mixed motives that had no place at all in his own make-up – and oh! people didn't believe that!') The Movement had a man of undoubted authority as its Superindenent. He was not called 'The General' for nothing! But he was a Shepherd too, who kept close to his growing flock and knew their time of need.

Where it all happened

The Movement saw more long-term success in the seaport towns of South Wales than in the industrial hinterland of the valleys. The seaport towns were high on Pugh's agenda. They were a stiff proposition. Their population was more racially mixed and their pattern of sin and crime rare in the valleys. It was estimated that over 2000 seamen were found in Cardiff alone every day, 'and many foreign and British seamen have met with salvation in our halls and tents,' Pugh was able to write. At the turn of the century he quoted a *Daily Mail* report which said that Glamorgan was the black spot of the British empire for crime and this was due to the arrival of 'wild spirits' from all over the world.

Newport

Parts of Monmouthshire were not far behind – Newport for instance. To meet it Pugh turned to the tried team of Seth and Frank. Even Seth knew when things were daunting. 'He went there weak in faith with no members or listeners in sight, starting from the barebones.'[11] But in August 1895, accompanied by his brother who was on holiday (!) from his own church at Neath, they placarded the town with posters – 'The brothers Joshua are coming.' Their advent was not agreeable to certain respectable professors of religion, but Seth was proof against cold receptions when on the king's business. He tells of the early moves to make contacts.

'We secured the temperance hall for the next twelve months which possessed a very fine three manual organ. On Sunday August 4th, like my namesake of old, I determined to walk around Jericho. Worshipped at Havelock Street (Presbyterian Church) and in the afternoon I walked around the park, distributing tracts to young men, but an official soon told me it was contrary to the rules, so I gave one to him which he threw away. I came to a lodging house where scores of men were seated in a large room. I gave them a couple of songs and a short address.

'In the evening I attended the YMCA and gave a gospel address and two solos to about 400 young people. On the Saturday morning Frank and I took the temperance meeting and on the Sunday morning I went to the temperance hall, not knowing a single person who would stand by me. There was a congregation of three hundred; in the afternoon five hundred, at night the hall was packed. The collection amounted to £5. 6s. 0d.'[12]

Overflow meetings were held in the corn exchange for an hour and again, when those congregations were dismissed, fresh congregations composed of street loungers were admitted for another service. Ebenezer Welsh church gladly lent its premises for week night meetings for a month and every evening the old chapel overflowed. This proved a great blessing to the Welsh church bringing it into close contact with the Forward Movement and communicating to it a revived evangelistic spirit. 'It was just what Pugh had longed to see.' During those twelve months of sustained evangelism Seth estimated that about one hundred became Christians and were constituted into a church. When the colossal Central Hall was built in 1895 Seth took charge for some years. Among the crowds one night was found a local reporter who gives us a view of Seth and his ministry that has the spice of someone known to be critical. *The Torch* published it in full as 'An Opponent's Opinion':

'Mr. Joshua's personality is somewhat peculiar ... if he were walking towards you, you might judge that he had been a sailor; his arms and chest are those of a typical blacksmith; his head gives one the impression that nature hesitated between making him either a great scholar or a great fighter and effected a compromise, for the brain cavity is large and the forehead lofty which would account for the scholar, while the jaw is square and massive, which might account for the fighter.

'Imagine the Hall absolutely full of people; the singing of the fiery Welsh hymns is over, Mr. Joshua steps to the front of the platform and gives his text. His dissection of it and explanation of the context and all matters which he considers relative to it ... show that the man is not merely a copyist. He betrays remarkable originality of thought. Up to this point the sermon promises to be an ideal one, there is, however, a subtle change.... The weapon of sarcasm has been handed out to Mr. Joshua, and he has apparently taken a vow never to let it rust in its sheath.[13] I know as well as anyone the wrongs which at present exist in this land of ours between the poor and the rich, but I must candidly say that when I hear him denounce from his pulpit all that is selfish, or mean or artificial or unreal or dishonourable or vile, and then sneer – and he can sneer – at the rank or class of society where such things may be winked at, it sounds very much as if he were sneering at rank because it is rank, at culture because it is culture, at science for what it knows and at the rich because they are rich; but of course I am aware that he is a man of too much natural good sense to intend any such thing for a single moment.

'When this part of the sermon is over, he applies himself to the personal harpooning of every soul in his audience; he has the invaluable gift of making his appeal a purely personal one, and I always feel as though I were the only individual to whom his message is directed.... There is one aspect of his preaching which is as telling as his oratory, and that is his dramatic power. His pulpit is the entire platform and conceals nothing of the man, and as he preaches the gesticulations with which his words are accompanied merge into acting scene after scene in the sermon, until you begin to wonder whether, after all, it is one man who alone produces the marvellous effects which bring the old gospel truths home to men and women Sunday after Sunday. For one thing Mr. Joshua does and that is preach a simple Scriptural way of salvation. I believe that for reaching the masses with the gospel there could not be found a better man in the whole of South Wales. I said of his appearance that it combined the thinker and the fighter; I say the same of his preaching ... he has, in reality, made the Forward Movement the success it is in Newport.'[14]

Malpas Road, Newport

In another part of Newport – the Malpas Road area, a large hall seating eight hundred and costing £2000 was opened on February 4, 1897. This was a sheer venture of faith for here was not the smallest nucleus of a church in the area. It was one of those moves that brought down obloquy on Pugh's head from time to time. To every one's relief a fine congregation gathered on the first Sunday. At the end of five months there were thirty members, one hundred and twenty at the Sunday School and at the Band of Hope. In October 1905, Pugh looked forward to the coming of a new minister to Malpas. The church had gained from the revival days. 'He is entering upon a field and going to a work with some of the most spiritually minded people we have ever known. The love of Christ constraineth them, to a wonderful degree, to go forth after those who are ready to perish.... This young church is full of the Spirit of Christ – and hence as free from a self-seeking spirit as any church we know of.'[15]

Sandfields, Aberavon

In the same year 1897, the erection of the docks at Aberavon (Sandfields) and the flood of navvies who gathered to construct them, led to a call from the local Calvinistic Methodist churches to the Forward Movement. A school hall was built and opened by John Pugh on 13 June 1897. In 1927 it was to put the Forward Movement on the map once more through the vigorous and transforming ministry of Dr. Martyn Lloyd-Jones documented in detail in Ian Murray's thrilling biographical account in *Martyn Lloyd-Jones: The First Forty Years, 1899–1939.*

Saltmead, Cardiff

The Saltmead area of Cardiff was a formidable challenge to any Christian presence in the 1890s. Richard Burgess, an evangelist who joined Pugh from Beckenham, reported: 'It was not a safe place to visit, nor a safe place for open airs. In one house I found several men, husbands and brothers at war. They were in the kitchen, arms and legs flaying, engaged in a scrimmage. As most were drunk I was able to get one at a time and lock them in some other room. When the police started moving women from disreputable quarters they began to hive off to Saltmead, to new streets. There were whole rows of crowded houses and streets of prostitutes. It was a veritable inferno.'[16] This was soon to launch the Forward Movement into work among women as we shall see.

Pugh always attacked the strongholds. A piece of vacant ground was found. 'Pugh and I plunged our umbrellas into the soil and perched our coats and hats thereon. We started clearing the stones so that a tent might be erected. I preached the following evening to the accompaniment of those stones hurled at the tent from the outside.'[17] 'By 1948,' writes Williams, 'Saltmead, generally believed to have been beyond redemption, is now one of the most respectable working class areas in Cardiff – a transformation begun by the work of the Forward.'[18]

Crwys Hall

In the north of Cardiff the rapidly growing areas of Cathays and Heath were also short of churches. Where the Whitchurch Road, Heath, runs into Crwys Road we enter the Cathays area of the city. In these areas two large Forward Movement Halls were to be built. First, Crwys Hall. Pugh had had his eye on this new residential area for some years. A large estate of 700 houses was going up and, in 1898, while he negotiated for a site, he hired two large rooms in the neighbourhood to begin evangelism and prepare a congregation before he built a home for it. We shall go into some detail about this site, because it shows the birth pangs of new developments like this and also has an encouraging modern postscript of closure and reopening recorded in the last chapter.

He hired, at 17 shillings a week, a large room over a stable in Dalcross Street, Cathays, seating several hundred. The second was in nearby Fitzroy Street. This was opened in premises once belonging to a Sunday Drinking Club, the transference 'dislodging the forces of darkness from their headquarters in Cathays, transforming the old shanty of a hall into a place of blessing' as Pugh put it. It was stated at the time, 'if a man wants to know the rough side of the Forward Movement mission, let him go to Fitzroy Street for three months'.

In the meantime the builder at the Crwys estate gave up an excellent site, at a stiff price, on Monthemer Road. Now began a massive building programme as the large Crwys Hall[19] with a lesser hall began to rise. Day after day, as the work proceeded in Cathays, a gentleman was spotted walking around, keeping the work of the Movement under careful observation. People began to feel suspicious about his movements. But the day came when the mystery was revealed. As a direct result of this 'spying' Pugh received a letter from a Mr. Charles Pierce, J.P. of Bangor asking how he could help. They told him they needed to furnish the Dalcross Street room where hordes of children were turning up. 'When,' wrote Pugh, 'we were at our wits end about what we were to do for money to pay for the seats, Mr. Pierce sent a cheque for £20. He wrote, "If you are short, please wire as soon as this comes to hand." We wired that we were short of £9 and it came next day.'[20]

On 21 March the memorial stones of Crwys Hall were laid. The excitements of the start of a new century were in the air and a big day was made of it. The new brass band of the East Moors Hall marched up through the district inviting people to attend. The weather was glorious. The first stone was laid in memory of Edward Davies, Llandinam – his memory perpetuated in the first Forward Movement Hall to be erected after his death. Five were laid in all, including one by Richard Cory's daughter and another by Mrs. Pugh, the first time she had been persuaded to do so. She acted on behalf of the Sunday school. Her words to the crowds are a good example of the way the Forward wanted ordinary people to see the Halls as their building: not daunted from attending by the respectable formality which was beginning to afflict noncomformity, nor intimidated by the churchiness of a growing ritualism:

'Past success was largely due to the fact that we recognise the truth that the house of God is really the house of man; and the more we make it the house of man, the more it becomes the house of God. This fine building will be no sanctuary unless it is always regarded as the home of the people. Here human life should be interpreted, its pain alleviated and its awful tragedy explained. Here the outcast and the fallen should be able to come as to a father's arms. Here the perplexed and distressed should come as to the light of home; and here all conditions of men and women should be able to come with the assurance that whatever their anguish, their disappointments and sorrow, they will find love, rest and peace. If it will not be all these then it will not be the house of God. To do this has been the great purpose of the Forward Movement – to bring sin-stricken men and women to a saviour who can take their burdens away, to sweeten lives made bitter by the disappointments of life, to keep children from the darkest and saddest side of life. And because I am trusting that this place will help in that work of God, I have the greatest pleasure in laying this stone.'[21]

The Crwys Hall was opened for worship at the end of May 1900. The huge Sunday school constantly grew and was to exceed a thousand children. A large donation from Charles Pierce made it possible to complete the lesser Pierce Hall. Donations came in large and small sums for the double hall project, chiefly through personal appeals by Pugh who himself collected £1,800. The Crwys/Pierce Halls cost £3,500. Towards this Charles Pierce donated £1,100.

Pugh's daughter tells us that a large space of land between the Crwys and Pierce Halls had been set aside for the erection of a Women's Training Institute. Young Christian women in Wales who offered to train for work among the needy were forced to go to England or Scotland for a training course. This worried Pugh. At the opening of Pierce Hall in 1906 he made a plea for £1,500 to launch the Institute. But he died the following year and it remained one of the many dreams he did not see realized.[22]

The day following the opening, *The South Wales Daily News* noted how, like the Salvation Army before it, the Forward Movement had survived pointless criticism because of the practical nature of its work and 'we report with pleasure the spectacular growth ... of a Movement whose aim is for the good of society'.

Heath Hall

In February 1900 the *Torch* reported that a third branch to the Crwys Centre, as it called the meetings at Fitzroy and Dalcross streets, was doing well – 'Heath is another wing to the Centre, divided from the Cathays site by the large Cardiff cemetery.' 'Upon my return from the United States in 1900,' says Pugh, 'a deputation of mothers, who had waited upon my wife in my absence, appealed to me to do something for the salvation of the neglected people and children of the Heath district.' After the usual open airs and house and tent meetings, agreement was arrived at on the request to build a Sunday School Hall to hold 350, to be followed by a large hall. Meetings were held for soldiers from the nearby Military Barracks. The present building, on Whitchurch Road, seating 900 and costing £4,300 was opened on June 20, 1906 by Mrs. Frank Jones, daughter of John Jones, Tal-y-sarn. By the close of the day £1,030 had been given towards the debt. Heath became one of the first of the Halls to be self supporting. Its evangelical witness has remained consistent and vigorous throughout the century whereas the Crwys Hall declined and closed in 1996. But that, as we shall see later, is not the end of the story....

Kingsway Hall, Cardiff

There is one ex Forward Movement church, that of Kingsway Hall, Cardiff that has bucked the trend. After being tended until recently by Sister Heulwen Jones as the last 'Sister of the People' to remain in ministry, it has, in 1998, been purchased by a Cardiff Welsh Evangelical church under the leadership of the Rev. Gwynn Williams. There is a certain pleasing irony in it being the only Forward Movement building that has ever been taken over by a Welsh-speaking congregation! Despite all the anglicizing trends of the past century, it speaks of continuing evangelical witness in the Welsh language.

Mission Hall, Neath

Nearly forty miles to the west of Cardiff, Frank Joshua was continuing to do the work of an evangelist and pastor. All that the

Forward Movement stood for saw classic demonstration in the Neath mission. By 1900 its membership stood at three hundred and fifty. By 1902 it ran out of space. It was to increase further to eight hundred and fifty in the wake of the 1904 revival.

But by 1900 Frank was concerned about the future. It was not as though he was not blessed in the work, for the Mission was never more prosperous. But he was convinced that an independent mission had little security for the future, as it depended largely on the lives of one or two people. After discussions with John Pugh and John Morgan Jones the Mission Hall was received as part of the Forward Movement, and Frank was ordained. The one accepted the other. It was also agreed that the Forward Movement would help to provide a large permanent hall to meet the needs of the expanding church.

As usual they did not let the grass grow under their feet. Pugh and Jones heard that the following day, in the same street as the old building, a plot was to be sold as freehold. Many were keen to buy. The selling price was likely to be £2,000. 'We were to be pitied,' says J. M. Jones. 'We did not have that sum between us and we had no church authorization. Yet either from presumption or from faith we went to a builder and gave him the freedom to bid up to £1,500 pounds. He managed to get the site for £1,000 ... the church has been self-supporting from then on.'[23] The building, seating over two thousand, was erected in eighteen months and every Sunday night was crowded. The men's Bible class, which had begun with five members had grown to one hundred and eighty and, until the new building, had been in 'a kind of bondage through restricted space'.

In 1905, *The Torch* wrote 'the Revival has kindled a new interest in Bible study'.[24] It carries a photograph of 110 young men gathered to honour their Bible Class teacher, Mr. R. A. Williams. His comments are reported. 'When he began the work he had no idea it would have risen to such magnitude, or he would have hesitated to accept the post.... There was a fear of danger in increasing numbers if they did not grow in grace; then let them be as a tree shooting forth branches and bearing good fruit for the Master.... There was only one who should be prominent in their work and that was Christ. He was the teacher; Him they should honour, serve and exalt and crown him Lord of all.' (Loud applause)[25]

Frank gave his all to the Neath Mission, a ministry as large as any in Wales. It was said that if Frank had no time to study apologetics, his apologetics were conversions to Christ!

Dinam Hall, Barry

For our final example of Pugh's strategic planting of halls in the sea port towns we turn our eyes to Barry. Its ultimate demise tells the other side of the Forward Movement story which was itself to be wound up as a separate organization in the 1970s. Overlooking the now derelict part of the dock at Barry, is a huge statue of David Davies of Llandinam whose family continued financially to support the Forward Movement in a massive way until its debts were finally paid off. He stands, like his great contemporary Principal T. Charles Edwards at Aberystwyth, facing the sea. Both of them are at the scene of their great accomplishments. Edwards stands in front of the University College where he was the first principal. Davies stands in Barry Dock which he built as an outlet for the Rhondda valley coal that his company mined. T. C. Edwards has a Bible in his hands. David Davies is studying a roll of financial accounts. Edward Davies, his son, was a leading constructor of the docks along with his father. As a compassionate Christian and an enthusiast for the Forward Movement, Edward had a heavy burden laid on his heart – aware that he and his family had brought thousands to Barry from all over the kingdom. 'Be sure to do something for Barry Dock,' he said to Pugh before his early death.

Dinam Hall, Barry, was opened in 1903. The evangelist during the First World War was the Rev. Griffith Griffiths who had already had twenty nine years as a medical missionary in the Khasai Hills as the first of the denomination's medical missionaries. On returning home for health reasons he laboured for the Forward Movement at Barry, turning down a lucrative government war post, preferring to continue to preach the gospel. He used to dwell on the fact that the cosmopolitan character of the Hall at Barry Dock was more pronounced than he had ever experienced in India. People from all four home countries were joined by French, German, Norwegian and black sailors. But Barry Dock is now almost a ghost. Its life gone. And so too has that of the church, a reminder that churches that rise can also fall. It became a repeated story in later years.

Pugh, ever more busy, began to show increasing signs of exhaustion. 'Even ministers of good things,' says Richard Hooker, 'are like torches, a light to others, waste and destruction to themselves.' 'Preaching,' said Joseph Parker, 'is self murder.' A man of herculean proportions and to all appearances healthy and robust, the task was slowly sapping Pugh. The responsibilities he bore in the last decade of his ministry were colossal. Debts piled up in thousands on the dozens of massive buildings. A complacent opposition from the cautious brethren meant frequent battles on the floor of presbyteries. This caused a lion-hearted yet sensitive leader much pain and many a sleepless night. He continued to be in constant demand as a preacher.

Overseas Visits
In 1896, in his 50th year, he accepted advice and went to South Africa for a break, though he preached often to Welsh settlers there in Welsh. In 1899 he went as Wales delegate to the pan Presbyterian World Alliance in Washington. 'We hope,' wrote the *Torch*, 'that Mr. Pugh will enjoy what he knows hitherto only by hearsay – a real holiday.' He certainly made a real impact. 'It is not too much to say,' says John Morgan Jones, 'that he shook the Alliance assembly with the amazing facts of the success of the work. He managed to get them to sing a Sankey hymn – they usually praised God by singing psalms. After referring to his venture at Tredegar and to the service held under the clock he added – "and this is the song I sang". After he had sung the first verse he said "and now join in the chorus". The response was feeble at first but soon cold Presbyterians hearts warmed up and by the second time round they were singing so heartily that the walls of the room resounded...'[26] A report on his contribution appeared in the *Washington Post* of 6 October 1899. 'The Alliance is good, solid, but it lacked somewhat in brightness and enthusiasm. There was not sufficient Methodism in it,' were Pugh's own

thoughts on the gathering. His experience of Welsh churches in the U.S. reaffirmed the importance of his own work back home. 'To think that a country so small as ours can influence a country so large as this for good should make us doubly diligent to prepare our people for their grand vision in life.'

He went to the White House and was introduced to the U.S. President – 'a gentleman in plain black clothes, with no provision for his protection.'[27] This particular scene, with its lack of ceremony, seemed to make more of an impression on him than anything else in America. When he landed back in this country the news greeted him that the University of Kentucky had honoured him with the degree of Doctor of Divinity.[28]

CHAPTER SIX

POVERTY AND PROSTITUTION

Pugh was as painfully aware as any in the city of the hundreds of homes in Cardiff harassed by sickness, poverty and sorrow, apparently unheeded by organized Christianity. Moreover, he was much concerned about the drifting girls and prostitutes roaming the streets, either spurned or exploited.

One of the barriers in the way of those trying to help such women lay in 'the conspiracy of silence' on sexual matters which prevented things being mentioned in polite society. Talking about such things offended the Victorian sense of modesty. Most in the churches therefore acted as if the problem did not exist. However, evangelical societies in England had been to the fore in breaking through this barrier. Though Wales was slower in this, a more understanding and kindly attitude towards the prostitute had already come from the rescue attempts of many evangelical agencies in mid century. This compassion was a working through of our Lord's example. After early concentration to help girls who were already into prostitution, the emphasis in the 1880s was moving towards preventive help for 'friendless' girls, especially the wild, undisciplined girl from a poor home whose schooling was over but who had not settled down into any suitable job. They were

vulnerable but had not yet succumbed. Pugh seemed fully aware
of the need in Cardiff to help in both these respects.

Scotland points the way

He had first to overcome the chosen blindness to the problem that
prevailed. In this he enlisted the help of his wife and daughter. In
1893 he took his daughter, then still not twenty, to the Cowcaddens
Convention. She explains why. 'He wanted me to see the Sisters
of the people at work there. It seems that William Ross had spoken
one day to a poor lady about her soul, who, looking pathetically in
his face, had replied, "Oh Mr. Ross, if you were as hungry as I am
you wouldn't have time to think about your soul." That woman's
face and answer left such an impression on Mr. Ross' tender nature
that was never to go away. He plunged deeper than ever before
into deeper friendship with the One who "when He saw the
multitudes had had compassion on them"'.[1] He told Lord Overton
about the incident. His response was to influence Pugh's own action
years later. He promised to support six experienced Christian nurses
to go among the poor of Cowcaddens and six Sisters of the people
who had been taught in the Bible Institute, Sauchiehall Street,
Glasgow, who in their turn went out at night to contact the
prostitutes. These dedicated women lived among the people in the
crowded closes. Their work was so successful that they provided
Cowcaddens church with a constant flow of new members and
eventually the local police reported that the Missions had helped
to improve the overall tone of the Cowcaddens area itself.

Ann Pugh's reminiscences must be unique among young Welsh
Christian women of the time:

The White Flower
'One night I dressed in a Sisters uniform for safety and went with
Sister Jessie on her nightly round. As we walked through the streets
I saw sights that made my blood boil with anger. I should have felt
compassion and sympathy for the women. Maybe it wasn't right, but
the feelings that were uppermost were those of shame and fear. All
my sympathy went out to the young men who were placed in such a
vulnerable position and open to temptation. I longed to go to them
and remind them of their mothers and to talk them into more

appropriate and noble thoughts of what a woman should be. As I went past them in the lamp light I raised my helpless cry to God – "Oh God, give these young men strength to withstand temptation". But the Sister did more than that. The answer to her prayers came through her own hands. A girl stood in a doorway of a house, touting for work. The sister went up to her – "here is the last flower I have left" she said, "Would you like to have it?" The girl in the doorway took the simple gift and replied, "It's been a long time since anyone gave me a flower" and then she added, "It's been a long time since a respectable girl even spoke to me at all". Sister Jennie looked at her and said, "You're not very happy are you. Can I do anything for you?" "No! There's nothing that can be done." "There might be. Think about it – anyway you know where to find me, don't you? Come in to see me and let me be your friend."

'We returned to the Sisters room in the Close and spoke of the great need for a work which could prevent what was going on. The door bell rang. There was the girl with the flower in her hand. "When you asked if you could do anything for me I said you couldn't. But you said perhaps you could and invited me. Well, I've come now. I want you to help me. It was the white flower that you gave me that made me come here. It wouldn't leave me alone." '[2]

Back in Cardiff, after a fairly thorough study of the similar plight of people there and in other industrial towns Pugh evolved a three fold plan.

Firstly, he sought to concentrate the concern and get the massed support of the women of the church. In 1894 'The Women's branch' of the Forward Movement was formed through Mrs. Pugh's initiative and with the support of three hundred women at a church Association at Llanrwst. They proposed securing trained nurses at Cardiff, and encouraged members throughout the populous districts of Wales to meet together for Bible reading and prayer and to arrange regular visits to the neediest homes.

But the problem demanded more than part time voluntary endeavour. The second part of the plan was 'to inaugurate a new order of (full time) women workers to be called "Sisters of the people" whose chief work would be to assist the evangelists at the big centres and who were fitted by training and character for work among women either hardened or broken by friendlessness and desperation'.[3] In *The Torch* edition of May 1898, Pugh wrote:

'I am persuaded that a bird could as soon fly with one wing as the Church of God can evangelize the great centres of population without Christ-possessed women to go in and out among the suffering poor. There is a work no-one can do for Christ but them. It must be left forever undone unless they turn to do it by providing the means or volunteering to do it themselves.'[4]

The leadership of a 'slow moving church'[5] hid their faces from the facts. It took five years for it to be taken seriously. But in 1903 Pugh achieved his object at Amlwch General Assembly. A searing speech from Sergeant Barker, one of Pugh's most zealous and original evangelists who worked in notorious Saltmead, Cardiff, crushed opposition. People sat appalled as the wraps were taken off life in an area of Wales' largest town.

'From three hundred to four hundred fallen women reside in my district. There are more than one hundred houses empty of families because they have been occupied for immoral purposes. I know girls going straight from sabbath school to the streets and thirty of them have gone since I am at Saltmead. These girls are expected to adopt this life even by some of their parents.'[6]

That settled the question. It was unanimously passed that a Bible woman be appointed for protective work at the Saltmead Centre. By 1909 there were eight Sisters who were engaged both in rescue and preventive work.

The third part of Pugh's plan was for a Home for single women especially those trapped into prostitution. It would also provide for single mothers and their babies. With the Women's Branch now officially part of the denomination they accepted their role with determination and Pugh gratefully left it to them. In 1903, Mrs. Tydfil Thomas of 6 Shirley Road, Cardiff, became organizer of the Women's Social wing. In comparison with women pioneers in England, Mrs. Thomas is a late comer but she deserves attention as a Welsh evangelical pioneer in social work. Her appointment came at the right time. It was the 1904–05 revival that brought middle class church women face to face with a new challenge – the unusual presence of converted prostitutes in their church congregations. 'Were it possible for us to publish the details we receive, and how the daughters of Zion are slain, the hardest heart would melt.'

Mrs. Thomas wrote in *The Torch* for April 1905: 'How pressing the need for a Home is, this incident will show. Recently at a revival meeting in the centre of Cardiff, fifteen women were drawn by the cords of Christ's love to abandon their life of shame. They met together in one room. What shall we do with them? The Nonconformists in Cardiff have no home, no shelter to offer them. Accommodation was found for two in the Salvation Army Shelter while the other thirteen, precious souls for whom Christ died, had to retire to their old haunts.'[7] Whether to their old habits as well we have no record.

This was too much for four Sisters. Distressed at what looked like abandonment of young lives given fresh hope by the gospel, they requested authority from the Forward Movement to establish a preventive home with facilities for two sisters to live in among women in need of protective care. Soon Mrs. Richard Davies of Treborth Hall, Menai Bridge, wife of a leading nonconformist politician, gave £440 enabling the Forward Movement to purchase outright a property in Grangetown. A Home named 'Treborth' was opened on November 30, 1905, the public meeting being chaired by Sir Alfred Thomas MP. In the next two and a half years under the leadership of a wise matron, sixty-three girls were given residence, retrained for jobs, many of whom went on to do well in domestic service. These placements had themselves to be carefully arranged as sometimes girls found themselves in danger through 'living in' as domestics. The immediate success of Treborth led to a much larger four-storied house situated in its own grounds, being opened in Cowbridge Road, Canton in 1907. It was financially supported by John Cory and by the widow of Edward Davies, Llandinam, who continued to contribute hundreds of pounds annually towards its upkeep. This was a culmination of Pugh's three-fold plan for a Christian social service for destitute women.

The new home was placed in the charge of the pastor of Saltmead Hall. For the first twelve months he and his wife undertook the extra work of management of the home free of charge. A resumé of the first year report reveals some of the reasons why Pugh had a burden for this work. The report's 'Victorian' language, which makes us uncomfortable today, must not hide from us the loving, sacrificial, practical concern shown in these homes by this dedicated couple.

1. Fifty-three friendless, fallen women have found shelter.

2. Fourteen betrayed women have found their way back to virtue.

3. Seven girls restored to their parents, two to their relatives, three wives to their husbands and families.

4. Six women deceived, have been cared for with their babies and later found situations.

5. Suitable arrangements were made for their babies so that the mothers might be free to earn their own living and support their children. A total of one hundred and twenty-six women, girls and babies sheltered and rescued during the year.

Comment, too, on the work of the Sisters highlights the practical effect of Christian truth and care. 'What an amazing story these Sisters could tell of the wonderful works of God silently performed in the homes of the people, such as reconciling parents with one another as well as with their grown up children, settling age-long family disputes, persuading the unmarried parents to enter marriage were it only for the sake of the children!'

The approach of the Sisters, based on earlier experience of women's societies in England, was to visit, possibly a brothel during the day to try and reach women individually, and when they had won their affection and trust, provide them accommodation at Treborth, treating each case singly as its special merits required. Newspaper photos of the Home show attractively dressed young women engaged in various tasks.[8]

As the movement became more empirically aware of the social conditions of the people it broadened its activities. Barker, whose report on Saltmead had been the catalyst for action over child prostitution in Cardiff, moved to Merthyr in 1905. In August of that year *The Torch* reported that he was beginning to storm evil strongholds in 'that metropolis of South Wales' steel and coal fields'. Pugh was always quick to castigate landlords of slumdom. In a letter written to the *Merthyr Express*, Barker of the Forward Movement is thanked for his kindness in caring for the people caught up in the following horror story. Pugh carries the letter in *The Torch*. It refers to a poor family in 'one of the smallest houses I have ever seen – a living room, a place (which is very wet) for keeping coal, and a small bedroom – for which the charge is 16s. a month. The proper rent ought to be about 5s. or 6s. at the most, but I suppose the owner wants about 500 or 600 per cent on his money.... I found that because one poor woman was five weeks in arrears with her rent, an execution was taken out and her furniture was taken, and because she would not leave her house (no legal notice had been given her to leave) the door had been taken off its hinges and the window taken out. This poor woman and her children (one little girl a cripple) were left at the mercy of anyone who might like to walk in. I should like to mention that this house is kept beautifully clean by this poor woman, and it is a pleasure to see how well kept the children are.'[9]

Seth Joshua was engaged in evangelism along with Barker at Merthyr in April 1905. He wrote to Mrs. Jessie Penn-Lewis about it, imploring her prayers. 'A very hard fight is going on with the forces of darkness. Nearly every error under the sun finds root in this place. There are strong spiritualistic societies, ethical societies, agnostics, Christadelphians, and the last importation would be the Pentecostal Dancers. Strange to say they are drawing a strong following at Dowlais. We ourselves have seen the temperance hall crowded for the past fortnight and every service we see victory in conversions. Still I never felt Satanic forces so strong as at this place.'[10] In July he was back at Penydarren, Merthyr after a trip to Scotland.

The Forward Movement had just built a Hall and had sent a new evangelist there. Seth rarely wrote with such anguish.

'It was a great change from near the "Banks of Allan's water" to the cinder tips of Dowlais and Penydarren. Our Forward Movement hall is in the very centre of a district degraded by drink and its natural effects. Merthyr is a district covered with the blotch and scab of sin beyond any other in the whole of Wales. We had some profitable meetings and many came forward to seek the Lord. Victims of drink! How they need a prop here and support there. The most depressing thing here is the sight of so many in the grip of the drink habit. Would that someone would support a Sister worker among these poor fallen mothers. The future of this Forward Movement cause lies with the young, and yet the material here is the most crude it is possible to imagine'[11]

Similar conditions agitated the Rev. Watkin Williams who began a Forward Movement work in Pontypool a few months before the revival began. 'Our great need at present is a Sister of the people. There are women here by the hundreds whose redemption seems hopeless, unless the gospel will be taken to them by a sympathetic, God-fearing woman. The environment, to use a big word, of these women is terrible. I know that surroundings will not save, still, they tell upon the life, and to see the places where human beings have to live here is sickening. I would rather stand in the shoes of the publican on the day of judgement than in those of some owners of property here. But the leaven is in the meal, and this place must be permeated with holiness.'[12]

Williams reported great evangelistic encouragement in the space of twelve months. 'During the last fourteen years God has wrought many and great miracles through the Forward Movement ... but none greater than in Pontypool. A few had been toiling here through a long and dreary night and had caught nothing, and the general opinion was that, for our Connexion, these waters had no fish. But in the beginning of this year the Forward Movement laid hold of the net and cast it on the right side of the ship, and lo, the net is being filled. There is now a church of one hundred and fifty members ... those who are best fitted to judge speak in the language of the old saints – to whom deliverance had come – "When the Lord turned again the captivity of Zion we were as them that dream".' Annie Pugh writes: 'My father's wish was to name one of the Forward Movement Halls, St. David's, after Pontypridd where he had spent nine happy years.' So they called this new Hall at Pontypool St. David's. Many came in through the revival. It would be impossible to find a seat there after 5.30 pm on a

Sunday evening, with many turned away. Many of the converts worked in Pontnewynydd tin-plate works. I well recall how I was struck by the prayer of one of them who worked with the 'cold-rolls' (a process which flattened out the tin plate). 'Mangle us Lord. Iron the creases out of us.' These men were quick to enrich the language of prayer and speak to God in the new tongue of industrial life!

Relief given by Forward Movement halls, especially to children, was usually indiscriminate. In the winter of 1907–08 which had severe frosts, hundreds of children at several halls were provided every day with soup, articles of clothing and other necessaries of life.[13] 'Some of them attend Forward Movement services, but they brought others as hungry as themselves. However, no questions were asked and no distinction was made: all were treated in the same manner.' The 1909 report of the Sisters work tells of eight Sisters making weekly about a thousand visits to the homes of the non-churched, to factories, workshops, prison cells, in furtherance of their general work of befriending the friendless as well as seeking to lead women and children to Christ. Brave stories emerge, such as the Sister at Pontypool who exposed herself constantly to infection during a typhoid epidemic in order to continue her work among the poor. Her ministry led to many new faces turning up at the hall. Later, owing to the shortage of evangelists of the right stamp, some of the Sisters were put in full charge of the smaller centres – occupying the pulpits regularly and were the spearhead of the Forward Movement in its later difficult years.

Testimony to the commitment to social work among the Sisters and the halls in general comes from *The Times*, 16th May 1907. Reginald Mckenna, Monmouthshire MP and First Lord of the Admiralty, reported (to the House) on the issue of disestablishment of the Church of England in Wales:

'The question has been asked here, "If the church be disestablished who will minister to the poor?" In this House with an audience consisting almost entirely of English and Scottish members, when that question is put, immediately the picture is conjured up of some Church of England missioner going down into the slums of our great cities preaching and winning the poor over to the Christian faith.'

'But is that a picture of what has happened in Wales? Who does the slum work in the cities of Wales? We have a movement in Wales known as the Calvinistic Methodist Forward Movement. (Hear, Hear) The object of that Movement is described as "to get at the non-church and non-chapel goers and lead them to Christ, to provide Christian nurses for the sick and poor, and to get all to abstain from the use of strong drink." I take the City of Cardiff and I ask you to compare the work of the Welsh Calvinistic Methodist Forward Movement with the work of the Church of England. When you speak of the work of ministering to the poor, you have to conjure up, not the work of the clergymen of the Church of England, but the work of the nonconformists.'[14]

CHAPTER SEVEN

SETH – WALES FOR CHRIST

The final sharp spur to the Forward Movement to provide pastoral help for women by women had been provided by the conversion of prostitutes in the 1904 revival. Our task in the next three chapters is to tell how the years before and during that revival, 1903–5, were, for Seth personally, the most memorable in his already exceptional experience. He was granted more blessing as missioner than he had seen for some years. Conversions were constant. Busy schedules had kept him from keeping a diary for many years. But the loss of three friends by death in 1903 somehow sobered him to vow to keep a record of his journeys and work during the following year. It has left us with a rich record of divine visitation. It also gives us a graph of the spiritual heartbeats of one of God's athletes as he ran the race, looking to Jesus.

In August 1903 the first Keswick in Wales Convention was held in Llandrindod Wells. Its memory still remained with him at the end of the year. 'I received a definite spiritual blessing at Llandrindod. My heart had been prepared for this by deep trial and experience. This year has been deeper and fuller in all kinds of experience than any former year of my life.'[1]

In 1904 he entered upon his work as evangelist for the connexion as a whole. In 1901, Ross had been appointed to a special position as evangelist to the Highlands, leaving him free of his duties at Cowcaddens. Pugh had seen that a similar arrangement would set Seth free to exercise his unique evangelistic ministry on a wider scale. By 1904 he was able to lay down any local pastoral tie. A packed preaching programme took him all over Wales and well beyond. How did that year begin?

The first entry for 1904 finds him relaxing – and reflecting on his need for more of it! Having been so accomplished a sportsman in his youth he no doubt hankered a bit after physical diversion. On January 1st he enjoyed himself at a New Year's party at Langstone Court near Newport. 'I managed to shoot a snipe, a pheasant and several rabbits.... I feel that a day like this is a great help to me. I have been religious overmuch in not taking reasonable recreation. Now that I begin my work as connexional evangelist and must work at high pressure I must insist on breaking away from my toil in order to give mind and body proper rest. My one strong desire is to live out the consecrated life in 1904.'[2] Much more – 'joy unspeakable and full of glory' lay ahead of him.

His first engagements of the year saw him at Shrewsbury, Montgomery and Newtown. After a Sunday at his former pastorate, Memorial Hall (they obviously wanted to hang on to him!), he was taken ill on his way to Ystrad Rhondda. It was a fever that kept him in bed for a week and was to trouble him again in the future. This illness tried him sorely as he was due for a mission in Cowcaddens, Glasgow. His reflections after being kept out of the fray are notable. In fact his whole diary shows such honest talking with himself and God that they provide us with spiritual fragments worthy to stand alongside much more famous journals of the soul.

'How strange it is to spend a day at home without preaching. Yet it cannot be a waste of time. The lessons I need are being driven home to me. Pride is brought low. Humility is being deepened. My frailty is made so clear and my dependence on God increased. How easily the Almighty can dispense with the cooperation of so weak a worm. I see it all; yet I remember that the Lord once said: "Fear not, thou worm Jacob ... thou shalt thresh the mountains, and make the little hills like chaff."'[3] Meditation on that particular passage was to bear fruit in busier times, as we shall see.

Scotland Again

He left for Glasgow over a week late and after a long and tiring journey, was still weak from a high temperature when he arrived. He stayed a fortnight, over one hundred professing conversion. His admiration of William Ross, whose ministry he regarded as prophetic, was boundless. The Editor of the *British Weekly*, J. M. Ross, William's son, also gave strong testimony to the ministry of both Seth Joshua and John Pugh at Cowcadens. At the last service of the mission Seth preached on Isaiah 62:10. His diary invites us to follow along with the congregation's response.

The command of the text was 'Go through, go through the gates' – that is, the gates of conviction, the gates of pardon, of consecration, crucifixion, Pentecost, abiding joy and service. Step by step the whole congregation seemed to go through into these experiences, some into one and some into another.

His own New Year's desire to live out the consecrated life saw him exploring more widely in his reading. For the next few months we find him probing critically his own inner life, testing for the authentic and, for a while, varying in the paths he took as he sought the Lord's presence. Strangely it was in the land of reformation theology that he was introduced to the mystics. While in Glasgow he read *A Model of Prayer* by Madame Guyon. When we recall that his formal education had been absolutely zero his capacity for independence of judgement and his wisdom in 'taking the meat and leaving the bones' of different traditions is impressive.

'She is a great mystic and I cannot say I can follow her in every particular. But I have lived long enough to know that there is room for many varied experiences in God's kingdom. God manifests himself to his chosen in different ways. As for myself, I find that I am being starved from all visions, emotions and sensations. Nothing comes to me by the observation of the senses. I am driven to bare faith.' Again he wrote: 'I was much blessed today while reading *An Appreciation of Santa Teresa* by Alexander Whyte, DD. She was another mystic of the type of Madame Guyon.'[4]

His recent introduction to the teaching of Keswick on 'holiness by faith in Jesus', his even more recent dip into the mystics were now added to his more long term reading of the Puritans. The resulting uncertainty seemed to leave him cautious for a while about the place of experiences in the Christian life. '(Though) I find an increasing power to turn inward for communion ... my one great difficulty is to free myself from looking for emotions, feelings and sensible manifestations. I see it will be a long struggle to starve all these things in order to live by faith.'[5] Yet before the year was out he was to be overwhelmed with an overpowering sense of the presence of God both personally and among the people of God!

Seth, the Hunter

Seth, of course, was not a student of spiritual experience for its own sake. It is a privilege to have access to his inner life as he prepared himself to face the crowds in their spiritual needs. It was the evangelistic task and God's enabling for that that ever absorbed him. In February he was shocked by the state of people in Blaenycwm. 'Satan seems to have made it his own hunting ground. Lord, help me to hunt also.'[6]

Seth, the Hunter! No better name could describe him. He found so much of his inspiration among the hills and valleys. Before a visit to Treherbert he went to the Common, Pontypridd, and stood on the rocking stone. It flooded his emotions with memories of the time when the hound of heaven had hunted him there. 'All the valley lay before me and I saw the Egypt out of which God had brought me. I was much affected by the vision of the past and found relief in prayer and praise. This seemed to fit me for the meeting....' Inner wells of gratitude flowed in such evocative terrain 'and I never remember speaking and singing with more spiritual freedom'.

Seth and Frank, who were both peerless for their open air preaching among great crowds, also looked for open air solitude to prepare many a sermon. Seth would wrestle with his text by a stream or among the trees. A sincere effort to use original material brought him great satisfaction. In March he enjoyed a walk up to Trevethin and was able to prepare a message on 2 Corinthians 5:20. 'Now then we are ambassadors for Christ, as though God did beseech you by us, we pray you to be reconciled to God.' He did not often jot his sermon thoughts into his diary. But this text carries the burden of Seth's ministry and so we share his thoughts on it that afternoon. He was struck by the fact that he, an ambassador, though invested with authority, was a stranger in a strange land and that he was present to look after the kingdom he represented. That he did so in Christ's stead filled him again with the dignity and responsibility of his calling. He saw how he was called to reconcile where there had been the quarrel and rebellion of sin. He felt again the power of the word 'beseech'. It means tenderness, he reminded himself, it means tears. In a man of such tender spirit tears were never very far away. The tender note was often heard amidst his firm authority and was one of the factors that so compellingly drew sinners to Christ when he engaged with them.

Not so long after he went to one of his favourite spots for meditation. 'I enjoyed a blessed time of reading and prayer in Sophia Gardens under a tree. Being wet there were no people to disturb my meditations. From experience I find freedom in prayer and readiness of matter largely depends upon Bible study. Communion with the written word seems to be a staircase up to communion with the living word.'[7]

These retreats were indispensable for life lived at full stretch, constantly facing new challenges and face to face too with the anxieties of being a worthy ambassador of Christ. In March at Wrexham he wrote: 'I am very anxious about this mission and can only lean on the divine strength for help. The circumstances demand much wisdom, caution, self control. I shall need to be self contained and to withdraw in order to seek a secret pavilion.'[8] In May, before a mission he wrote: 'A great weight came upon my soul today and remained until the night. After all had retired to rest I was compelled to stay up and wrestle in prayer. This continued till about 2 o'clock, Sunday morning, when I felt convinced the Lord had become my helper.'[9]

On the way back from Prestatyn he was impressed with the expansive scenery, with the river through the lovely Towy valley. The thought of a break came over him. No doubt his wife Mary would have reminded him of his resolution on New Year's day 'not to be religious overmuch'. At the end of May he and his wife rested among their old haunts at Pontnewynydd and they felt refreshed together before he was off again on missions in the

Rhondda and Machynlleth. At a mission in Cinderford in the Forest
of Dean open air services were held in different parts of the town
before a procession to the tent. 'One man who came out as a
Christian tonight will pay for the whole mission. He heard us in
the open air and followed to the tent. Hundreds of such cases have
I seen to prove the power of open air work.'

Sad news from Glasgow

At the opening of the 44th Forward Movement Hall in South Wales
– where William Ross also preached – fifty people openly
confessed Christ. 'This is the second time I have proved prayer
effectual in a definite manner this year.' Ross had come to Cardiff
for health treatment at Houghton's Hydropathic Home. Not long
after Seth was deeply saddened when, awaiting a train at Newport
station, he heard the news that 'dear Mr. Ross had passed away at
Glasgow ... he was the most loving man I have ever known and
therefore the most Christian man I have known. Poor Cowcaddens.
There will be tears there. Ross gave them his very life-blood. How
rich was his experience. His voice was not the voice of a novice
on any subject.'[10]

The Llandrindod Convention

As the year wore on a strange unrest and foreboding came over
him, somehow feeling that a change was forthcoming. He had a
long confidential interview with F. B. Meyer in London on 17th
June. 'The result of today's consultation may mean much to me
and to thousands more. Guide me, O thou great Jehovah.'
Thousands? What could he have meant? An intriguing silence rests
over the episode. Seth knew when to draw a curtain over God's
dealings with him as well as to be open. The statement is all the
more tantalizing because in August he attended the second of the
Llandrindod Wells Conventions where the Keswick teaching of F.
B. Meyer would have been warmly embraced by many. But though
Seth had recorded his own gratitude for the personal blessings of
the previous convention, his reactions this time were more reserved.
Again, his remarkable gift of seeing to the heart of things emerges
here. His words could have been written by J. C. Ryle:

'My one fear is that many people are in danger of cultivating holiness at the expense of service. It would be a thousand pities to see people make holiness a substitute for work. Even prayer can be made a substitute for honest work.' 'I am bound to record what appears to me another danger in connexion with the teaching I heard. Not with the doctrine, but with the manner in which the people were invited to reach the experience. I consider it a dangerous thing to become too dogmatic with regard to the steps leading into the blessing of spiritual fullness. My opinion is that this land of milk and honey is reached by many separate paths, and that the Holy Spirit leads into this in his own way. The theory sounds right when you listen to it, but each soul must go onward in his own way. Preach the truth and leave it to God's Spirit.'[12]

His own preparation for preaching at the convention is a model correction for any who are given a platform at any large gathering and are tempted to use it for a veiled ego trip. He certainly had no tendency to allow the 'holiday spirit' to put him into 'entertainment mode'. 'The preparation of the heart is of the Lord. My one desire is to adjust myself rightly – to become passive in the divine hand. Hindrances to service in mental distraction, heart severance and disturbance of spiritual balance can only find their readjustment by the calm which follows whenever there is a passive state obtained through fellowship with Him.' Tempted as he was to select such topics as would be considered popular by the holiday visitors to Llandrindod, he overcame it and preached from the words: 'if any man will come after me, let him deny himself, and take up his cross daily and follow me.' He, the most natural and exuberant of men, became more reticent in conversation 'believing there is a divine art in profitable conversation'. He who had a fund of dramatic conversation stories from his own ministry could write: 'I am thankful to find that my determination to avoid the repetition of stories and tales (without real profit) is now bearing fruit.'[13] It was as if the Lord was preparing him to handle much more dramatic events, and, in some ways, the personally disappointing turn to events that were to come, by bringing him to a place of more selfless servanthood so that he could handle both.

Humility, of course, is not to be confused with a colourless style or presentation. He had a memorable way of getting things across. 'This morning,' he said at the Convention one year, 'I rose early and went for a walk around the lake. The Lord said: "Seth, you are not going to preach that old traveller this morning." "Very well, Lord, give me another text then." "Let this be your text: 'Fear not, thou worm Jacob ... I will help thee'" .... "What about the sermon, Lord? He has given me the sermon also," said Seth to his captivated audience.

'Firstly, the worm need not fear any fall.

'Secondly, the worm has no back to break, etc..'

Sometimes God gives specific messages for specific people. Some time afterward a Liverpool merchant told him that that remarkable sermon at Llandrindod changed him altogether. 'There my proud, stiff back was broken and I thank God.' It was at the year's commencement, shut in by fever, that Seth had felt the power of that text in his own soul. One of the highlights of the Convention was the open air where Seth was especially in his element. After another holiday and ministry at Burry Green, Gower, among a delighted country congregation, he wrote on August 23rd, 'My holiday is now drawing to a close, and I long to *strip* for mission work proper.'[14]

Little did he know what he was stripping for.

Where better to start again than at Neath with dear brother Frank. He spent a fortnight of September 1904 as special missioner at the Mission Hall. Fifteen hundred attended the opening open air meeting on Saturday. He found this time touching as many of the people were his spiritual children from 15–20 years before when he and Frank had been in harness. But these days of celebration and splendour were soon to be surpassed.

CHAPTER EIGHT

THE FULL TIDE OF REVIVAL

On Friday, 16 September 1904, Seth packed his bags yet again, bade his heroic Mary and the children farewell and set out this time for a trip west to New Quay, Newcastle Emlyn and Blaenannerch. 'I shall be away about a fortnight.' As usual he asked the Lord to go with him. The Lord had already gone ahead.

His mind must have been somewhere else, because, experienced traveller though he was, he forgot to change trains at Llandysul and went on to Newcastle Emlyn by mistake. It gave him the chance to have tea with the Rev. Evan Phillips. In view of the events about to unfold and Seth's work with the Forward Movement, there was something symbolic about the encounter. Evan Phillips had been converted during the 1859 revival. He was the grandfather of young Ieuan Phillips, who, some months later, along with his little sister Bethan – Mrs. Martyn Lloyd-Jones to be – were to be put on a train from London to go and stay with their grandparents, in order to experience the 1904 revival for themselves. Some twenty years or so later Lloyd-Jones was to begin his time-honoured ministry at the Forward Movement hall at Aberavon. Some forty years later Ieuan Phillips was to become superintendent of the Forward Movement. Neither Evan nor Seth could have glimpsed any of that as they talked around that tea table, and Seth had one thing in mind. How was he to get to his preaching destination? On his return to Llandysul he boarded a horse-drawn carrier and endured a cold drive of fifteen miles to New Quay. The mishap and the misery hardly foretold the marvels of the morrow.

Evan Roberts – God's instrument

Seth's mission to these Cardiganshire towns that September has become historic. For four years he had prayed definitely that the Lord might take a lad from a rough background like his own, from the coalmine or from the field to revive his work in Wales. He prayed that God would choose an instrument that would humble human pride. Though he did not realize it at the time, this was the week when his ministry was used of God to help set that man ablaze.

It seems that Seth knew nothing on his arrival of an unusually powerful though local spiritual stirring that had accompanied some young people's meetings in Blaenannerch, not far from Newcastle Emlyn, where there was a preparatory school for men training for the ministry. Among them was an ex-coalminer from Loughor – Evan Roberts. When Seth preached there on the first Sunday he became immediately aware of what he called 'a remarkable revival spirit'. 'I have never seen the power of the Holy Spirit so powerfully manifested among the people as at this place just now.'[1]

From then on God was in the midst of his people. Those scriptures that speak of the nearness of God were fulfilled. 'Shout and be glad, O daughter of Zion. For I am coming and I will live among you' (Zech. 2:10).

His diary entries take on a new dimension:

Monday, 19 September. The revival is breaking out here in greater power. Many souls are receiving full assurance of salvation. The spirit of prayer and testimony is falling in a marvellous manner. The young are receiving the greatest measure. They break out into prayer, praise, testimony and exhortation in a wonderful way.

Sept. 20. The revival goes on. I cannot leave the building at New Quay until twelve and even one o'clock in the morning. I have closed the service several times, and yet it would break out again quite beyond the control of human power.

Sept. 21. Several souls. I don't know the number, and they are not drunkards or open sinners [his usual clientele!!] but they are members of the visible church not grafted into the true vine – not joined unto the Lord – not baptized into the Spirit ... They are entering into full assurance of faith, coupled with a baptism of the Holy Spirit. The joy is intense.

Sept. 22. Group after group came out to the front seeking *llawn sicrwydd ffydd* – (the full assurance of faith). Every person engaged in prayer without one exception. The tongue of fire came upon each. We lost all sense of time in this service.

Sept. 23. 'About forty conversions this week. It's as near as I can fix it. I think that those seeking assurance may be fairly counted as converts, for they had never received Jesus as personal Saviour. Being constrained by the people I stayed this evening again, and a precious time we had. The affection and love of the people is touching to behold. I thank God for His blessed time to my own soul. I am saturated, melted, made soft as willing clay in the hands of the potter.'[2]

On Saturday he did not get to bed until 2 a.m. and was up at six to get to Newcastle Emlyn. He had been given to understand that his presence there might not be so welcome and the note of apprehension that sometimes crept in to his willing spirit and consequent cry to God comes through. 'What shall I find there? Lord, come with me for I hear that Thou art kept outside the door in that town as at Laodicea.' At first that seemed to be the case:

Sept. 25. Tried to give them an account of the revival at New Quay, but I broke down under the emotion. There were signs of a deep desire. Nothing has moved as yet. I preached four times today.

Sept. 26. There was a touch of power in the service tonight, and a few moved towards the cross. I find scarcely a soul here in the joy of assurance. It is a pitiable sight to me. When I tested the meeting only a small handful among hundreds would stand up to confess a present salvation. The witness of the church is nothing in this state.

Sept. 27. A large number were blessed this evening. Some students received blessing and confessed salvation. The name of one is Sidney Evans [he was from Gorseinon and as an old man was known to the author. He was later to play a significant part in the revival]. 'The Lord will certainly move this place.'[3]

The way he chose to do so was to be a common means of the spread of the blessing:

> *Sept. 28*. About fifteen young people came from New Quay. I did not preach [a very unusual decision for Seth. It shows how convinced he was that the group from New Quay would convey a genuine experience of God], but I allowed them to pray, sing, exhort as the Holy Spirit led. The fire burned all before it. Many cried out for salvation. Many knelt in their seats, but I cannot know the number. The Master knows.[4]

Then came an even more significant move to Blaenannerch where blessing had begun before Seth had left Cardiff.

> *Sept. 29*. Grand meetings today at Blaenannerch. It was a remarkable thing to hear one young man, Evan Roberts. He caught at the words and prayed 'Bend me, O Lord.'[5]

From his lips it became one of the most frequent prayers throughout Wales in the days ahead. Seth's ministry had been blessed to Evan Roberts at the crucial time in his dealings with God. Sure now that revival had come, Seth wrote to Mrs. Penn-Lewis, describing 'the cloud as a man's hand' which was coming over Wales. On 9 November, 1904, she began a regular contribution in *The Life of Faith*, chronicling the advance of the blessing.

When Seth returned home to Cardiff from west Wales his first thoughts in the diary, even after such halcyon days, were for the family: 'All my dear ones well after these days on mission work.'[6]

From now on the young ex-miner, Evan Roberts, who returned to Loughor soon after Seth's meetings, was urgent and compelling in his desire to win Wales for Christ. In retrospect it seems a strange providence that the younger man, with immense power under God throughout the whole land, should have been burned out in the next eighteen months and become a recluse for the rest of his long life, whereas the older man, strong as an ox, mature, experienced, balanced, spiritually anointed, a preacher of enormous power and evangelistic fruitfulness, with still twenty years of fire and faithfulness to the truth ahead of him, should have become a secondary figure in the spreading fire of the revival.

Seth, however, was deeply conscious that God had given what he had prayed for. A lad from the mine had been raised up to humble human pride. And when Seth had prayed, 'O Lord, give me Wales', God had instead given it to the young man decisively blessed through Seth's ministry. 'And now,' Seth wrote as the revival spread, 'he who sows and he who reaps can rejoice and say, "Not to us, O Lord, not to us, but to Thy name be glory, for the sake of Thy mercy and truth." '[7]

For a generation or more after this time, 'Evan Roberts was the prime mover of events in a multitude of lives – the miner's son who became a doctor, the steelworker who became a minister, the schoolboy who still remembered.' Loughor was to become a place of pilgrimage from all over the world.

The continuing work of revival

But don't get it wrong. Seth certainly was not set aside. We have still much to see of his exploits. Generally speaking the revival had not had much effect in North Wales in the first month or so. But by the beginning of November 1904 Seth and Frank were in Llandudno town hall. They began taking converts out into the streets to invite friends in. He noted over fifty saved, with crowds turned away. The Presbyterian magazine *Y Goleuad* observed that their prayers to the Lord to have compassion on the people had borne fruit.

Back home in Cardiff he went from his home at 28 Talbot Street to his favourite patch at Sophia Gardens, near where the Glamorgan Cricket ground now is. He wrote on 18 November: 'This path alongside the River Taff has become sacred to me. I have seen the hawthorn blossom three years in succession, and fade again, as I have prayed along its shady path. I have wrestled for a personal baptism of the Spirit, and for a national revival. It has come and I rejoice.'[8]

The Ammanford meetings were a high point:

20-27 November. This has been one of the most remarkable days of my life. Even in the first morning meeting a number were led to embrace the Saviour. In the afternoon the blessing fell upon scores. At seven the crush was very great – a surging mass. Some most remarkable conversions. Impossible to count. At one time in the service there was a hush such as I shall never forget. The power was divine.... Again the people sang in the streets, and the service went on till nearly midnight, although the snow lay thick on the ground. *Diolch I Dduw*.[9]

Nantlais Williams, the young minister of Bethany Welsh Calvinistic Methodist Church, Ammanford, only very recently converted himself, found Seth's ministry to be crucial in providing a spiritual shepherd for the scores of converts. He noted that Seth knew every spiritual step in the spiritual life 'from the sawdust of the taproom to the heavenly places in Christ Jesus'. He benefited himself from the quality of Seth's ministry and was to follow his example in defending clearly basic biblical doctrines that were under attack.

Then, moving on to Llandeilo and marching through the town before a meeting at the town hall, he caught a chill which led to a highly debilitating illness. He writes: 'I went straight to bed upon arriving back at Ammanford. Very ill today. Temperature 103. I find myself talking, singing and praying while in a half-awake condition.'[10] He was ill for three weeks with influenza and tonsilitis. Mary came to Ammanford and took him home to Cardiff. It was a hard blow and he had painful struggles over the strange providence of being out of the fray when such blessing was engulfing the land.

Saturday, 10 December. Every day I have been able to read of the Revival going on. The Holy Spirit is doing wonders. Satan has made many a special mark on me recently. Fearful conflicts. His fiery darts have pierced my armour at every point. The coward has been fighting me on my back.[11]

But by 14th December he was up on his feet again and rejoicing especially that the revival had come to Cardiff. Dr Charles Davies, the minister of Tabernacle Welsh Baptist Church, The Hayes, the city centre area where Seth had held the open-airs ten years before, invited Seth to exhort the people in the after-meeting. Over fifty came to Christ. It marked the point for Seth of the beginning of revival blessing in the city. At a further meeting at Tabernacle two days later the church suddenly emptied: 'at one given moment [by an inspiration] the great congregation poured out into the street to sing, pray and speak. I have never seen such a sight in my life.'

Now well into his stride again he decided to travel to Loughor and Gorseinon where Evan Roberts had burst upon the public scene and which were, in that sense, the cradle of the revival. On the way he called at Neath and rejoiced with Frank. Up to five hundred people had professed conversion through the Mission Hall and it saw another long-term leap in the numbers attending and the building up of the church.

Gorseinon fulfilled his expectations: 'Held a blessed meeting. Wonderful fire.' On Sunday he led three: 'I can't describe the power and the liberty in these services. At times it is overwhelming.'[12] At Brynteg Chapel where John Penry and Henry Rees Penry were two of the earliest revival converts (Christian teachers of mine in their later lives), Seth had a very strange experience. It has added interest in view of the fact that the chapel turned against the revival and its converts some time later. 'A prominent man stood up at the start of the service and declared that he had prayed that the Holy Spirit should not come to that service. "Try to get the Holy Spirit," he said. "I will go outside and when you have failed I will come back in, and the Spirit will come." He went outside and a wonderful sight I saw. The people confessed Christ on every hand. Prayer, praise and testimony and prayer flowed without stop for over two hours. Glory be to God.'[13] The following night showed no bad influence, 'and great liberty came to the people to follow the promptings of the Holy Spirit. It is impossible to watch these wonderful scenes and not remember the apostolic times in the church as described in 1 Corinthians. Most of those gifts are to be observed.'[14]

The following night was of particular interest to Seth, it being now three months since that eventful night when he had heard Evan Roberts pray 'Bend me, Lord' in Blaenannerch.

22 December 1904. A most profitable service tonight in Moriah Chapel, Loughor ... this is the chapel in which the revival began in this part of south Wales, and in which Evan Roberts first began to declare his experiences.[15]

The following evening Seth gave the story of his conversion in Moriah. 'Strange to say I was able to speak at one time in Welsh, translating from English into Welsh. It came naturally.'[16]

With Christmas Eve upon him he was off home. His heart lifted as many trains passed him laden with colliers going home for Christmas. 'In every compartment they were singing the hymns of the revival. No drinking and no swearing.'[17] Seth esteemed the miner. 'I think the collier a fine type of man, with the exception of the drunkards and the blasphemers, I believe the colliers to be the finest body of working men in Great Britain.' It can safely be said that many colliers would travel far to hear Seth preach the gospel.

If the colliers had Christmas Day off, not so Seth. He preached at Barry Dock, beginning a week-long mission, 'but never did I have a harder day. Against wind and tide all day.'[18] He snatched a family time on Saturday, New Year's Eve, holding a watchnight service at home at which young Peter was present. They reconsecrated themselves to the Lord's service. At the close of 1904, he wrote, 'God be praised for the most wonderful year. It has been the most fruitful in conversions of all past years, and in personal experience the richest of all. Answers to prayer have strewn the pathway. Definite answers.'[19]

On New Year's Day, 1905, blessing began to flow at Barry Dock. 'I enjoyed a good day and preached with freedom. In the evening service three people came to the front. The prayer of one man when he found the light was touching. Thus the Lord has stooped to use me at the start of another year.'

The next day he was joined by 'Dr Pugh and his brother Edward, who had been converted at Crwys Hall, Cardiff, on Sunday night. He told me he had seen a vision of his family in heaven, all complete except himself; and his mother called him, saying, "Come, Edward, we are all here except you." This broke him down and he came.'[20] There were several examples of vision experiences leading to genuine conversion during the revival.[21]

Seth's greatest desire was to see the revival take a strong hold in Cardiff. He was encouraged by the signs, but his best expectations were not realized. On 3rd January he preached at

Salem Church in Canton which 'was indeed a revival meeting'. A unique entry the following day speaks of his wife Mary going to Tabernacle, the Hayes, with him. It was one of the advantages of a growing family and Seth preaching in Cardiff. 'Wonderful audience and many conversions. It is indeed blessed to see the Revival going on so powerfully. Cardiff will certainly be moved before long. The flame is burning in six or seven churches now.'[22]

But revival, because it is a time of heightened responses, could also show more overt opposition to the offence of the cross than in less intense times. Sometimes this could show itself in passive resistance, sometimes in active. In Pembroke Terrace Church, Cardiff, Seth 'felt a hindrance. The older people do not throw themselves into the tide of blessing, and the young are timid to move. I was helped to speak to them on the conditions of receiving the Holy Spirit.' When he returned to Salem, Canton, the next day 'there was much opposition and most bitter scoffing.'[23] A spiritual battle was on right there in the church. 'But,' commented Seth in a revealing phrase, 'the power over-ruled. The meeting was not fruitless, two men came out for Christ.'[24]

A day or so later there was a similar encounter in Hoylake, North Wales. On Sunday the 8th of January he wrote: 'a divine touch came into the 6.30 meeting when three or four stood for Jesus. Also at the 8 pm meeting the power fell upon many and there were surely fifteen conversions.'[25]

But the enemy of souls hit back the following night. 'At one time there was a strong satanic power among several young people. They laughed and scoffed among themselves and yet many were sobered before the end.'[26]

A fortnight later, when he was back in Cardiganshire and God met them and they knew extraordinary times, he encountered a different barrier to blessing.

I had liberty to preach from the last clause in Leviticus 17:11. About thirty people came forward, when the people showed signs of vulgar curiosity. The Holy Spirit was grieved and left us in great darkness. I was utterly broken down and wept. After about an hour the people who grieved the Spirit gradually went away and about 11 pm a mighty rush of power came back. A crowd of sinners came weeping to the cross. Everything broke up into praise, prayer and great thankfulness. This experience taught me many secret things of the Spirit.[27]

On one occasion at Rhyl, when it seemed as though the power had left him, Seth found it was his own attitude over a fruitless evening that had to be dealt with. After a night of no conversions he wrote with a keen regard for a right spirit within him: 'Very disappointing; I feel dreadfully heavy of heart when a service passes without conversions. Hard to preach, hard to pray and hard to restrain an outburst of testimony against the unspiritual state of the church. Love must conquer. Love must guide. Lord, forgive me if my words burned in the heat of any other passion.'

Then, in late January, another incident occurred which saw Seth goaded into further passionate response. It was just after he had ceased to keep a diary, and in days when he seemed to be borne along by powers not his own. But that did not prevent a direct and public rebuttal of one of his preaching aims – to bring church members from a position of nominal belief to a personal acceptance of Jesus as Saviour and a consequent assurance of salvation. The incident, ominous for the future of the revival, occurred in Tabernacle Church, Cardigan. The minister there was the Rev. Dr Moelwyn Hughes (1866–1944). He had received a masters degree and a doctorate from the University of Leipzig in Germany. When Seth preached in Tabernacle he asked, in his customary manner, for all those certain of their salvation to stand up. Few did so and Moelwyn Hughes, the minister, intervened, saying 'that he was representing the feeling among the deacons of the church' that 'many of them were believers but they could not be certain of salvation'. Seth, long used to taking on the interrupter in open-air debate, could not resist taking on the learned doctor. There ensued a dispute between them about the 'doctrine of assurance' which was not brought to an end until one of the deacons intervened.

Whether or not it was wise or right for Seth to endeavour to persuade the minister of his error before his own congregation, Seth was the one in line with the Confession of Faith (article 33) of his own church,[28] and he was deeply worried that membership based on nominal belief was eating at the heart of the church's effective witness before the world (recall his entry for 26 September). He was to have further opposition in Cardigan as we shall see.

In his January report to *The Torch* he touches on a related topic. 'In our intellectual pride we have been making the pulpit a kind of professor's chair from which to preach the ethics of Christianity. We are trying to reach men's natures from without. This revival has produced better ethical results in one day than we have done since the day when this false light led us astray.'[29]

By the end of January 1905, his discipline in keeping to a diary in such hectic times fell away. But not before we have cameos of him enjoying a rest day on a farm where they caught fifteen rabbits. One whole precious day and evening he spent with the children. Another day to be remembered was when a whole family of six came to the Lord at Hoylake. Across the border in Liverpool he found things 'exactly like our Welsh revival. The same spirit, the same fruit and the very same manifestations.'

He had fellowship with other significant Christian leaders: 'At Liverpool I visited Torrey's meetings [Dr R. A. Torrey, the American evangelist]. He asked me to give them an account of the work in Wales'; 'Went to Pontypridd. Spent much time with Gypsy Smith. Took the overflow service in the evening. Gypsy is having a wonderful mission. Praise God.'[30]

His diary ends on a note of quite breathtaking spiritual splendour back in New Quay, the town of his first touch of the day of God's power that he was still enjoying. As the first time, he arrived late, though for more serious reasons.

Saturday, 21 January. Journey to New Quay. On the way from Llandysul the van upset on a steep hill covered with ice. We were nine persons in a covered van, and were all upset. It was a most providential escape.

Sunday, 22 January. Wonderful day today. Yes! One of the days of the Lord upon earth. Scores sought full assurance. The people prayed and praised as I have never seen done before.

Monday, 23 January. Tonight there was a wonderful scene in the Tabernacle chapel. Indescribable is the only word I can use. Even in the afternoon at 2.30, a crowd came seeking the blessing, but at night it was a general breakdown. About fifty or sixty came forward and all prayed aloud. The congregation also broke out in audible prayer. People praised aloud in all parts of the chapel. I shall never forget the sight. 'Praise the Lord, O my soul.'[31]

Then on the following day came the earlier quoted incident of 'vulgar curiosity' when a huge overflowing crowd turned up having heard of the blessing of the previous night. But the full tide could not be held back as Seth describes.

> *Wednesday, 25 January.* We have had indescribable meetings. It would be impossible to record in writing the scenes witnessed. Hundreds are blessed. The power at times overwhelmed strong men. It will never fade from my memory. Over and over again the front became crowded with weeping, praying people, especially old people. Praise the Lord, O my soul.[32]

On Thursday we leave him, still wisely and obediently preaching the word of God in a time when some other leaders had sadly left off amidst the surges and upheavals of deep emotions. 'Today's two meetings were even more wonderful than those of yesterday. The power swept the chapel. God gave me power to preach on the house built upon the sand, "and it fell" etc. Crowd after crowd of seekers came to the front, while the great congregation burst out into shouts of praise. It was like a boiling sea. Hallelujah! My soul is melted like wax.'[33]

Those are the final diary entries. But the closing of the diary does not draw a final veil over his personal reflections. In a shoe box in the Bristol Office of the Overcomers Movement in 1995 there came to light a few of Seth's letters written to Mrs. Jessie Penn-Lewis. Mrs. Penn-Lewis had been born in Neath in 1861 into a middle-class Calvinistic Methodist family. Her father was a civil engineer and her grandfather a Calvinistic Methodist minister. Because it had English speaking classes, she attended Sunday school at the church of John Griffiths, rector of St David's. For a woman of frailty she kept up an astonishing ministry in Europe, Russia, the States and India. She was influential in the work of the YWCA and Keswick, and was a prime mover behind the beginning of Keswick in Wales, though she cut her links later with the Keswick movement. She is most identified with the Overcomers Movement. She also became a close friend of Evan Roberts and cared for him at her home after his dramatic exit from public life. She stressed the experimental side of the cross and the Spirit. Seth, who became increasingly unhappy with excessive subjectivity of holiness teaching such as Penn-Lewis advocated, nevertheless had a sympathetic correspondence with her over the period of the revival. He wrote from Aberporth on 12 July, 1905, in between visits to Aberporth and Cardigan.

Dear Mrs. Lewis,
A most gracious work has broken out in this quaint Cardiganshire town or village. It is a little over a mile from Blaenannerch and there are many small places not far away. The people gather from far and near, so that the blessing is carried into adjoining districts. The fire had not reached this place although it had burned in other churches not far away. On Sunday there were a few touches of life, but on Monday the cloud broke when over two hundred came forth to the front to bend, weep, pray and confess. Now you could not call these converts – and yet it is with us as in Scotland [he had recently been there, of which more later] – the churches are full of nominal Christians whose lips have never been opened in prayer or testimony, and who believe that assurance of salvation is not possible in human experience. Last night again the meeting took the form of passionate prayer, and for a long time it was like the noise of many waters. If you refer at all to this you will know how to distinguish between these scenes and that of out-and-out sinners at a penitent form. These people know their Bibles and live simple, unworldly lives but they lack vital religion. They lack the knowledge of a personal Jesus and a personal baptism. But see how real Jesus is – here is a translation of a young woman's testimony: 'The flowers speak to me of Him now, the leaves of the trees whisper to me His name, the mountains seem to talk to me about Him. I listen by the brook and the water sings to me about Him and so do the birds. It is Jesus everywhere now.'
    You notice the poetry of it and the pathos. Add to this a pathos indescribable in the voice, a tenderness in the eyes of the speaker and tears like dew drops falling, you have a picture over which the angels weep.[34]

It is difficult to recall that the man rejoicing like this was known as Satan in his early work days, a boxer on the Monmouth circuit, and a bundle of uneducated trouble till Christ claimed his drifting young life.

Seth also reported on this trip in his 'Notes from my diary' in *The Torch*. Except for the problem of drunkenness among some church members, he writes in a more general way for the public eye.

Again the swing of the arm of providence brings me to this beloved county. At Aberporth we hear again the lap of the waves of Cardigan Bay, and there are golden sunsets in the sea. Nature is at its best here. From the outset the meetings were a success and in every service there were tokens of pentecostal fire. Silent believers received personal baptism and became eloquent in prayer. Grave clothes were removed from the risen Lazarus, and the voice of praise rang out. Barren fig trees received sap to bring forth the fruit of thanksgiving. I am confident that a tide came into these services and lasting fruit will follow. There was no opposition, no jarring note and no rocks to avoid in this place. The only painful thing I discovered was that a few good-natured men drank, at times, to excess, and yet were permitted to take part in Christian service. This should not be. For the sake of the church and for their own sakes it should not be; where these things exist there must be a need of a quickened conscience, and of a spiritual conception of what holiness means. God grant that this revival may bring this to every church. As many as could fill the vestry came forward to bend one evening, and these continued in prayer for a long time.[35]

A devastation of spirit

Yet what opposite extremes of experience high times of God's dealings with us can bring! Cardigan was his next call. Before going he summarized in a letter to Mrs. Penn-Lewis what he saw the stress of his ministry to be in these revival times among churches where formal adherence to the faith was widespread, but where confidence in salvation and confession of Christ were widely absent. 'My work is clear. My message is that of assurance, and a call to open confession by coming out before men. Here Satan is entrenched. It is a fight against long standing prejudice and spiritual ignorance. So far I have been kept' (Letter from Seth Joshua to Mrs. Jessie Penn-Lewis, 12 July, 1905).

As it turned out, this further trip to Cardigan brought a devastation of spirit. He is unable to share the details, but what he does write makes this the most disturbing note ever left us by Seth and seems to hide a battle more severe than he had ever fought in a boxing ring!

At once I was conscious of being in troubled waters – the devil put up barbed wire in all directions.... My spirit had no rest; it was perfect agony, so much so that I was obliged to beg the Rev. P. Morgan, Blaenannerch to allow me to sleep at his home. I cannot give the details of all this – they are written in the book of judgement – let them stay there *for a time.* 'Judgement is mine. I will repay says the Lord.'

The revival withers on the doorstep of some of our churches because of the attitude of a few! In the face of all this we saw victory, but the fire was largely imported. It came in the young people from Cilgeran, Llechryd and Blaenannerch. What a change again at Capel Drindod. Here in the midst of the hay harvest, the people filled the chapel until very late every evening. They were tender services; not one rock to bump against and a calm pervaded everything. At Cardigan they mocked us beneath the window as we prayed and sang in an upper room, but in Capel Drindod it would be impossible to find men to do it.[36]

In an earlier letter to Mrs. Penn-Lewis, sometime in March, which records neither date nor place of writing (was it Leicester?) we again see his exhausting work rate and his continuing humility in the midst of success.

You really must forgive me for not coming over to Great Glen. I have not had an hour to spare all week They have really worked me too hard and I am feeling very tired out today. Never more so.

Yesterday was a wonderful day indeed. Even at 10.45 am this big chapel was crowded and through the day it was a mighty crush. So people came to Christ and were dealt with by a body of the best workers I have seen among seeking souls. 300 people have been dealt with this past week. I hear that some 50 came out at Melbourne

Hall last night and 20 at the YMCA. Today is my last day.... I am at Colwyn Bay from March 18-25. Kindly remember me. On Wednesday and Thursday we have a conference at Pontypridd for Ministers, and Dr Pierson is there with us, and I have promised to take some part there in consequence of the unfortunate illness of Mr. Inwood.

I shrink from this for I feel my unfitness, being only knee deep in the river at the best.

With kindest regards to your dear husband though a stranger to me.[37]

This correspondence with Mrs. Penn-Lewis in the later stages of the revival gives us another glimpse of what was going on in Seth's personal walk with God. 'Never shall I forget the experiences of the past five years, and of the last two in particular. Outwardly my cross has been light, my crushing was an inward one. Now I am becoming a most lonely man. He leads me into a kind of wilderness. Bless God for the sands of the desert and Jesus.'[38] 'I hope we may meet some day that I may compare notes with you as to my inner experiences lately. I fear to speak of them publicly. It is dangerous these days to speak too freely. Never was Satan so on the alert.'[39]

Revival and Evangelism

We have now had sufficient evidence from Seth's past four months to notice some of the differences between evangelism and revival. In Seth Joshua we have a vastly experienced evangelist who had constantly seen large numbers of conversions in the missions he had led.[40] But, up until his trip to New Quay it had always been in the context of meetings organized around a start and finish time and with very little, if any, alerting of the congregation as a whole into spiritual realities. Now God was intervening in a more direct manner. People felt the immediacy of it. It was he who was in control. Constantly people observed how time seemed to stand still so that the customary decision to close a meeting with prayer was overturned time and again by a resurgence of praise or testimony or weeping or confession. A depth of experience of the love and holiness and power of God came overwhelmingly upon people who had been Christians for years. People had a high awareness of the presence of God. In his evangelism Seth had for years seen God use his preached word powerfully to the salvation of many. But here Seth, although a participator and preacher, was mainly aware of being an observer of God at work. Revival shows God present and at work among his own people and upon a community too. In evangelism it is man who is the subject and the doer, dependent though he always is upon God giving the increase. But in revival God is the subject, man is the object. God himself acts, restoring his church to life and to an awareness of fellowship that was hardly evident before.

CHAPTER NINE

REVIVAL REPERCUSSIONS

Seth at Keswick, in Scotland, at Llandrindod and in the USA
Like most preachers Seth had unfulfilled ambitions. In July 1905, he wrote to Mrs. Jessie Penn-Lewis, telling her of his invitation to stay at the Keswick Convention with a party of Scots Presbyterian ministers. The Rev. D. M. Mcintyre of Glasgow, who was married to the daughter of Dr Andrew Bonar,[1] the biographer of Robert Murray McCheyne, had invited some United Free Church ministers to join them: 'Thus, after many years of heart desire the Lord has opened a way to this great convention of ten thousand believers.'

This had not entailed any plans for speaking, of course. In those early Edwardian days the Keswick platform was the preserve of people of a very different background from Seth's rough origins.

But, as we shall see, the revival dictated otherwise!

In Seth's report on the convention in *The Torch*, he first felt it necessary to reassure readers about the teaching at Keswick as regards any liberal tendencies such as were beginning to appear in some of the ministers of his own denomination. 'No Welshman need have any fear of Keswick on doctrinal grounds. It stands with unflinching attitude for the deity of Christ, the inspiration of the Book, the all sufficiency of the atonement and the personality of the Holy Spirit.'[2]

Seth was also happier than one might expect with the way it presented teaching on sanctification. Though Keswick was recognized by many as a potent spiritual influence, apprehension had been expressed during the Welsh Presbyterian English Conference of 1900 about some Keswick speakers 'who tended to look down from some towering eminence of experience and attainment upon other poor creatures. The true saint of God is the last to know of his own superiority.'[3] J. C. Pollock's history of Keswick shows that its leaders were well aware of these pitfalls at this period and sought to discourage such manifestations of super-spirituality. Seth certainly had no truck with any kind of cant. In his customary manner of openness to new experiences he listened for himself and made his own judgement:

> The teaching on holiness is sane, practical and scriptural. The suggestion that sinless perfection is a plank in their platform is one of the lies of Satan. Victory over known sin is certainly preached as a possible present experience. This is taught as being dependent on total surrender – faith in the blood, with instant and constant obedience to the guidance of the divine Spirit. You can feel no shock from the doctrinal side of Keswick.[4]

The 1905 Convention was a unique event in its own history due to the arrival of a large number of Welsh people and ministers who were experiencing the revival. The exceptional effects of the presence of this Welsh contingent caused a major debate both during and after the Convention. Seth was the only one of the Welshmen to speak from the platform and his personal memories are of special interest when compared with observations made by other leading speakers in *The Life of Faith*. He wrote:

> The prevailing note of Keswick was revival. It rang out in prayer, conversation, song and testimony. The swell and heave of the tide could be felt in everything. A large number of Welshmen were present and they were gloriously used of God among the people. The leaders of the platform were aware of it but there was evident timidity as to consequences. Several times the tide rolled in and threatened to carry away every preconceived plan, but the check kept back the tide until the last night. It was indescribable.[5]

One of the convention speakers who did try to describe the event was Dr A. T. Pierson.[6] During July 1905 he did a brief speaking tour of South Wales, visiting various centres where there were still revival evidences. He was 'deeply impressed' with what he saw and time and again his Bible expositions stirred congregations. He came to Keswick fresh from this experience. In *The Life of Faith* for August 1905, he wrote:

Certainly, after thirty years, something comparatively new has been seen at Keswick. There are two opinions already 'in the air'. One is that it was an impulsive, if not impetuous outbreak of Welsh emotionalism that became infectious and rapidly swept through the convention. Another is that the same Spirit of God who has moved so mightily in Wales, stirred those great audiences in the Keswick tents. Personally, I am entirely confident that we have had, not a visitation of Welshmen, so much as a visitation of God.... We thank God for the deputation from Wales. The brethren that came up were from the centres of the great revival and themselves God's appointed leaders in it. Such men as Rev. Seth Joshua; Professor Keri Evans[7], Rev. Owen M. Owen of Merthyr, Rev. W. S. Jones of Llwynypia and others came from revival scenes in their own churches. Apart from the special meeting on Tuesday afternoon, given up to testimony as to the Welsh Revival, only one of them spoke in the meetings; but they prayed ...[8]

Seth tells us of the Tuesday meeting. 'The tears, the laughter and the glow of that Tuesday remained as a benediction throughout the week. The Lord wonderfully honoured the Welshmen that day. I was given two opportunities to speak to the people.' There had obviously been misgivings among many as to what visibility, if any, should be given to the Welsh visitors. Rev. J. B. Figgis, one of the speakers, in an article headed *Diolch Iddo* (i.e. 'Thanks be to Him', the oft repeated congregational response at revival meetings) describes the background.

At the preliminary meeting of the convention, one of the speakers most valued amongst us had pleaded with might and main for a welcome for the revival. If there was a doubt that night whether he had done wisely, that doubt seemed to be dispelled next day at that wonderful afternoon meeting, when the Welsh pastors gave their testimony. We felt like the disciples of old – 'Who were we that we should fight against God?' The meeting, some thought, was too short. It would be simple ingratitude to God and man not to acknowledge that the new atmosphere the divine Spirit created owed its development largely to the Welsh revival and the testimonies borne to that wonderful work of grace. We pity the man who could remain unmoved while one bore witness that he and his fellow countrymen 'were like unto them that dream'. 'The devil had made me doubt the Atonement, then the Incarnation; and even God became merely a postulate. God brought me back to Him and back to Wales ... but I was still wanting something... Then the power of God came and laid me at his feet. It altered my preaching.'[9]

Seth was the only Welshman who spoke from the platform. It was not a scheduled talk. Seth tells how it came about. 'The Rev. Luce of Gloucester took me aside and told me the Lord had revealed it to him that he was to ask me to speak in his place.' J. J. Luce, MA, a parish vicar, had already visited Wales to test for himself what was happening in some of the storm centres of the revival. 'I saw no trace of extravagance or fanaticism.' His willingness to stand aside for Seth was based on confidence that the work was of God. The invitation 'greatly humbled me for two reasons,' said Seth.

First of all I saw my unworthiness; secondly I saw the deep humility of an aged vicar willing to obliterate himself. Just imagine our [Welsh Presbyterian] Association preachers taking the young preachers of Wales by the hand saying, 'We have decided to step aside in order to allow the Holy Spirit to use you in our place'. Would that not be an ethical fruit worth looking at?[10]

Seth used his platform opportunity to plead for the dropping of barriers to the Spirit's work. Figgis wrote:

At the meeting after Mr. Davies had sung 'When I survey the wondrous cross', Mr. Seth Joshua rose and said, 'There are breezes blowing from Calvary; shall we receive or refuse them? God can send a universal revival when we take away the stone... There are places in Wales where the Revival is shut out because they want it all in their own chapels.' Who could resist his calls to repentance, these appeals to charity toward one another, all punctuated by shouts of '*Diolch Iddo*' and made very real by the scenes of the last twelve months in Wales?[11]

On the following Wednesday night, the Keswick convention had an entirely novel experience when the main meeting was prolonged till 3.00 a.m. Dr Pierson stayed on in the tent to help guide a prayer meeting which many Welsh members had asked for. He noted at the start that 'some tumultuous elements were at work. There was, perhaps, undue noise, some intemperate speech and slight tendency to a fanatical spirit such as beget not order but confusion'. This element, however, 'voluntarily withdrew' according to Pierson,

and till 3.00 a.m. there was one anthem of prayer and confession and praise in which, though we passed from major to minor keys and reversely, there was heard not one discordant note! For three hours there was not a break in spontaneous exercises varied in character, but all uplifting and helpful, oftentimes half a dozen on their feet at once, yet no disorder. While some are trying to account for this by human psychology, we are constrained to look for explanation to Divine Pneumatology, as John Owen calls it.[12]

Then the Friday night brought another evidence of a new work of God. Dr Pierson was a Presbyterian, and one of the few Americans to speak at Keswick. He had been pastor at Spurgeon's Tabernacle from 1891 to 1893 and had then gone to teach at Moody Bible Institute. He tells how, on Friday afternoon, a company of about thirty had met on Skiddaw hillside for prayer. They had definitely asked that the Holy Spirit would sweep through the meeting in power, setting aside the appointed speakers, if he pleased, compelling confession of definite sins, bursting through all needless restraints of fixed programme, leading to boldness of testimony and keeping down all disorderly elements. Every specific request made that afternoon on the hillside was fulfilled to the letter, wrote Pierson. Seth was at that prayer meeting. 'We spent the afternoon with dear Dr Pierson on the mountain of prayer. We had asked the Lord to sweep away every barrier to the *outflow* of the tide and the dear aged brother said Amen with us.'[13]

Pierson describes how the first platform speaker for the evening, Rev. E. W. Moore, had spoken on the 'Ordeal of Fire' (1 Corinthians 3:11-15).

> I felt God's refining fire going through me, revealing the wood, hay and stubble of work and motive. When I rose to speak, so humbling and overwhelming was this conviction that it was quite involuntary that I should first of all make my confession. I did so[14] and asked others who, like me, had felt conscious of God's direct dealing, to stand with me before God as those who then and there besought him to refine us now, that worthless material might not accumulate against the coming day of Fire.... The whole tent full of people rose as one man ... not one word of the proposed address was ever delivered.... I stood there on my feet for about two hours and a half, witnessing the Holy Spirit's wondrous working. Scarcely any human guidance was needed. Christ was in the chair. A soldier confessed to desertion and theft and left the tent to write out his confession, and some of us saw later on the letters he had written. A commander in the Navy declared his purpose to make his ship a floating Bethel. Not less than fifty clergy, evangelists and leaders in Christian work confessed to sins of avarice, ambition, appetite, lust of applause, neglect of the Word, of prayer, of souls; there were hundreds of other individual confessions. No improper word was spoken ... Seldom has any such scene been witnessed by anyone now living. God moved in wholly unexpected ways and no one could think of interfering ... we closed with 'Coronation' and 'Diadem' ... with the profound sense that God had visited His people.[15]

Seth shares his reaction to that never-to-be-forgotten night. 'Dr Pierson was quick to see the hand of the Spirit and threw away his address. Never did he serve God more wisely. In that one act he revealed his inner character.' Seth viewed the spontaneous response of the huge congregation as 'the outflow of life. The inflow had been so gracious that the mighty mass of saved and sanctified humanity needed an open door of utterance. I found myself shouting over and over again this text: "And they overcame him by the blood of the Lamb and the word of their testimony." God is my witness that I am writing in tears at the very memory of it.'[16]

The Keswick records give no details of this dimension of the 1905 Convention.

Scotland once more

Seth was no stranger to the train journey north to Scotland. He valued his links. In a letter to Mrs. Penn-Lewis he tells how touched he had been when a letter came inviting him to visit the General Assembly in Edinburgh. 'They desire me for ten days, and this will throw open doors.'

As much as he enjoyed stimulus from Christian gatherings Seth was primarily an evangelist, a hunter of souls, and not essentially a conference speaker at all. From Keswick, Seth passed on up to Scotland for a brief evangelistic mission in Callander. There were also meetings at Alloa and Bridge of Allan. On 31st July he sent an open card, post-marked Callander, to Mrs. Jessie Penn-Lewis. Mrs. Penn-Lewis had spoken at a women's meeting in the convention. Rarely can a postman have read such a card:

> The fire still sweeps over my soul in waves after that Keswick Pentecost. I can laugh, I can cry, sing, shout, just as the fire moves me. Something has broken in my nature, something is crucified. I am ashes – *Dim ond llwch y llawr* ('nothing but the dust of the earth') – Praise the Lord. Watch my soul, for a wilderness may not be far away. We had a prayer meeting for Scotland in the train on our way to Glasgow. Scotland is to have it. Joshua.[17]

Glorious things were happening in his life and how he celebrated and rejoiced in God. But Seth was never triumphalist. He knew his nature and the likely trials ahead. Thus his humility and the note of caution too in that card. His ministry at Alloa, which he entered into through his friend D. M. Mcintyre, reminded him that not all would take to the fire. He found, as he had in Wales, that the Presbyterian church was full of unawakened, nominal members. In a letter to John Pugh he wrote:

> My one burden at Alloa was to bear a message to the churches. A mighty opening came there. The spiritual condition was simply lamentable. Sinners were converted and backsliders restored, but the bulk of the work lay among nominal Christians. Hundreds of them

came out to the front, many in a broken condition of heart. Over two
hundred did at one meeting, one hundred and fifty at another. Please
do not use this in the shape I give it to you should you ever refer to
my work there. You might refer to it in general terms. I am getting to
tremble at publicity of results. In a letter Dr Moffat informed Rev. D.
M. McIntyre that a clerical member of the Bridge of Allan Committee
has resigned on account of the irregular proceedings on the day we
met there. I suppose this explains what Mr. Hamilton whispered to
me after that breakdown. He said, 'And now the devil will kick.'[18]

By breakdown he probably means public evidence of
brokenness of spirit shown by many in the meetings, which to
formal eyes would have appeared irregular. In a touch of humour
about the rumpus he wrote to Mrs. Penn-Lewis – 'You are as much
to blame as I am!'[19]

In his public report in *The Torch*, Seth confines himself to the
positive side of the visit:

The meetings here ended with gracious showers. I think the Scotch
are a great people to move in a body. They are clannish in religious
habits as in most other things. They hang together in a wonderful
way. It was therefore a blessed sight to see great crowds move out to
the front at the same moment. It was not possible to deal with people
individually. The work was beyond human power, and so the bulk of
those who came forward to pray could only be left to themselves, to
their tears and prayers.[20]

A familiar friend is missing from these Scottish events. William
Ross would have delighted so much in these exceptional days of
visitation from his Welsh friends, touched now as they were with
that baptism of fire he so prayed for.

Llandrindod Convention, August 1905

In August, Seth joined the Forward Movement team at the Keswick
in Wales Convention. John Pugh found it helpful to have his
workers mix there and get more widely known as well as it
providing them a holiday and a refreshing ministry. Each year this
benefit came as a result of the generosity of Mrs. Davies of

Llandinam. With Wales still in revival the third conference attracted people like moths to a flame. Brynmor Jones captures the atmosphere:

> They flocked in from every part of Wales but more especially from the thickly populated mining valleys. They came to share and impart their own rich experiences of revival days and they came to receive every possible bit of instruction. As one man said, 'We were like bees looking for honey.' So great was the demand that five men shared each bedroom in the lodgings and over large parties filled each guesthouse to bulging. Then the excitement was further intensified by the arrival of a large party who had been to the main Keswick and had caused quite a stir there ... many gave thanks to God for such an 'exhilarating visitation'. In this spirit the Welshmen came back to Llandrindod and were greeted on the station by crowds of believers, who were expecting some still greater climax.[21]

At one meeting Evan Roberts rebuked the people so starkly about the lack of love and reconciliation in the churches that many broke down. Roberts himself again felt the power of Seth's ministry as he had done at Blaenannerch. Pugh tells the story.

> The powerful sermon which preceded the Communion by the Rev. Seth Joshua so filled all hearts with the divine presence, that our young friend Evan Roberts – who sat on our left – prayed God to dim the vision of the cross which crushed him, and which largely overwhelmed all present. Truly it was a time of refreshing from the presence of the Lord.[22]

The 8 p.m. open-air meeting at the Rock Park, where Seth Joshua and Sergeant Barker were scheduled to speak, drew an immense crowd and 'the power which accompanied those who prayed and spake was simply divine'. 'We found it impossible however, to confine the meeting to the planned speakers – for others felt constrained to testify to the love of Christ; and the meeting went on till nearly 11 p.m. The glory of God seemed to rest upon the place. 'At the great closing meeting in the tent, again Forward Movement speakers like Watkin Williams and C. L. Perry preached. One of the most touching things, apart from the decision of some to take Christ as their Saviour, was the wonderful testimony given by Mr. A. Rees, an elder in our Welsh Church at New York. His testimony to the joy in his soul at obtaining assurance of salvation melted the great throng to tears...' 'They were days of heaven upon earth,' wrote Pugh.[23]

The speakers themselves marvelled at the response to their messages and all over the tent people were confessing past disobedience, making fresh vows to serve and give. With spiritual realities pressing powerfully on people in a context where holiness and obedience were given prime stress, it required wise leadership to keep people from emotionalism and imprudent vows. In general it was so. But in his report to *The Torch* in September Seth once more showed how he could be both wholehearted in his ministry while objective in his assessment of tendencies of which to beware.

> The convention will never be forgotten. It reached a higher mark than Keswick. The spiritual conflicts were fearful. One of the first utterances of this convention was 'and now is the judgement of this world, now is the prince of this world cast out'. *It was literally fulfilled.* There were demon possessions at Llandrindod this year. I know it – but Satan was bruised under the feet of the saints. These things are too sacred to write about, and I am sorry that in one instance an unsanctified pen wrote an incorrect account, simply to dish up a meal for a dirty appetite. But who will ever forget those wonderful meetings.[24]

It is worth noting here that the Rev. E. H. Hopkins, a founder of the Keswick movement, in his write-up on Keswick 1905 commented on his experience of spiritual conflict at that year's convention. 'The present writer has lived in a heathen country, and is familiar enough, as all spiritual workers are, with the sense of the presence and hostility of the principalities of darkness. For the first time, he had a similar experience at Keswick this year and on two occasions.'[25] It is interesting to link this with Pierson's observation that the Keswick of 1905 had, in a new measure, at the Monday, Wednesday and Friday gatherings in Skiddaw street tent, 'a Pentecost – the new wine of the Spirit, undoubted and striking movements of God's Holy Spirit, growing in intensity and power'.[26]

Aware of, and never dismissive of this dimension, Seth's main concern after Llandrindod was in another direction and highly perceptive.

'The one thing I feel compelled to write about is that the objective side of truth was too much in the background. People were overdosed with subjective truth. They were driven to introspection to such a degree that many were in the pangs of despair. I do not attach blame to the platform in this. The speakers were not aware of it. This crop of despair came to light after the convention was over.

Let me speak a word in love – a word of caution even to my superiors. Let us remember we have entered upon a conflict with dark spirits. Their victory depends upon getting the eyes of the soul off the blood and all objective truth. Beware lest the very cross may be used to crush a sensitive soul instead of being the very symbol of comfort.

It is quite true that the cross has its sword side to cut to the death, but there is a balance of truth and to rightly divide the word of truth is a great need of the moment. Evangelical truth on its objective side can never be omitted without danger.[27]

Seth does not name names. It was becoming a feature of some ministries, for example, F. B. Meyer's, to stress phrases like 'let the cross of Christ cuts deeper and deeper into your life'. Seth seemed to sense that the work of the cross in taking our guilt away and being the basis of our justification and assurance had slipped from its health-giving centrality. By January 1906 he was even plainer in his criticism of how tendencies both in the revival and the holiness movement had slipped into existential excess. 'Sanctification [was] made the basis of assurance in Wales, instead of the finished work of Christ.' This led, in his view, to a subjective instead of an objective faith, obscuring the desire to save others. As an evangelist he saw this as a device of Satan. In a comment on R. J. Campbell's *New Theology* in July 1907, which showed the same subjectivist bug at work in more academic circles, Seth showed where his deepest theological roots lay. 'The tonic for this anaemic age is Calvinism.'

For three weeks he was away on a mission in Belfast. And so things continued in the ways we have now become familiar with.

The extraordinary experiences which had so thrilled and motivated him were now fading away as the revival phenomena departed. But his evangelism still bore the fruit of the Spirit's blessing. In 1906 he was given a new challenge – an invitation to preach in America.

Seth in America

He was accompanied on his trip by Mr. Sam Jenkins, a singer of the gospel, and was involved in three months missions work. They were given a special sendoff from Liverpool by the presbytery there. A few words on Sam Jenkins will help us to see why he accompanied Seth. It was not just an aping of the American habit of sending evangelist plus soloists to Britain. Sam Jenkins had played a nationwide role in the revival:

> He had received a great deal of publicity from the journalists because of the songs associated with him. Sam was a 25 year old tinplate worker when the revival took him up and carried him into singing from town to town. He was soon called the 'Sankey of Wales'. The song that caught the mood of the revival was 'The song of the rebel'. Wherever he went he sang about 'the old rebel' and it invariably brought blessing.[28]

I can still recall the moment of stillness that came over the congregation at my grandmother's funeral in the 1950s when Sam Jenkins entered the church.

Seth and Sam sailed on the *Berengaria* on 26th September and Seth had his first experience of preaching with an interpreter when he addressed a party of Swedes on board. Arriving on 3rd October they visited first Dr A. B. Simpson, founder of the Christian and Missionary Alliance, and then the Welsh church. Powerful services were held at the Mid Granville *Cymanfa Ganu* (Hymn Singing Festival). He preached in Massachusets and Pennsylvania. In Wilkesbarre he saw the other side of the pastor's heartbreak over the Welsh emigration from Neath when he met a large number of people who had been brought to Christ through his brother Frank. It would be instructive to have more detail of his comment, 'Satan fought every inch of the ground traversed by me in the States.'

The pages of his notebook after 5th November are missing and we know that something prevented him from going out west. A mystery exists as, in 1906, Sam Jenkins brought back a teapot and stand from Patagonia which has the head of Michael D. Jones, the founder of Patagonia, inscribed on it.[30] Presumably therefore one or both of them went down south to Argentina during this trip. Sam was not with Seth on his return.

By the time Seth returned to New York in late December he was showing deep signs of Hiraeth. He saw the *Corona* ready to sail, which would take him home in time for Christmas, but he was told, alas, that all berths were booked. He prayed an oft repeated prayer: 'Lord, please, I want to go home.' As he wandered on the quayside a stranger came up to him and asked:

'What are you doing here, Mr. Joshua?

'I want to get home on that ship, but it is full up. But say, how do you know my name?

'I'm a Welshman and I heard you once in a Welsh church. You want to go home in that ship, do you? Well, I'm the master of the berths. I'll fix you up.'

He gave Seth a first-class cabin free. As he explored the ship he soon found a young student from the Moody Bible Institute who had been longing to meet him. The voyage home was a joy.[31]

But when he got back he found his great soul mate, John Pugh, ominously unwell.

CHAPTER TEN

A GREAT VICTORIAN
and his loyal lieutenant

For some time Pugh's health had been causing much anxiety. No doubt revival times, with the long hours, crowded halls and hundreds of conversions recorded from among those attending, though vastly encouraging, meant also great additional demands. Pugh's energies had ebbed. He was forced to miss much of the battle for most of that year.

Details of his personal involvement in the blessing of the revival are sparse. But his perspective on it comes from a few surviving extracts in *The Torch*. The growth of the Forward Movement he wrote

> did much by way of preparing the way for the present gracious revival which is proving such a blessing: (i) By calling the attention of God's people to the desperate spiritual needs of the populous towns of South Wales; (ii) By urging upon them, by precept and example, to seek the baptism of the Holy Ghost for Christian service and soul-winning.[1]

Without evidence of Pugh's explicit teaching on the baptism of the Spirit it is risky to speculate, but two things seem clear. First, he interpreted the power of the revival in terms of an extraordinary work of the Spirit – 'the baptism of the Holy Ghost.' Secondly, he also believed that 'by example' the Forward Movement evangelists had manifested this power in days previous to the revival when they had witnessed phenomenal evangelistic success. This is borne out by the comment of Principal T. C. Edwards in the Annual Letter to the churches in 1899 on the preaching of the Forward Movement evangelists:

> Possibly [their] chief characteristic is the insistence on the necessity of the full assurance of faith. The evangelists also believe in a second baptism distinct and separate from conversion. It was believed to be a necessity if the gospel is to be preached with irresistible power.[2]

Edwards phrase 'a second baptism' is more commonly rendered 'the baptism of the Spirit'. It has been associated by some Puritans, some of the leaders of the eighteenth century revival and by the later Forward Movement preacher D. Martyn Lloyd-Jones both with 'the full assurance' of faith and with 'irresistible power' in preaching. Edwards had himself been overwhelmed in the 1859 revival under preaching that demonstrated that power of the Spirit. It would seem that the exceptional power in evangelistic preaching shown by Pugh at Tredegar and Pontypridd and later by the Joshuas, H. G. Howells and others, is being attributed by Edwards to this exceptional blessing of the Spirit ('a second baptism'). If we search for streams leading to the flood of the 1904 revival we certainly can trace one here. The empowered preaching that enabled Seth to gain inroads into the lives of the apparently unreachable are advance showers of the cloud-burst that was to come. Pugh spoke in August 1905 of 'the glorious revival with which our land has been favoured and which, as a Movement, we have been experiencing for the past fourteen years. We rejoice that the people of God throughout the Principality have participated in this glorious revival.'[3] It is intriguing that he uses the word 'revival' of the work of the Forward Movement since its inception. This may be a simple reminder to his readers that the source of the exceptional preaching power of the evangelists was a touch of the same quality of spiritual power that was demonstrated in the revival.

A further reference to the revival by Pugh is also in *The Torch*.

The magazine carries an extract from the Annual Report of Professor Ellis Edwards, the Vice Principal of Bala Theological College, on the effects of the revival on the college. (What he records is also true of Trevecka and gives us a rare picture of what had happened in circles of theological learning at the time).

> The revival was experienced here in a marked degree. The students' ministry has been greatly influenced. Preaching has now quite a new power. The meetings held and the convictions awakened during this searching time could not leave College studies in the same position as before; it was impossible for students to do what they deemed to be their duty by the gifts and calls of the revival and to the old number of hours to their studies. The Senate judged it wise, in the exceptional circumstances, to omit the Christmas examinations. It was a time when something more valuable than all college instruction was plainly given from on high. That which was granted to college this session will leave, I hope, long effects. Indeed we ask and crave for some of that outpouring, whose character cannot be mistaken.[4]

Pugh's response to the letter cannot veil his longstanding dissatisfaction with the kind of preparation the colleges were giving for preaching that would reach the ordinary public. 'These have been our sentiments since the inauguration of the Forward Movement and it is not surprizing that some young men who come to us during their vacation have felt disinclined to return to their studies.'[5]

One wonders whether that was the sole reason why some students were reluctant to pick up academic studies again. Was Pugh making any veiled allusion to the further worry that men like Ellis Edwards, though early firm supporters of the Forward Movement, had already begun to show the blight of modernism in their teaching as early as 1900?[6] It is an ominous pointer to the rapid departure from evangelical truths among many ministers which the revival only delayed rather than offset, though that drift has outstanding exceptions among ministers.

Pugh also picked up another cause of concern regarding the later stages of the revival – the superficial and merely emotional, and therefore temporary, nature of many religious experiences resulting in a reversion to former loose patterns of behaviour in many people. There had certainly been a considerable reduction in the number of criminal cases as a result of the revival influences, and this social purging had been well attested in the courts. But Pugh quotes a Judge's observations on the effects of the revival to make his warning

In the Grand Jury at the Summer Assizes for the county of Glamorgan at Swansea, July 25th, the number of cases had not been a long one. But Mr. Justice Phillimore said 'at Denbigh he had been able to congratulate the County on the very great good which appeared to have resulted from the Revival, and he had hopes of observing the same effects in Glamorgan. He believed it had been so in the county, but he could not help fearing that there had been a great reaction since. A great many cases came from the Colliery districts where the Revival had been very strong and very effective. Of course there were a certain number of cases which no one would expect to be touched by this religious revival, such as the foreign population, and visitors to our seaports.'[7]

Pugh responded to this emerging evidence that there was a 'kick back' effect.

Most earnestly would we call the prayerful attention of our readers to our Saviour's warning: 'When the unclean spirit is gone out of a man, he walketh through dry places, seeking rest, and findeth none. Then he saith, 'I will return into my house whence I came out, and when he is come, he findeth it empty, swept and garnished. Then goeth he and taketh with himself ten other spirits, more wicked than himself, and they enter in and dwell there, and the last state of that man is worse than the first. Even so shall it be, also, unto this wicked generation.' 'He that hath an ear, let him hear what the Spirit saith unto the churches.'[8]

The Torch's report on the occasion of Memorial Hall, Cardiff's anniversary in 1905 acknowledges a waning of power as well as an awareness of it. 'We felt at times a real touch of true fervour, indicating that the Spirit of the revival has not yet left us.'[9]

Every judicious writer, from a religious or a secular perspective, sees two sides to the coin of the revival. John Morgan Jones, Pugh's successor, saw it as a great blessing, when religion became the top topic in a nation's conversation, and when numbers at Forward Movement halls increased dramatically. But there was the downside that many who joined were never born-again and from them came a later falling away when Forward Movement numbers declined. 'The revival brought a lot of dangerous elements of wheat among tares.'

Dr K. O. Morgan, certainly a detached analyst, is able to give many positive comments on the phenomenon. He describes the chapels in 1906 as still 'in flood tide', enjoying 'a halcyon period'.

> For eighteen months, chapel life all over Wales was galvanised by spontaneous Bible reading and prayer meetings and revivalist passion. Evan Roberts ... had become a major national influence, one to whom even Lloyd-George had to pay obeisance.... What the revival had done was to provide countless men and women with a new hope and comfort in the face of brutalising conditions. The cause of temperance in particular made immense advances.... Social life became that much gentler and more civilized. Debts were paid; family feuds were healed overnight.... Certainly the Independent Labour Party was one beneficiary of the revolutionary impact of the revival.'

He shows the downside by noting that in 1914 all the main denominations were recording decreases. 'But still, the Evan Roberts revival did give the Welsh chapels a temporary impetus, unique in the western world.'[10]

Burdened with the care of all the churches under his direction even Pugh, the man of steel, was beginning to fracture. For years he had tended to neglect himself, sometimes not eating properly and cutting down drastically on sleep to keep abreast with administration. Though he was unwell during much of 1904 he continued to overwork. When he failed to attend Forward Movement directors' meetings, a much overdue move was made and John Thomas, a trusty co-worker, was appointed his helper to try to lighten the burden.

Controversy over the building programme never went away. Some criticized Pugh for not building in some key areas. Others called for a halt in building altogether. 'Some people, like old Pharoah, expect the Forward Movement Committee and evangelists, to make bricks without straw.' When, again under the stimulus of revival growth he did purchase a central spot in Swansea, there were those who still cavilled even though it was a freehold site which he described as 'the greatest bargain we have ever had'. He went on:

> This is saying much, for some marvellous pieces of good fortune have fallen to our lot and properties have become ours that have amazed shrewd business men who know the value of such things. Instead of carping that we are plunging into unreasonable debt, it would be well if some of our short sighted critics would first consult men who know something of the value of our splendid property.

His motive in seeking new sites was always the same: 'Pray that from the start this work may prove a mighty impetus to all the evangelical churches of Swansea, and that thousands now perishing in that great town may be led to Jesus Christ for salvation.'[11] These words could serve as an epitaph.

His deep worries about debt on the properties were now a shadow over his life, especially as some said it reflected badly on the good name of the denomination. A series of strange providences decreed that several crucial men of money and influence died in 1905. They were body-blows to Pugh. The first was Richard Davies, Bodlondeb, who had given more than anyone knew. He had a passionate zeal for mission and Pugh had a way to his heart. Soon after promising to give £500 a year extra to waylay debt he died unexpectedly. In the same year came the sudden death of the Rev. David Lloyd-Jones, a mainstay of Forward Movement pulpits, and a man who was able to rally support for the Movement from among other influential men. Then it was the turn of the Dr William James of Manchester, a key figure in gathering a large support for the Forward Movement in the north and someone who was relied on heavily for his organizing skills. He, like Lloyd-Jones, had become fearful and cautious about the future.

Then in that same year Pugh had one of the biggest disappointments of his life. The denomination announced a collection to mark the new century. On 5 August 1899 *The Torch* reported the founding of 'The Twentieth Century Fund'. 'Let us pray for the protection and guidance of the Lord during the century which is about to begin.... This fund is for the immediate relief of places where we have lost and are losing ground at home. It is a rescue work, first and foremost.'[12] In the light of this expressed purpose of the denomination Pugh was confident that it would provide a major contribution to clearing outstanding debt. But, as it turned out, the Movement was given only £15,000 towards the borrowing fund, a large donation, it is true, in contemporary terms. But it did not lift the basic load of concern. These 'changes of fortune', which were becoming almost portents of later decline, were capped one morning in 1907, just after Pugh died, when a cheque of £500 arrived from John Cory, promising another £500, only for the Forward Movement to discover that Cory had died the night before and the cheque was not, for some reason, cashed!

In her reminiscences Pugh's daughter paints a picture of her father at his most stressful moments:

At midnight on a New Year's Eve, a man was to be seen sitting hunched over a desk in his study, writing laborious letters to people whom he believed could be moved to help the work, and to send it on its way for another year. Nobody was allowed to disturb him, because this was work which had been postponed for a long time and it simply had to be done. Every now and then he would pause, as if unable to carry on, but shortly he would again take up his pen and continue writing, but again with the same inexplicable difficulty, as if he were striving to the utmost to complete his task.

'Every body thinks,' he said 'that I am fond of asking for money, because I am always doing so. God knows how contrary it is to my nature, and I hate it more each day, especially when I am forced to write confidential letters to people.' Perhaps it was the element of dismay that the ministers of Christ were unable to make both ends meet in Wales because of the lack of a mere thousand or more pounds that effected him more than anything. The sum he needed he always described as 'tiny', 'trivial', 'small', because he compared what people spent on themselves with what they gave to the church of Christ.[13]

In late January 1906, to help him fight his escalating ill-health, the Forward Movement directors sent him and Mrs. Pugh to Egypt and the Holy Land for a holiday. The trip was plagued by bad weather in the Mediterranean. As they sailed from Alexandria to Jaffa, stormy weather conditions prevented the ship docking. It had to proceed to Beirut. From there they took a train to Damascus, but as they were returning a bad snowstorm occurred in mountainous country and Pugh's chest condition took hold again. Mrs. Pugh thought his end was coming and persuaded him to cut short the trip and not go on to Jerusalem. They returned home in time for the stone-laying ceremony at Heath Church on 4th April 1906, which was also his official welcome-home service. People were struck with how very weak he looked, cheerful though he was in their presence. At the end of September 1906, the Pierce Memorial Hall was opened with a golden key by Mrs. Richard Davies. Once more Pugh rose to the occasion: he appeared better and preached fluently. But it was obvious that as the winter came on 'the mists of the valley were descending on Dr Pugh' ('*yr oedd niwl y glyn yn dechrau amdoi Dr Pugh*'). Against doctor's orders and the advice of family and friends he fulfilled a preaching engagement in Acrefair, once more appearing to demonstrate great strength and giving the impression of being in top form. But this was his finale. For the rest of his time he was confined to home, signing his name when necessary to Forward Movement business and struggling to edit *The Torch*. But he was at peace.

His text for that last service had been 2 Corinthians 13:5: 'Examine yourselves whether ye be in the faith.' This last preached message of his life, under the title 'Proofs of Conversion', was a simple summary of the concerns of his ministry:

1. Surrender of the will to Christ.
2. A consciousness that our sins, though many, are forgiven.
3. A taste for the word of God.
4. A delight in speaking to God.
5. A desire for the salvation of others.
6. A desire to be like Jesus Christ.

Pugh's final words appeared in the March 1907 edition of *The Torch*, the month of his death. He was sixty-one years of age. His words revealed the foreboding of a man who was reading the signs of caution around him about the future expansion of the Forward

Movement, perhaps half aware that there would be a failure of nerve when he passed on. He looked for an example of resolution to leave to others:

We won't go back; Prince Henry of the Netherlands' pluck encouraged the life boat men on the Hook of Holland in their heroic attempts to rescue the perishing on board the ill-fated 'Berlin'. 'We won't go back before we save them, we must get them somehow' were his determined words. And they saved fifteen. The Prince of Peace is with us in our attempt to rescue perishing humanity. Must we go back? The cry from Liverpool, London, Bristol and from two dozen densely populated areas in Glamorgan and Monmouthshire for the help of the Forward Movement is heart rending to those who know their moral and spiritual needs. Are we to retreat owing to lack of funds? Some of the most talented and Spirit filled ministers have joined our ranks recently. We need more. With loyal support and the cheer of God's people we won't go back.[14]

Some special moments of good cheer came when Seth, his right-hand man, returned from the States just in time to have a few talks with him. 'I would not have liked dear old John to have gone home without seeing him. His chats meant so much to me.'

Pugh's death

Pugh's daughter Ann describes the end:

And now, as I come to his last days I write with his diary before me. 'Sunday January 6th – very poorly and confined to my bedroom. Perfectly content in the Lord...' and so on until March 24th. A short while before he left us I was sitting with him in his room when the Rev. F. W. Cole came in. He prayed with us, and when he had finished my father said, 'Francis, will you take charge of Heath Hall? They are without a minister and there is a great opportunity for the Kingdom of God.' He promised to do so.

The same evening Dr Cunningham Bowie, the doctor who attended my father and was his great friend, came in and told me in his hearing, 'There is no reason that your father should die; with his constitution he could live another twenty years, but he has completely burned himself out. If your Connexion had given him a telephone and a car, the bare necessities to enable him to accomplish the more easily all he has done in less than fifteen years, he could have lived.'

'But,' said my father, taking hold of my hand, 'the Saviour died when he was 33 and I am 60. Don't "rust". Wear yourself out for His sake, my child.'

And so, on Palm Sunday, March 24th, he entered the New Jerusalem.[15]

His funeral, to quote *The South Wales Daily News*, 29 March 1907, 'was one of the largest, as it was one of the most impressive and representative, seen in Cardiff for many years.' The Lord Mayor of Cardiff and six MPs were joined by many other leaders of church and national life. 'It was a great public testimony to a great personality and a remarkable organizer in the religious world of the Principality – the greatest religious organizer modern Wales has seen.' He was a born leader of men and one of the great Victorians – he had become a household name in Wales.

The Crwys Hall was heaving with people many hours before his coffin was carried there. The assessments of his life and work ranged over a wide canvas: the first man to see the need and act to rescue his land from a flood of irreligion; the man with a heart always kindled by a love for God and love for men who were down in the gutter; the warrior who fell like a soldier cut down on the battlefield, having spent himself out, fighting ceaselessly in unrelenting attacks upon sin. Lord Pontypridd, who had watched his work from the beginning, spoke about his unquenchable courage. He remembered what he had had to meet with when he had faced people feared by the police. He had no fear of them because he loved them so greatly. He loved Wales and desired to present her as a gift to the Lord. His single eye for the advancement of Christ's cause and not his own comes out in Pontypridd's view that, had he been a self-centred man, he could have founded a new denomination.

Yet, to his daughter, his real funeral service took place around the grave in Cathays cemetery before the cortege arrived from the church. Many hundreds had come there and especially some of the poorest friends from the Forward Movement centres. Many had walked a great distance, ill able to pay the fares. They lined the edges of the path and their funeral service was entirely spontaneous. It was very fitting for them to form the guard of honour. Long before the procession arrived the great crowd sang hymns. Then came an extraordinary moment that seemed to encapsulate the grace, the grit, the gumption, the genius of 'the Forward'. Jack Turner, a member from Saltmead Hall shouted with a loud voice:

> 'Brothers, the one thing that John Pugh loved us to do above all else was to present ourselves to Christ. If we haven't done that already, let's do it now, and afresh, and utterly, as he taught us to do, so that we may be worthy to stand at his graveside. Now, my brothers, as for being able to live a worthy life in our own strength – a life similar to his – that we cannot do. But in Christ we are able and all we need do is to respond to his promptings in our hearts. May this day be a turning point in our lives and the start of a better life.' 'Amen,' said many of the listeners, either to themselves or aloud, and they wept afresh.[16]

As Seth Joshua struck up the familiar Welsh hymn *O fryniau Caersalem*, the effect among the huge crowd was electrifying. The most moving sight of all was of the thirty or so Forward Movement evangelists, Seth standing prominent among them, weeping and singing 'like children who had lost their father'; the Three and the Thirty united in grief at the loss of one of the Three.

The crowd had left. The grave-diggers took to their task. Even they could not avoid the man and his message. 'Why is there such a commotion?' they asked. 'He wasn't a bishop or anything.' And one of Pugh's people, still present, replied, 'No he wasn't, but he was more than a bishop. He spoke to me about Jesus Christ and what he could do for me – that's what he told me.'

The man and his work

The Movement saw marked, even amazing, success in the brief period of sixteen years (1891–1907) that Pugh was involved. Pugh was a special gift to meet the special needs of his day. Principal Prys commented that if he had had the job of creating John Pugh, doubtless he would have made him a little different to what he was, but he questioned whether his Mr. Pugh would have started the Forward Movement. 'Heaven created him – hence he started the Movement.'[17] Howell Williams, the Movement's official historian, highlights the New Testament features evident in Pugh which help us account for his work.

Pugh was a conscript of God; necessity was laid upon him to preach to the masses, having heard his marching orders. John Morgan Jones tells how he could stop men in their tracks over the matter of their eternal destiny.

> He was an attractive figure on the open streets. His well built, athletic frame, his light step, his bright sunny face and that dark coloured beard in striking harmony with his body frame, would compel the passer by to turn and look, and possibly respond to a cheery 'Good day to you'. It might be said of John Pugh as he strolled along one of the Grangetown streets what a Boston newspaper said about Phillips Brooks. 'It was a dull, rainy day, when things looked dark and lowering, but Phillips Brooks came down through Newspaper Row and all was bright.'

He was unable to meet with misfortune in others without feeling it to the quick and doing his utmost to seek to remove it. Often his hand would find its way to his pocket almost unwittingly. He was completely at home in the middle of a crowd of ordinary folk and they in turn felt he belonged to them and identified with them.

Pugh was a great lover of people and of the Lord. 'Christ for all and all for Christ' was his ministry motto. His preaching was supremely evangelistic with a heart full of compassion for the unchurched thousands 'without God and without hope in the world'. Surrender to the Lord Jesus Christ was the one and only end of preaching. That passion consumed him. He could say with Jeremiah, 'His word was in mine heart like a burning fire.'

Pugh's biographer, writing in 1946, at a time when the doctrines of grace were no longer in the forefront of the church, was keen to underline this key to Pugh's success:

> Behind all this was Pugh's assurance of his own personal salvation with its accompanying joy, even hilarity, which could neither be suppressed or restrained. This doctrine of assurance, was his favourite doctrine of grace. He would fully agree with Dr James Denney that, 'while assurance in Roman Catholicism was a presumption, and in

Protestantism a privilege, it was, in the New Testament, a fact'. He was animated by the thought: 'He loved me, and gave himself for me.'[18]

He was a great prayer–warrior, especially in intercessory prayer for the salvation of souls. Frequently his prayer was the means of conversions. And at more than one open-air meeting his prayer checked threatened violence or silenced a crude interruption.

He was a man of courage who did not shrink from theological controversy when he saw the gospel at risk. He singled out for public criticism two tendencies of his day.

Firstly, he singled out the increasing ritualism of the Church of England which he dubbed 'religious foolery'. When this was coupled with pathetic preaching his comments could be withering and embarrassed the more irenic type who found Pugh's straight talk difficult to take. Here is a sample, sent back to *The Torch* while he was bound for America.

Divine service on board ship was conducted by one of the High Church Fraternists of Montreal. I never in my life heard such a miserable attempt at preaching. His text was – 'no one putting his hand to the plough and looking back is fit for the kingdom of heaven'. Never did I see such a greater contradiction between text and parson, for he certainly looked everywhere but to his text. A week old convert of the Forward Movement would have done better than this august successor to the apostles. From such successors good Lord deliver us. How such a noodle had the impertinence to attempt a sermon is beyond me, except on the presumption that 'fools rush in where angels fear to tread!'

The use of such dismissive language ought not to hide the fact that Pugh was not blind to the sincere compassion and pastoral care shown by many ritualists. During the strong anti-ritualist crusade led by John Kensit in 1898,[19] Pugh admired his courage and embraced his Protestant principles, but because he felt Kensit's tactics smacked of extremism and could be counter-productive, he took the opportunity to highlight the humanity of many ritualists:

It is well to remember that the High Church party show great devotion in the social department of christian work. By their sympathy and active help they have won over a large mass of people. And if the term 'East End Curate' is synonymous with a ritualist, it is synonymous too, with a man who has power and is loved by the common people. When will we Nonconformists learn this lesson? When we think of Father Dolling of Portsmouth, of Father Adderley and many others, to whom humanity is greater than the church, it is well that we should be charitable in our judgments. Many ritualists are as sincere as the most enthusiastic evangelicals and, taken in the bulk, they show a more genuine, self sacrificing devotion to their church than do Nonconformists. If we had half as much devotion to the church's Christ as they have to the church, we should have little to fear.[20]

But Pugh never lost sight of the fact that one of his purposes in founding *The Torch* was to resist ritual advances and the Rome-ward tendencies they represented. 'As things are,' he wrote in 1898, 'we mean to quit ourselves like men in the sharpest conflict in religion since the days when Martin Luther posted up his famous ninety five theses on the door of the castle Church at Wittenberg.'[21] A year later the paper saw it right to make a call for action. 'Once to every man and nation comes the moment to decide,' it wrote. The time was ripe 'to meet Puseyism[22] with Pughism everywhere. Plant a mission hall next door to every ritualistic church.'

The second tendency of his day that he singled out for criticism was connected to the first: the returning tide of Romanism. Pugh was alarmed by this for he saw ritualism as a movement of terrible force to drag England Rome-wards, leading the Church of England to deny the faith she had so long cherished. He comments:

On what sorrowful days have we fallen! We protest, that it may be known, that even as of old there were seven thousand who had not bowed the knee to Baal, so there remains a great multitude – loyal and faithful to Paul, Luther, Wyclif and the noble army of Protestant martyrs.[23]

And, 'the only antidote to the present bold and open attack of Rome is aggressive evangelistic effort. If we merely stand on the defensive we shall be swamped'. He grieved when he saw the seeming impotence of Catholicism in Irish areas of South Wales towns where the drink problem was rife. 'There is not sufficient of the living and soul saving Christ in Romanism to quicken the dead in trespasses and sins and then to elevate ordinary people.'

He spoke out time and again against slumdom and the toleration of prostitution by the Cardiff City Council. The liquor traffic he saw to be the biggest source of social evil among the people he was in such close touch with. He identified *The Western Mail*, still Wales' national daily, as the 'publican and papal champion in Cardiff.' The conflict between them on the 'evils of the trade', as *The Torch* saw it, was public and therefore read nationally (see Appendix 2).

Protestantism did not escape his whip. He wrote from the States: 'the danger of Presbyterianism here as in England is to be crippled by respectability and to die of starch. O that the spirit of Knox, Calvin, Whitefield and Harris might fall upon us.' He was aware of how much more could be done if the complacency of the wealthy, well-housed churchgoers could be lifted. 'One of the greatest needs of the church of God today is a baptism of consecrated giving of its substance to God's work.' It was said that he was not always acceptable in the homes of the rich for they knew that if he cornered them, their pockets would be much the emptier. But Pugh did not find this an attractive part of his task.

> It pains us to plead to carry on a Christ-like mission, and, if we possessed the means, we would never ask a single soul to share with us the great privilege of carrying on this God-given mission. Some friends told us recently that an honoured servant of Christ died penniless. To which we replied that our surprize would have been very great had he died otherwise. How any Christian can hoard up money in this dying world, to save which the Son of God though rich became poor, is a mystery.

Neither did Pugh mince his words when it came to colleagues inadequate to meet the changing challenge of the times. For example: 'men who are unqualified for the great work of the Christian ministry should be urged to go back to their daily calling,'[24] he said in 1892. He really did mean it when he called for grit, grace and gumption. In his frustration he sometimes so forgot professional etiquette as to call some ministers 'namby pamby' and 'jellyfish'. One wonders what words he would have found for the modern television 'vicar'.

Marking time

It is not our task to follow the future fortunes of the Movement as such. But a brief assessment of the policy of Pugh's successor from 1907–1922, the Rev. Dr John Morgan Jones, will show some of the immense problems ahead. Jones was a convert of the 1859 revival and had wholeheartedly supported the Forward Movement from its inception. He had great gifts and was faithful to the gospel. But he was already in his seventies when succeeding a man who had died, exhausted from his exertions, at sixty-one! And his was now a different world. He was an influential figure in education, a member of the Court of University College, Cardiff, and of the governing body of the University of Wales. Pugh's death deprived the Movement of an 'in touch' leader. He knew at firsthand the people and the problems of the industrial areas. 'It could be said that the succeeding Superintendents lacked something of this close personal involvement...(there was) a certain distancing effect upon social attitudes in the movement.'[25]

Jones' motto from the outset was what Pugh had feared: 'Consolidate.' That was regarded as the first necessity. In many ways this was very understandable and it is difficult from all normal views of financial prudence to see what alternative lay open to him. There was a huge debt of £86,000 on the Forward Movement halls building account. From then on his more cautious hand steered away from further building expansion. Pugh's achievement was undeniable. He had, generally speaking, got the halls he appealed for. Some of his contemporaries, however, had felt that his impulsive temperament had led to almost irresponsible initiatives. His failure to win secure financial support to resource it, partly the result of the untimely death of Edward Davies, had left a sense of crisis. The only possible solution seemed to be to put the brakes on. Unfortunately the slowing down of the building programme also seemed to affect the priority given to virile evangelism. Pugh's drive had impelled both. The new consolidation seemed to lack urgency. Howell Williams sums up the dilemma facing the Movement at this time: 'The populous industrial areas were loudly calling for expansion, while the Connexion on the whole was calling for a halt, deeming it unwise to travel fast in view of her limited resources'.[26] The financial constraints were worsened by the falling off in the support of the wealthy, though with the notable exception of the Davies sisters of Llandinam. And the increasing shadow of social and industrial unrest which seriously worsened after the War tended to effect the Forward Movement centres most immediately because of their social composition.

Seth's tribute and change of track

Having got to know Seth and felt his yearning for reaching the lost we will not be surprised at his reaction to this slowing down. He found that the new policy did not suit him. He prayed about his future as an evangelist and from 1909 until 1921 he became a full-time missioner to the Federation of Evangelical Free Churches. He was set apart for this work at the Methodist Chapel, Tonypandy. Within two years the Forward Movement had lost its two greatest evangelists. Link this with the increasing difficulty in finding evangelists anyway and we see another crucial weakness that was to overtake the work.

At the time, and until his death in 1925, Seth had his own clear view of what attitude should have continued. He was all for the daring spirit of Pugh. He made this point, forcefully when interviewed by the *Cymro* newspaper some years later (1924). His replies to their questions are best dealt with at this point, before we continue with the story of his later years of ministry.

Seth was asked whether the Movement made a mistake by appointing someone so different to occupy Pugh's place. He was the soul of propriety. While never for one moment disparaging an old campaigner whom he respected deeply, he does raise a serious question as to how the appointment was made.

It is too delicate a question for me to answer. Many reasons constrain me from stating an opinion. The old Calvinistic view is that 'all things work together for good'. There can therefore be no mistake when the ultimate harvest is reached. But suppose it was a mistake. Even then, the Connection [i.e. the church members] is not to blame. These matters are not determined by the rank and file who have no voice in the matter. The Rev. John Morgan Jones had his own personal qualifications and they were great. I am not prepared to say that any mistake was made, but I do say that it was not the mistake of the Connection. One of the greatest dangers for today is for an inner autocratic few to be permitted to legislate for a democratic church.[27]

On hearing that, the question arises as to whether Seth might have succeeded Pugh. No doubt the members of the halls would have been unanimous for him if their opinions had been tested, though he certainly would not have wanted office work to keep him from the highways and byeways of evangelism. Such an appointment would have been highly unlikely anyway in early Edwardian days. Seth, despite his enormous talents, would have been regarded as a 'footsoldier' or 'NCO' by most leaders of the Connexion.

It struck the editor of the *Cymro* that seventeen years after Pugh's death no biography had yet appeared. He asked Seth to comment on this omission.

'This is a question for the Connection to answer. If you should shout the question through the valleys of South Wales and Monmouthshire, the mountains would echo back "Why not?"

'Is a biography needed.'

'Yes. And print it on the best paper ever made and bind the book in the best calf skin binding. Print the title and the name in gold letters. Make it so beautiful that even Ruskin would say "Well done."'

'Who would write it?'

'Someone with a blind eye to his few small failures and an open one to his many golden qualities. A writer in touch with his ideals and in sympathy with his ambitions. One who could hide himself, and reveal the subject of his biography. The most thrilling chapter would contain the story of his first struggles, and when out of tears and prayers, emerged what afterwards compelled his critics to stand in wonder. Only a few are now alive. Mrs. Pugh was an eye witness of all this.'[28]

Seth's style and personality give added weight to his warm-hearted tribute to his old colleague and mentor. We also sense how deeply he felt that the next generation, which had swiftly turned away from the virile evangelical distinctives of the early Forward Movement men and sisters, had conspired to underrate Pugh's gifts and stature. When asked of his opinion of John Pugh as a preacher, he stood foursquare in Pugh's defence:

> A critic would answer this question by saying what he was not as a preacher. I can only write my opinion as to what he was. What he was looms up in my memory and I see the mountain peaks cutting through the drifting clouds. He often preached and wept at the same time and his tears were as eloquent as his words. His sermons glowed with a passion for souls. Sometimes it would reach a white heat. He preached with one arm clinging around the cross, and with the other outstretched to snatch souls from the wrath to come. As an open air preacher he ranks with Wesley, Whitefield and Howel Harris. He found his way to Calvary from every part of God's word. If a man can be measured as a preacher by his passion for souls, his tears for sinners, his heroic open air testimony and his fruit in the salvation of men, then the Rev. John Pugh was truly great.[29]

A preacher indeed. But not, as Pugh's daughter helps us to see, how his generation defined a preacher.

Annie Pugh acknowledges that it was

> quite a common opinion amongst the ministers of his connexion that he was no preacher, although others who went to hear him thought otherwise.... When my mother was asked what it was that she considered to be the greatest spiritual victory in my father's life, she replied, having thought for some minutes, 'that he was willing to forgo being a preacher in the general sense. He had the ability, the power and the intellect to be such, but he was willing not to be one, and to count himself as nothing so that men did not hear him, but rather Christ.'[30]

It seems to come down to the fact that Pugh faced up realistically to his calling to reach out to previously non-church-going, maybe poorly-educated, labourers and artisans. In this context plain speaking and urgent appeal reached hearts. In contrast, the drift of many in the Welsh pulpit around him was to be ever more literary and polished, so that preaching became a self-conscious performance, with a display of flowery imagery. This drift produced a sermon-tasting attitude in the hearer. Many could afford to preach like that in their generation because chapel attendance was still high and they did not have to win or keep an audience. If that is what is meant by 'being a preacher in the general sense' and therefore being recognized as one by colleagues, Pugh and the Joshuas and others were well rid of it.

In *The Torch* for December 1900 Seth took up the cudgels to defend the Forward Movement evangelists against the critics of their preaching. The point was made that they played to the gallery. Seth responded:

Just so, so your fear is that of lack of reverence and pulpit dignity. But if you call sanctified wit and sarcasm playing to the gallery then go to Mount Carmel and heap your condemnation on the head of the old prophet Elijah. By all means uphold pulpit dignity, but if it does not spell the word A-D-A-P-T-A-T-I-O-N there will soon be no more admiration than can be bestowed by the hideous vision of empty seats. Have you ever noticed that there is an indissoluble union between a certain type of pulpit dignity and empty seats? This Movement was raised by God to reach the masses, and it is supported for no other reason. Who would not admit that the very material to be wrought upon demands a wider freedom than that which is needed in ordinary church work? Every angler knows that certain fish must be played with before the final jerk of the hook. The angler plays to the gallery here. You must do so, even to win the affection of a child reluctant to come to your open arms. But in preaching must everything be made subservient to a certain stereotyped plan that cramps originality, creates an insipid tameness which becomes too familiar, until at last it breaks on the ear like the sound of an old played-out tune?[31]

That is not to say that Pugh or the Joshuas encouraged 'off the cuff' preaching or that adapting to your audience meant superficiality:

Pugh always maintained that being a 'missionary' preacher (which is how he saw the evangelists) called for the whole of a man's intellect and understanding. This would not render him at a disadvantage but rather would give him the greatest qualifications for his work. To those who would excuse themselves from the effort of thought and meditation with the argument that they wished to be evangelistic preachers instead he would say with emphasis – 'if God does not want your brains, He wants your ignorance even less'. When a 'respectable' church argued that the work of evangelising was only for the uneducated or for just one class of people he would strongly reject such an idea. He saw preachers in whatever context they were in as 'debaters for Christ, calling for a verdict.'[32]

There is another factor about Pugh's preaching that is worth mentioning. Along with all this he would talk of an extra factor – the 'giveness' of a message. His sermons, he said, would 'come' to him, so that he rarely then had difficulty in thinking about them and planning them. His week was full of travelling, committees, building business and speaking. 'For some reason I don't have difficulty. I am convinced God gives the text to me so that I have no anxiety on the matter.' This continual belief that God was with him, prompting him, sustaining him, driving him on was a prominent trait.

When asked by the *Cymro* journalist if Pugh had left an abiding mark in the places where he preached, Seth waxed hot, eager to show that what had not yet been officially preserved for posterity in print was still recognised where it mattered – at grass roots:

Certainly his memory is green. The stones, the bricks and the rafters in scores of buildings all cry out and his works follow him. The children of his day, now grown into manhood and womanhood, speak of him with admiration. 'His leaf shall not wither.' No grave is deep enough to bury his memory in. Not even the grave of neglect dug by the hand of ingratitude. Not even the grave of prejudice dug by the ghoul of envy. God is pledged to keep his memory blessed, and it will be so, for it is written by the pen of iron on the fleshly tablets of human hearts.[33]

The main reason why Seth left the Forward Movement emerges in his reply to the next question of this determined journalist, who evidently saw his role as investigative. 'I should very much like to have a little of your experience with the work before and after the

death of John Pugh.' Seth's reply breathes the urgent sense of attack
in images taken from the recent World War:

> There is the greatest possible difference. In Pugh's day the bugle was
> always sounding 'The Charge'. The command was 'Up and at them'.
> We were always 'going over the top'. It was an offensive, an attack,
> a rush to attain an object. The enemy was kept on the alert. He was
> not permitted to rest, but kept in dread suspense as to the next surprise
> attack. After Pugh's day the command was 'Mark Time'. This military
> term was literally used. The result of this was that only one set of
> muscles were exercised, and the fighting muscles lost the power of
> motion. The army was kept marking time on the parade ground, close
> to the canteen. The nostrils of the warriors were no longer extended
> and trained to smell powder, but to smell the soup. Another pet phrase
> used, the moment Pugh passed away, was 'consolidate'. Then there
> set in a frost, and there followed a consolidation similar to that known
> in the North Pole. We need the fire of the old days.[34]

The bugle's sound

Seth kept his fire to the last. Twelve strenuous years of nationwide
evangelism lay ahead. Information about them is intermittent and
inadequate. The hand of the diarist grew tired, though the voice of
the preacher did not. We have a few samples from 1909, Seth's
last year with the Forward Movement, of mission reports sent in
to *The Torch* by churches after Seth had been among them.

One comes from Newlyn in Penzance in April.

> Twenty years have passed since Seth Joshua last visited our church
> ... many still remained who eagerly looked for his coming to us again.
> To these Mr. Joshua had lost none of his power as a preacher, singer
> and soul winner, while to the younger generation who knew him for
> the first time, his ministry was appealing and convincing. This quiet
> old fishing village of twenty years ago, with its band of zealous,
> godly fishermen has given place to a more cosmopolitan fishing port
> and the crews are, for the most part, indifferent to spiritual things. In
> consequence Mr. Joshua found very different material to work upon
> and the people much harder to move, but as a result of the mission
> one hundred and five souls have been added to the church, for which
> we praise God.[35]

Other excerpts show the deep affection, even awe, of people for his ministry:

'We call him "Seth" because he is a national favourite. Have you heard Seth? He is worth hearing for his loving humanity – a great heart full of throbbing sympathy for sinners ... a visitor said after the evening service – "That preacher is a real man," and I could not help adding "and that man is a real preacher".'

'Many years have lapsed since we heard this sturdy preacher but his preaching is as powerful as ever. Men who we have thought indifferent were enthralled by the power of the messages ... "many shall come from the east and the west when the nations assemble before the throne of God and call him blessed".'

'His visits to some of the centres have been almost a resurrection to life. Invariably confessions of conversion were made. In his mission to Clive Road, Cardiff, a fortnight ago, seventy-three came to the front, mainly young people who must live in surroundings and houses where poverty, drunkeness and immorality prevail.'[36]

His two main prayer-supporters when he changed his work were the secretary and the treasurer of the Free Church Federation. The three became great friends. They met every month at Rogerstone, near Newport, or Maesycwmer or Llandaff, Cardiff, where missions were planned and prayed about. The missions conducted were self-supporting but sometimes contributions were made to the work of the federation. At a series of meetings in Caersalem, Llanelli, for example, although no collections were taken, money flowed in like a river. Such blessing accompanied the missions that new invitations constantly poured in for Seth's services from districts adjoining those where he had been. Seth prayed for open doors and wherever they occurred he entered into them jubilantly.

As in his days with the Forward Movement he roamed wide through England and Wales and Ireland. His description of a visit to London gives us an insight into his style and gusto.

I went on a Sunday afternoon to Hyde Park. Here all the cranks of creation come to let off gas. A policeman said to me, 'Bless your heart sir, if they didn't come here to blow off steam there'd be an explosion in the city as sure as eggs.' It is Babel let loose; the blatant infidel with vulgar blasphemy, the city tongued agnostic, the shrill voiced socialist, the bulldog Christian Evidence lecturer who scream out their facts; all these mixed up with Church Army and Wesleyan music. We got the most extraordinary mixture of theology and crack brain creeds in all creation – O London, London, you do need a Forward Movement.

His comment unwittingly testifies to the public impact of the Forward Movement in the streets of Cardiff.

Seth's preaching continued to be honoured by the Spirit of God. His visit to Leeds Road Baptist Church, Bradford, in November 1912 saw 108, ranging in age from ten to over sixty, profess conversion. All 'hand picked fruit' according to Seth. In Rhyl in North Wales, where he dealt personally with all the converts, and in Brynmawr and at Abercynon in the South, over one hundred crossed the line in each place. In Watford, Hertfordshire, in January 1919 whole families came to the Lord. A complete Bible class of thirty came forward and confessed Christ.

Nothing thrilled Seth more than seeing his 'children' going on with the Lord. At Treorchy mission, Rhondda, the local pastor, the Rev. T. M. Lloyd, had been brought to the Lord through Seth's ministry years before at the Welsh Calvinistic Methodist church in Cardigan.

At Cwmdare the services were chiefly in the Welsh language and Seth found great freedom preaching in both English and Welsh.

Sometimes Tom Phillips, the treasurer of the Council, was able to accompany him, for example, to Portsmouth and to the Channel Islands. He saw at first hand and behind the scenes the tremendous work accomplished by a servant of God of exceptional power and dedication. He witnessed the cost and pain to Seth as family reconciliations were effected, as when he sat far into the night with a prominent business man, entreating, praying that he would accept Christ. The man's home was about to be broken up, but Seth saw it saved that night. His capacity to reconcile was exceptional. Mr. Phillips never found him downcast but always displaying the courage of a lion. Often missions were conducted entirely single-handed, for many churches expected the missioner to do all their work for them! Seth arrived at one place to be met at the station by a boy and he soon discovered that the church was dead, split by animosity. But God used him there to quicken people so that instead of being enemies, despising one another, the church was drawn together. Seth's companion, Mr. Phillips, could not but notice how he left the place drained dry and spent. Such close touch persuaded him that as a combination of urgent evangelist and patient pastor, sane and sound in judgement and doctrine, Seth was unequalled.

Behind Seth's own practice lay clear views of what he was aiming to do. He saw a vital distinction between the work of pastor and evangelist in the life of the church:

> The two gifts do not always go together. They are usually the separate gifts of the Spirit to the church. But the pastoral gift can be cultivated. A man may be a giant in the pulpit but a dwarf when dealing with the individual. The secret of success as an evangelist is to reach the mass, but the secret of the pastor is to reach the individual. In my judgement there is no better way than that of being a man amongst men. Move among them, mix with them, disarm them as to their conception that you are standoffish....
>
> The primary work of the church is to exist as a testimony to the world and to set forth the truth of their family relationship one to another and to God. The church is a home for saints and its work is to cultivate saintship. The members of this family are to bear one another's burdens and so live in love together that, like the church of old, they may have favour with all the people. The work of the pastor/ shepherd is to go among his flock and help to cultivate this unity of the Spirit, this family relationship and make his church a home of saints on earth. He is needed with the sick and dying. His eyes are keen to watch a sheep go astray. He is a man able to render first aid and with enough patience to render it seventy times seven.[37]

Undergirding all Seth's efforts was his endeavour to make preaching impact on his hearers. 'I think that the work of the true preacher is to aim at a mark and hit it. His preparation, his text and his sermon should all bend in the direction of the mark aimed at. The one purpose in fishing is to catch fish. To win souls is therefore the mark.'[38]

There were fellow ministers who were glad to learn this from Seth, such as one honest fellow-worker who had seen him at work in his area:

What struck me was his nearness to the people. His message had a definite aim. Many of us string together a number of harmless platitudes or try to impress with our learning. And as for understanding our preaching, many may ask, like the old fashioned Scots woman – 'Would I hae the presoomption?' Or others parade their doubts and deal with controversies – 'Our Bishop is an uncommonly clever preacher, but yet I cannot but think there's a God after all.' I am glad this mission taught us how to bring the living truth to bear upon the living lives of men.[39]

CHAPTER ELEVEN

'SAINT FRANCIS OF NEATH'

It is time to catch up with Frank and recall the character of the man who until his death in 1920 had been a radiant ambassador of Christ at Neath. During these years the Mission Hall in Neath was probably the most successful evangelistic church in Wales. We have seen how thrilled Seth was to discover how the church had grown during the revival. A closer look at the minister at the helm will help to show why it continued to thrive.

The inscription to Frank in the Mission Hall gives us a clue:

A faithful minister
A friend of the poor
A great singer in Israel
A winner of souls
Faithful unto death

The scripture 'Look to me and be radiant' found expression in 'Happy' Frank who carried sunshine everywhere, even though his work brought him into contact with some of the most tragic cases conceivable. 'Such a heritage points to a source other than that of natural endowment,' said Rev. T. Mardy Rees, who knew him well. 'Temperament might account for much of "Happy" Frank's

cheerfulness, but it was chiefly the gift of the Holy Spirit to him
that he might do his difficult work. He was never weary of saying,
"Receive the Holy Spirit. Breathe him freely, for he is your life
and heritage". In his sermons and work he emphasised the
importance of the Holy Spirit.'[1]

The Spirit gave him touches of his near presence. For instance,
while engaged in a mission at Neath with a Church Army captain,
they knelt together and prayed for a fresh outpouring of the Spirit.
Between the two stood a table with a candle and a Bible. After a
long agony of prayer together they opened the Bible and to their
amazement read a passage from Zechariah Chapter 4: 'What are
these two ... upon the right side of the candlestick and the left side
thereof? These are the two anointed ones that stand by the Lord.'
Following on such reassurance (which incidentally Frank kept to
himself for most of his life) they found the next Sunday morning
prayer meeting packed with expectant people.

> Frank might have been a poet for he had a playful fancy and a good
> deal of invention and an ardent heart. The spirit of romance was in
> all he said and did. He lived his poems in a life of joy and achievement
> and therefore did not attempt to write them. He might have won fame
> as a singer but he was content to use this moving gift to commend
> the gospel of grace. It was not just a public ministry to crowds. He
> would sing for a whole evening in his home to cheer a solitary
> individual who had just repented and returned from the wilds of sin.
> 'Gwynfa' ('A Place of Blessing'), the name of his home, was
> peculiarly fitting. Many were delivered from bondage to sin as he
> sang and were made secure by uplifting joy. Those who came under
> the spell of his personality could not forget the experience.[2]

The affection which the mere mention of his name evoked still
lingers in people's memory. The Rev. Peter Jeffery, a recent minister
of Sandfields Church, who grew up in the area of the Neath Hall
in the 1940s, recalls the esteem and affection which older people
had for both Joshua brothers. The poor turned to him for comfort
in bereavement and his ministry at funerals was remarkable. On
such occasions his sympathetic feelings found full play. Even in
his joyous moments there was, as in many gifted Welshmen, a
minor undertone which was most attractive. This was all suffused

by a selfless spirit. To many his selflessness appeared a weakness, but to Mardy Rees, it was the secret of his greatness.

The welfare of the mission hall was his all in all. As a life-long bachelor he lived entirely for it. He was a reformed pastor in the sense that he gave himself to the Word as he did to his flock. His expositions were original and he took great pains with preparation. Rees recalls occasions when he discovered him seated on the banks of the Gnoll woods brook, committing his Tuesday evening message to memory. As a nature lover he was helped by outdoor meditation. Seth, too, when in Neath, had his 'beech tree' at the Gnoll. A visitor to Wordsworth's home in the Lake District asked to see the poet's study. 'I can show you his library,' was the reply, 'but,' pointing to the hills, 'his study is yonder.' Frank too often had his study outside and 'stole from active duties' amidst the solitude and beauty of the Gnoll woods. 'The joys of nature,' he once said, 'should be taken to Jesus that he should bless them. We need Jesus in nature, if nature is to unfold her charms to us.'[3]

Our age needs a 'renaissance of wonder'. Life had not lost its wonders for Frank, either those of the old or the new creation. His favourite hymn was 'Great God of wonders, All thy ways are matchless, godlike and divine,' sung to the tune Huddersfield. He could never get over the wonder of his own conversion and he overflowed constantly with gladness before the Lord who had done great things for him.

Along with the awe-filled joy of wonder there came humour. His humour was a local fable. He never laughed at the weaknesses of other people, but the incongruities of human character and speech kept him bubbling with mirth. Humour in pulpit and conversation helped to drive home the words of soberness and truth which were his basic coinage. The gospel was never handled more reverently or earnestly, yet his unfailing good humour could not be smothered. He knew how to surprise his large congregations and laughter and tears were sometimes not far apart. John Bunyan says that 'some things are of such a nature as to make one's fancy chuckle when the heart doth break'. Frank, as an evangelist to sinners, knew the chuckle and the heartbreak of the true soul-winner.

His humour, of course, endeared him to young people. He entered heartily into their lives. In the field on a Whit Monday when the church turned out in large numbers no-one entered into or got more out of the games. Full of initiative and tact Frank kept things lively. He could entertain young people for hours and well might he thank God for the comical bone he had placed in his body. He gladly admitted his need of relaxation, and laughter renewed his spirit and was contagious to others. He knew well how heavy responsibilities bring weariness and need a 'diet of sunshine'.

Wonderful asset though Rees considered Frank's humour to be, he felt he ought to defend him by recalling this capacity in other notable evangelicals. Someone who had heard Rowland Hill for the first time was shocked because he made people laugh during a sermon. 'True,' was the rejoinder of a friend, 'but did you notice how the next moment he made them cry also?' Spurgeon confessed that rather than let his hearers become drowsy or inattentive, he would have recourse to that *wicked* thing called humour. Frank knew as much as any what the ministry of tears implied, but he preferred the ministry of smiles. His messages were interspersed with good humoured comments from church history or personal experience. Good humour saved him more than once but never made an enemy. His words were like oil on troubled waters and a tonic to the downcast. One Sunday evening the congregation was singing with gusto, 'Count your blessings, name them one by one, and it will surprise you what the Lord has done.' Frank noticed a prominent tradesman and friend silent. ('Listening to the volume of praise I was, to tell you the truth,' said Bill later.) 'Bill! hasn't the Lord given you a blessing? Sing up, Bill.'[4]

Such a relationship between pastor and people showed how well they knew each other and how honest they were with each other. If members had a disagreement at the mission they were invited up to the front and make it up. This method never seemed to fail. In a prominent place in the vestry was a card with the inscription that it is quite as much a Christian duty not to take offence as not to give offence.

Frank could turn the tables on self-excusers making biblical theology light as a rapier. Once he was remonstrating with a man involved in a rather shady deal. In self-defence the man said: 'You know, I am good at heart.' 'No,' said Frank, 'That is just where you are not good; if you were good there you would be good all over.'[5] And in the midst of his warmth his friends felt his honesty. One evening he turned to a brother minister and asked seriously: 'Have you been converted, Tom?' 'Yes,' was the reply after a little reflection. 'Good, but I have *never* heard you say so. That is why I asked.'[6]

He could show righteous anger too. He had become an influential man of the community and he soon learned what corruption in local government could be. He was approached by a man of dubious integrity to support his candidature for a seat on the Borough Council.

'Why do you come to me for your support? You know my principles are opposed to your way of living altogether.'

'I hope you will work a little, Mr. Joshua, to get me on the council. I will write you a cheque for £50 if you promise support.'

'How dare you offer me a bribe.'

'Well, if you won't have it for yourself have it for your Mission.'

'I could never support you, and certainly not after such an offer.'[7]

In the opinion of some, Frank, a strikingly handsome man, was vain as regards his personal appearance. 'But we believe,' says his loyal friend Mardy, 'that what was called vanity was only a high estimate of his body – "the temple of God" – and a desire to hallow it. There was no speck of pride in his makeup, as a thousand kindnesses revealed. The outward man was but a reflection of the artist in his soul, for he was an artist to his finger tips.'[8] And he was no pulpit showman. His pale countenance 'told of the preaching passion which consumed the bloom of health in him. He did not spare himself in his ministry. If he did not preach with the abandon of his brother Seth, his intense and earnest passion burnt him in the socket.'[9]

His popular title of 'Saint Francis of Neath' stemmed from his big heart for the poor. He died a poor man himself, for money had no fascination for him: he freely gave it away. Such a generous nature was often taken advantage of by professional beggars, for he could never steel himself against appeals for help. Every gift was enhanced by the cheerful spirit with which he parted with what he had in his pocket – usually leaving enough to get home! Fortunately for him the church treasurer paid his stipend weekly, for he never began a week with a surplus. There were those who, when they knew he had been away for a week or fortnight's mission, speedily relieved him of his rewards when he returned. Francis of Assissi is reputed to have said that he was 'plighted to poverty. No one seems to have wooed poverty for a bride since the Master himself, and I will woo her.'[10] In a sense Frank did the same, and the manner in which he was sustained reminds one of primitive Christianity. He gave away his only pair of boots one night to someone who called at his home for help. The following day he was in a predicament for he had a funeral to attend and the shops were closed. He had to wear the (too big!) boots of his niece's husband!

He was the hands and feet of his Master to many. One day he met a soldier from the local War Hospital who had lost both his hands. He invited him to his house. We don't know what powers he had as a chef, but he managed to make a pudding for the soldier, and when discovered in his room by his niece he was feeding his visitor with a spoon, and afterwards giving him a lighted cigarette. He was all things to all men and won not just some, but many.

His moral authority in the neighbourhood became such that he was able to constrain others to give to the poor. If on his pastoral rounds he found a family without food he would walk into a grocer's shop and order provisions to be sent to a house at once. It was his grateful boast that such a request was never refused. Not a few Neath grocers helped him in this way. One afternoon he called at a furniture shop and requested that they put a bed in a particular house within half an hour.

'It cannot be done, Mr. Joshua.'

'But it must be done. I am going for the nurse.' And it was done.

Frank was wont to say: 'I am not a theologian, never having been to college, but I preach Christ crucified.' 'His creed,' says Rees, 'was wrapped up in the name of Jesus Christ and his consciousness of God's condescending love for the world overflowed from him.'[11]

CHAPTER TWELVE

THE RETURN OF SETH

With the coming of the first world war the enormous load of pastoral responsibility which Frank had borne for thirty years took on another dimension. It took its toll even of 'Happy' Frank. As men left for the trenches and so left gaps in the church, so came the constant wearing news of sons, husbands, fathers who would never return. By the summer of 1919 he began to lose the battle for health. Vernon Mills, writing in his 91st year in 1998, recalls Frank's waning days. 'My only siting of Seth's brother was when I saw him being wheeled in a basketchair along the streets of the town on a Whit Sunday march of witness.'[1] Vernon was at that time a twelve year old onlooker, never having yet been to church. Frank's funeral the following year was one of the largest the town had ever seen.

Many months passed and there was no sign of anyone equipped to succeed him. This became a cause of deep concern to Seth who had, of course, been in at the start of the work. He confesses that he had never known such a time of wrestling with God. He was happy in his work as an evangelist and in comfortable circumstances in Cardiff. Ideally the Neath church needed the energies of a younger man. But the moment had come when Seth was compelled to say: 'My Father and my God. Take my life for Neath if it is Thy will. I will say goodbye to anything, provided I stay in thy will.'[2] The change back to local ministry in the church of his first love he never regretted.

Mardy Rees was present at his induction service on Sept 5th 1921.

> 'One thing in that enthusiastic service will ever remain with me – the evangelist's fine tribute to his wife: "Without my dear wife's self sacrificing love I would never have carried on my work. She tells me sometimes, 'Yes, Seth, it's all very well for you to go about the country and get the best welcome everywhere; but what of me? I have to stay at home and attend to the family.' Then, looking tenderly at his wife, he said: 'I know my dear, but the day of your reward is coming when the good Master will say, "Mary, come up hither; Seth, you stay there." '[3]

With a master hand and gifted with strength and energy well beyond his years he pulled the church together and stabilized his brother's work. In his early days he had been rather impetuous. But long since he had acquired patience. He discovered that self-sacrifice and not self assertion was the secret. On succeeding his brother he said : 'People ask me what I will do if they kick you? Well, I won't kick back. I have learned that a kiss is better than a kick.'[4] The last four years were as busy as any in his life. He worked hard himself and delegated work to others. He was a born organizer and had a firm grip of detail. The years of fruitfulness continued and there were people added to the membership at every communion till he died. (Even he, however, could not satisfy everyone. When a discontented member, who had belonged to several churches asked for his transfer Seth retorted 'My good friend, it's not a transfer you want but a tourist ticket!')

Yesterday and today

One of those who became a member at the Mission during Seth's ministry was able to tell his story seventy-three years after Seth's death. His recollections bring us right back into the atmosphere of the time. Vernon Mills writes:

As a lad of 16 years of age, I had never attended a church or Sunday School, and due to family frictions 'I was a little boy lost'. Then, one evening I heard singing emanating from the direction of Stockams Corner, opposite the Methodist Church, Windsor Square in Neath. There was an open piece of ground there, where various open air meetings took place, mainly of a political nature, but this particular evening, as I walked in the direction of the singing, lo and behold, it was a religious meeting. There was a travelling caravan complete with harmonium and I discovered the caravan was one touring the country under the title 'Open-Air Mission of London'. The leader of the mission began addressing the crowd and spoke of the Christ who went all the way to Calvary to sacrifice His life there as 'a ransom for many'. The man's description of the sufferings of the saviour touched the small boy's heart, cowering at the back of the crowd. But he so touched my heart that I went home, the house was empty and there, alone, I accepted Jesus Christ into my heart as Saviour and Lord for life! I knew not the speaker's name, but I thank God for the Mr. X who brought the gospel of salvation to Neath that day.

Therefore now my heartfelt desire was to attend a church and there was a boy in my street who I knew who attended some church. I enquired of this boy, 'Where did he worship?' He replied, 'The Mission hall', and I gladly asked, 'Could I go along with him?' So, the following Sunday we went together. When I entered – what an amazing sight and sound – over 1,500 souls packed into the church and the great Seth Joshua preaching. Glory! Hallelujah! I attended each Sunday and the sermons delivered by Mr. Joshua were soul searching and overwhelming. May I explain. It was not the 'luke-warm' message we hear nowadays. His whole body and soul went into the thrilling message. It was more a clarion call to salvation. Often times he was humorous too. I recall him once commenting on the claim that he was a landowner. 'Yes! I declare I am – I have a 6' x 4' plot of ground in Llantwit!!' (the local burial ground).

The sermon each Sunday was followed by the appeal, and without fail, three, four, five or six would respond and go forward seeking Christ. It was thrilling moment of victory for Christ and His kingdom. At one of these meetings I decided to be received into membership and I felt honoured when Mr. Joshua placed his hand on my head with the words, 'You have taken the finest step of your life my boy, in dedicating your whole life to your Saviour and His kingdom.'

Vernon Mills tells how the Mission hall had a preparation class for membership.

> I attended the week night meetings of the Young Converts Class. Mrs. Mary Joshua proved a great helpmate for her husband. She conducted these meetings which took place in the vestry. All the young converts had to kneel at their chairs and Mrs. Joshua expected us to quote a text or utter a prayer or quote a hymn. I recall how as 'a greenhorn' I without fail quoted the words of the hymn 'On Christ the solid rock I stand, All other ground is sinking sand.'[5]

Mardy Rees, in words written at the close of Seth's ministry notes how he had always loved things on a large scale, large halls, large crowds and he was equal to the challenge to the last.[6] His preaching was never above the heads of the poorly educated yet his messages furnished food for the reflective. He abounded in apt figures of speech and anecdotes suitable for the crowds he addressed. He was beloved of the crowd and his faith, love and joy gave him a majestic presence among them. He continued to lift up his voice fearlessly against vice and evil, in the open street and in the chapel. Yet he remained honoured as a Christian gentleman in the community and as opportunities came up, he helped every good institution in the district.

He was constantly appealing to the church for funds as the work continued to expand. They were generously met. In 1924 the church collected £3,209, a massive amount in today's terms. He remarked, good humouredly, 'Some day you will have that New Testament dictum inscribed on my tombstone in Llantwit; "And it came to pass that the *beggar* died."' His interest in the poor was proverbial as it had been with Frank. His last Christmas was celebrated by a tea for the aged, and each of the fifty present was given a ten shilling note.

When heavily burdened prayer was his relief. 'Make the valley full of ditches. There are plenty of surface workers in the religious world. What we want are diggers, those who prepare reservoirs for the living water.'[7]

America Again

In 1923 Peter, Seth's son, went to Grace Presbyterian Church, Brooklyn as assistant pastor. He persuaded his father to visit in August 1924. He sailed on the *Aquitania* and the six days on board compelled him to rest. Sunday on board, in contrast to his trip in 1906, grieved him sorely. It was the twenties and the sounds of the jazz age echoed round the ship's decks. Seth went to the leader of the band and asked him to play some Welsh airs. The selection left him feeling even more homesick! His preaching in America was precious to many congregations. He performed the opening ceremony at the new church of his nephew, Clifford Joshua's at Union City, New York. His final message was preached at his son's church, when Peter sang.

Peter was to spend a long life time in the States that extended into his nineties. His distinguished ministry included preaching at the college graduation of the young Billy Graham. The doyen of post second world war American evangelical scholars, Dr Carl F. Henry, acknowledges the way God used Peter in his own life.

> I heard him preach numerous times before and after I became a believer, in the days when modernism was regnant and he faithfully proclaimed the gospel. After I became a believer (I was a newspaper reporter and editor) he frequently prodded me toward the ministry. He would say that he covered Long Island for the Lord, whereas I covered it for the press. He was a fervent expository preacher of the gospel. He would kneel in prayer before preaching and on occasion would abandon his sermon for a time to sing an invitational hymn.'[8]

Dr Henry recalls how, in his teenage days, 'shortly after I became a believer I witnessed about the Saviour to a High School classmate of mine who was the son of the principal. I was unsure I could assuredly lead him to the Lord, and so took him to Peter Joshua, who did so. The chap later taught at a Christian college.'[9]

Many times during his 1924 visit Seth was also urged to settle and minister in the States, but his work at Neath called louder than the New World, despite its fair prospects. He returned home on the liner *Berengaria*. Within less than a year Peter would be making the same journey to attend his father's funeral.

For the time, however, the change and stimulus gave him renewed vigour. A large crowd awaited his arrival at Neath station. He could not resist a sound bite or two. 'Do not believe what you read in some daily papers about Prohibition,' said he. 'It is a great success and has come to stay. I did not see a drunken man during my stay in America.' His observations were widely shared at the time by others, and a year later the American president was saying the same thing. Deaths from alcoholism since the start of Prohibition in 1920 had spiralled downwards. But its future was fraught with gangsterism and bootlegging and in the end the move was a total failure.

'I have kept the faith'

He came home realizing how fierce was that other great controversy in the States – between fundamentalism and modernism. Although there was not the same stand up fight in the UK, even though the drift into modernism was as marked, Seth himself was severe upon those who, in the name of biblical criticism, despised the simple features of gospel grace. He would tolerate nothing that tended to remove the importance of the cross of Christ. He pulled no punches when asked in 1924 about the move away from the gospel in Wales and whether there was hope of it obtaining a hold on the masses again.

> The people are crying out for it. There is no grip in anything else. Can you blame the people for shrinking from the cold, bloodless touch of other substitutes? The people are sick and tired of the present day attempts to dress up the gospel in new clothes. A new tribe of theological tailors have wearied the people by forcing the gospel to become a quick change artist. Who would think of dressing the lily? Its naked beauty is its divine glory. It is those who lose faith in the gospel as the power of God who fly to new experiments. 'Go ye into all he world and preach the gospel' is still the standing orders for the church.[10]

When asked if there was a need to alter the style of preaching to charm the masses he could but answer according to his experience.

My danger in answering this question is that of judging things from our work here at Neath. During the past twelve months we have seen hundred confess Christ. As to the people coming to hear the gospel you may guess matters from what happened last Sunday. Our evening service commences at 6.30 pm, but the hall was crowded at 5.30 and a man counted some eight hundred people who could not get inside the hall. I have great expectations as to the immediate future. When the Greeks said, 'Sir, we would see Jesus,' the Master said, 'My hour is come.' We were never faced with an hour so pregnant with possibilities. It is come, brought to our doors wet with tears, stained with blood and with sobs of distress.[11]

As with Frank his ministry was meeting the neighbourhood's continuing hour of need. The church, through the gospel preached, was fulfilling its divine function as an emergency ward for spiritual casualties and material needs.

But soon the hour had come in another sense. Seth's next birthday was a solemn occasion, as his diary entry reveals. 'On this 10th day of April, 1925, I am 67, and the only one left of our immediate family circle. I am humbled before the Lord in my study now, and the silence of eternal things is resting on my spirit.'[12]

On Sunday morning 3rd May, 1925 this servant of the Master preached on the supreme passage for servants – John 13. The Upper Room, he told his congregation was: (1) A place of testing, (2) A place of cleansing, (3) A place of fellowship, and (4) A place of song. The last point came, not from John, but from Mark's rendering of the event, 'and when they had sung a hymn' (14:26). It is typical that his message left them with a song. The new song was never far from this pastor's heart or voice. It was said of him that his name – Seth Joshua – was not only biblical but musical.

In the evening he expounded with great gusto a rich uplifting passage from Isaiah. He entitled Isaiah 35:8-10, 'God's way'. He only leaves us his points, but they capture his eager life of evangelism. (I have put his texts into the NIV):

1) A clean way: 'The unclean will not journey on it.'
2) A plain way: 'The simple will not stray from it.'
3) A safe way: 'No lion will be there.' By paths – chained lions
4) A joyful way: 'Everlasting joy will crown their heads.'

5) A homeward way: 'They will enter Zion with singing.'
6) A free way: 'Only the redeemed will walk there.' All tolls abolished
7) Room for more in the way: 'Though millions have come, there is still room for one.'[13]

A few days later he passed this outline on to his son Peter in his last letter. 'When you get that sermon sketch on "God's Highway" mind you work on it. I consider it one of the best outlines that ever came to me. Preach it. It will suit any time.'

Mardy Rees recalled discovering these words in the first year of his ministry and filling them out in a sermon of his own. It led to the first conversion among the young people in the church. There was 'still room for one'. Seth, being dead, still spoke in the gospel he proclaimed.

'They saw no man but Jesus only'

This Isaiah message was a farewell to his people, though none knew it. The following Sunday he was taken ill in Swansea. In the agony of angina pectoris he returned to Neath. Even then, between spasms of deep pain his mind was still on his pulpit work. Always a man of discipline he knew that a new idea could flee from memory if not captured when it arrived:

'Mary, bring me some pen and paper.'

'You must rest quietly, Seth.'

'Bring me some paper dear, because I must catch these thoughts on the wing.'

He scribbled some thoughts, the last he ever penned. His text from the passage on the tranfiguration of Jesus summarized the motive of his ministry:

'They saw no man save Jesus only.' Peter, James and John were to taste death.

1) They saw the danger of spiritism. Moses and Elijah had departed centuries before – Christianity asserts the reality of spiritual bodies. Jesus only is the one safe communion.

2) They saw God's idea of Christian unity. Peter proposed division. God commanded them to find unity in his Son.

3) They saw Jesus taking pre-eminence

    (a) over Moses

    (b) over Elijah.

These were reformers. Jesus is a regenerator. Jesus abides. Others vanish.

    4) They saw the source of eternal life. Moses and Elijah were alive for ever more. Jesus is the secret. The life of the Body is Blood; Soul – Intellect; Spirit – Jesus.

    5) They saw salvation simplified i.e.

        (a) stripped of its trimmings

        (b) embodied in a person

        (c) all religious problems are simplified.

To see Jesus sums up the problem of conversion, eternal life, new birth etc.'[14]

Eager though he might have been to preach it, Seth had overtaxed his strength. In addition to his strenuous ministry at Neath he had recently taken missions at Llandrindod, Liverpool and Sheffield. Dr Lewis called in Dr Lancaster of Swansea for consultation. Seth's appeal to the specialist the day before he died echoed Hezekiah 'Give me fifteen years, doctor.' 'His heart,' says his friend Mardy Rees, 'was full of plans and generous purposes. His visions were too numerous and glorious to be realized in the flesh, but they remain as parables and prophecies of his heroic soul and are incentives to faithful followers.'[15] When the clock of St David's Church was striking eleven on Thursday night, 21 May, 1925, Seth Joshua said: 'I think I shall have a good night's rest'. He turned on his side and was 'forever with the Lord.'[16]

When the news broke, many throughout the country were staggered for he seemed such a strong man with many more years. God had given him a fine physique which had seen him through his arduous work as a pioneer. But he died in the midst of his plans and when the demands on his services were great and pressing.

The funeral service was led by the new Superintendent of the Forward Movement the Rev. R. J. Rees MA.[17] The Rev H G Howell had succeeded Seth in the first Forward Movement hall at East Moors in 1891 and spoke as someone who had known him longest. 'Mr. Joshua was a man with a large soul, a man of God and a man of the people. The great passion of his life was the salvation of the people. There were two Seth Joshuas – the one they were laying to rest that day, and the one who could never be buried. Thousands would praise and bless him.'

Hundreds of men, women and children lined the streets for he was the friend of all. Children loved Uncle Seth. The banks of flowers testified how greatly he was loved. Seth's body lay for several nights in the Neath Mission and throughout each night a rota of church officers mounted a vigil. Vernon Mills tells how, on one of those nights, they were startled at about 2.00 am when they heard someone entering, and out of the darkness a figure walked up the aisle and silently stood, facing the coffin. It was one of the Irish navvies. He raised his right arm, saluted the coffin and then left without a word. That act illustrated the love and respect which was held by all the navvies of the area for the pastor of the Mission.

Seth was mourned by his wife, four daughters and three sons.[18] His tombstone records, with that upward look that lifted others all his days, that he 'departed this life on Ascension Day 1925'. The scriptural verse was never more appropriate. 'I have fought the good fight.' He shared the same grave with Mary, who died in 1941 and one of his sons, the clever young Lionel, who preceded him in 1908 at the age of twenty-four. The memorial verse for Lionel reflects the heartache the parents endured at his passing: 'Sorrowing and sighing shall flee away.'

As a lad Lionel loved to correct his dad's occasional tendency to lose an 'h' or two in a sermon. The spirit of kindness was ever bubbling up within Seth and his genial smile made him a welcome companion who never stood on his dignity and who was accessible to his own and other children.

'Dad' said Lionel, 'You made a howler today'.

'What did I do, son?'

'You said "earthstone instead of hearthstone".'

'Well my boy, I will say hearthstone for the rest of my life.'

On another occasion Lionel said:

'You were wrong in your aspirates this morning, dad.'

'Aspirates, whatever are those?'

'You put an 'h' where it ought not to be and left it out where it ought to be.'

'Well, Lionel, what have you to complain about if I take it out from one place but put it back in another place.'[19]

His son Peter, who lived into his nineties and maintained a significant life-long preaching ministry in the USA, never forgot a day in Sophia Gardens, Cardiff when a lad. He had played truant from school and gone with a jam jar to the stream to see if he could catch some tiddlers. He spotted his father walking in the park and ran to hid behind some bushes.

> As he came near I was frightened as I heard that he was crying (something I thought my dad would never do) and as he went by he was saying 'Please God, give me Wales' and kept saying this as long as I could hear him. After a while I ran back home and while I had to explain to my mother that I had mitched school, I asked her what was wrong with dad, and told her I had heard him crying and saying 'Give me Wales'. She ruffled my hair and said 'You'll understand one day.'

Seth's constant roving, as he sought to reach to the far corners of Wales and wider with the gospel, meant that his stays at home had been brief. He loved these all too infrequent spells, but it meant that much of his communication with his growing family was by letter. Had his family letters when on his tours survived, we would have had further evidence of his striking and original personality. Three letters to his children do survive, two from the last week of his life.[20] Two are to his youngest daughter Phyllis. The first, written in 1920, after she had left home as a teacher, came at a time when a married man had tried to take advantage of her. Clearly she had not tried to hide the incident from her parents. Seth's letter shows his intense worry about her sexual vulnerability and his striving to be strongly protective and directive, yet not wanting to swamp her with the heavy hand of a 'Victorian' father.

> I have every confidence dear, in your common sense as to how you will deal with Matthias. But he will never enter my house again. You may trust me to convey this to him in a cool manner when I see him if we ever meet. To me he is a dirty cad henceforth. Possibly you will have the strength to look him dead in the face and tell him off. But be sure that you finish with him Phyllis. I would be proud of you if you

could do this. But if otherwise for reasons of your own, all well and good. No excuse as to drink will stand. Remember, he is a married man. He betrayed the trust of those in whose home he was entertained. He had no regard for your reputation. His estimate of your character must have been low, though he has never had a reason to think so.

You will be aware now my dear Phyllis of the perils that surround you. You have grown into a charming girl. This is no flattery and God protect you from receiving any injury by my saying this much to you plainly. You have your mother's lovely eyes i.e. when I first met her and loved her. Your life has been so beautifully simple and protected. You are now at a period when all the demon powers around you will conspire to rob you of your purity. Do you know, dear, that you possess in character, in intellectual power, in art and in refinement what is more value than any material gain you can think of?

Again I ask you, don't let this minister to your pride. These things are God's gifts to you. They are yours by virtue of parental sacrifices, many years of scholastic opportunity and of *your own* steady application. Mark this dear – read it more than once. The root cause of everything satanic is a jealousy of qualifications, moral, spiritual or intellectual and a demon desire to drag down the person possessing them.

I wonder did you need a rude awakening to this truth? Now you know, if not before, that as a burglar breaks in to plunder so there are demon powers watching to break in upon your more precious possessions.

Mark this also dear, and read it more than once. The root cause of every divine purpose is to create within you and to perfect the divine image of Christ. It rejoices in every addition to that end and in every growth into that image. I have told you of your personal charm, but that is physical and external. Your other possessions belong to the soul with its intellectual powers. But Phyllis, there is a spiritual realm. It is the inner chamber of your tripartite being – the only part of your being capable of communion with your Lord. He is a Spirit and can only have fellowship with spirit. When once this spirit power comes into your life it will be what electricity is to the dynamo and the engine to the electric lamp. The engine may be beautifully made, but it needs the spark of life. This is really what I am waiting for and praying for. The possibilities of your life then will be beyond all human thought.

Well dear I trust that this letter will not give you one bit of pain. I have no word of complaint dear. But I trust you will add this little petition to your prayers, if you have not already done so:

'Heavenly father, keep me from every snare and may the angel of God encamp around about, for Jesus' sake.' I shall hope to see you on Thursday but I can give no particular time. Dad.[21]

His other surviving letter to her, though written when he was within a week or so of death, is full of family banter and fun and something of a confession of his own, as well as a real attempt to relate to her as a teacher.

My dear Phyllis

I have been in bed since Sunday night – was taken ill in Swansea. I am a little better today. Perhaps it is just as well I am away in this bedroom. Mother has the spring cleaning fever on strong. I've the papering of one room with paste and paint, the chimney sweep rattling his brushes up the flues, Lizzie and Seth turning things inside out, and talking in spells about passing gall stones and tomb stones. I'm like the old (? *indecipherable*) in the cartoon, with my head under the clothes. The piano tuner came in also and helped to build up the Babylonian row, while old Jones' dog howled because the girl next door screeched out her top notes, playing on that old devil possessed piano of theirs. Then, to cap everything a brass jazz band came playing outside the whole afternoon yesterday. Do you know – no I don't think you do know – anything of the ease it gives you to curse and swear inwardly? If you let it out you lose caste but by keeping it bottled up you retain your respectability. This is where our standard of ethics go wrong. Men judge by outward appearances because his ethical standards are all outward. God judges the heart, but his standards are all inward. See how quickly I can turn from the jocular to the serious. It is a preacher's art, if he knows his trade. I have often wondered what is the true art of teaching in school life. Let me try and make a sort of guess, and you shall judge and let me know some other day.

1 The power to impart knowledge to others in exact proportion to their power of assimilation (sic).
2 The power to demand disipline (sic) without any undue severity.
3 The power to make children love you, because they are taught to appreciate effort to instruct them and benefit them.
4 A set determination (called patience) to plod on, in the face of seeming dullness and failiure (sic).

There are the qualities that seem to me indispensable. What say you?

And now, having joked, theorized and moralized I will end where I began, for Lizzie has just poked her face around the door and informed me that Tom's left leg swells up when he walks out of the house. She said it swells 'Hawfool'. Mother is gone out for tripe and onions. ? (*the cartoonist*) again!

Wonderful love from Dad x[22]

A week before his death Seth wrote his final letter. It was to Peter.[23] Peter was considering taking on a new pastorate in the States and Seth wrote to encourage him to do so.

Make the plunge Peter. Be not afraid. God will see you through. I am writing this in bed. I have overdone matters lately and on Sunday 10 May I was taken ill on Swansea St going to the High St Cinema Service. It was packed out but I preached and several conversions took place. I came home to bed and have been here ever since. Take care of your strength Peter. Work within your limit. Keep something in hand. I am good at giving advice...'[24]

He knew he was giving advice he had rarely kept himself. During the later Cardiff years, however, he had found time between missions to cultivate a plot of ground near his home in Llandaff. He was as heartily combative as a man of faith even here. The plot holders who worked on Sundays were challenged to produce such crops as he would by the blessing of God. It was said he proved his case.

This 'man of the people' ever remained so. On one preaching mission he could make little impression on his hearers and complained that they were all too proud to listen. Some retorted that he was proud also. This made Seth determined to rebut the charge which he saw as a damaging one. He sought some navvy clothes and preached in them, much to the astonishment of the proud and respectable congregation. It was reported that 'he brought them to their knees'. He could be even more daring. In earlier days, when visiting Maerdy in the Rhondda, he preached from the cross-bars of a street lamp 'to make them listen'.

He and Frank ever lived lowly before the Lord and so they did not find it artificial to live humbly among the deprived who made up so many of those who were won to the Saviour. A convert with very few possessions was determined to show his gratitude to God by having Seth and his wife and Frank to tea. 'It was a wonderful time of rejoicing, man, and a sumptuous table (borrowed!) A big dish full of cockles from Ferryside, and all kinds of tarts and Welsh cakes.' That man in time filled his house with furniture and became house owner and not tenant. That thanksgiving tea which he spread before the brothers in days of scarce resources, lived on in his memory.

Reflections and assertions
Seth had seen multiple examples of the way the saving gospel of Christ lifted men and their families out of the ravages and ruts of extreme improvidence, giving them a sense of stewardship of their little so that they managed their lives and homes well and bettered their living conditions. This of course, did not mean he was indifferent to public responsibility to help improve working and living conditions and often spoke out against those who tolerated such conditions. But he was outspoken too in his criticism of the growing expectation in the churches that better education and social reform would provide the answer to human sin. His words in some ways say to our own generation 'I told you so'.

> You can take your 'Institutional church' propaganda down into the valleys of dry bones. You may erect educational cranes for the uplifting of the bones. You may introduce every plank in the Socialist's platform. You may build garden cities and shout 'environment' until you are out of breath, and yet there will be reversion to type. The regeneration of the individual is God's plan. By all means let them go hand in hand, but regeneration must be the Jacob in the birth of these twins. It is a waste of energy to attempt dragging regeneration behind the chariot of social reformation. It is not a new invention, but a new obedience to an old command, 'Prophesy unto these bones, and say unto them, O dry bones, hear the word of the Lord' (Ezek. 37:4).[25]

As early as 1901, when addressing the English Conference at Merthyr Tydfil, he had said that the church of late had been giving an undue prominence to ethics with a strong admixture of socialism, but the multitudes remained obstinately outside the churches. He pleaded for a deep and continuing compassion for the souls of men and deplored how spasmodic and seasonal the work of evangelism had become. Was it inconvenient, he asked, for the Almighty to save a soul in the summer time? 'It was becoming an ecclesiastical close season.'

When asked a little while before his death by the editor of *Cymro* if he had any suggestion how to improve matters, his answer may have betrayed something of the sceptic's, 'I've seen it all before'. But what he said has the merit of life-long consistent confidence in the authority of God's word.

> Of what purpose is it to give suggestions, and give advice? This old world is pretty well choked with suggestions. Every committee, every monthly meeting, town councils, labour parties, socialistic meetings and every political party in existence, have been at this game of 'making suggestions'. Dear Mr. Editor, there is no material left out of which to make a suggestion. The thing is so overdone that there is no room for originality. What we need is not a discoverer of new suggestions, but a voice to command the army of God to fight the fight of faith. God never suggests. He commands – 'Do the work of an evangelist'. The only way to do a thing is to do it. Do not suggest to another how to do it. Do it yourself. Are our churches doing it with locked doors from Sunday to Sunday and 'Empires' open twice each night? Are we doing it with sleeves tucked up and coats off? I suggest the death of suggestions and the resurrection of practical activity.'[26]

One fact which he had to face in the mid 1920s was that building Mission halls in previously unchurched areas had not necessarily drawn in people over the longer term. It is the only time he seems tacitly to have acknowledgd that John Pugh and he may have put too much emphasis on a building programme:

> Years ago I would have said, 'Build halls for the people'. Now I see that halls may become empty or nearly so. The work within a hall may become dead and lifeless. It is not therefore a question of bricks.... The need today is the need emphasized years ago. It is the need of Spirit-filled men fitted to reach the masses ... the Connexion must now be prepared to spend more upon men and less upon bricks.

Say 'Mark Time' to the bricks if you like, but the cry from Macedonia is loud. The need is the need for men, trained in touch with the actual work being done.[27]

'Have you anything else to add?' asked the editor of the *Cymro*. Seth's reply combines a realistic recognition of the decline of Christian influence he saw about him with a word of burning conviction – a positive note entirely characteristic of the man and his ministry. Was he wrong to expect as he did? Or have we, his successors, signally failed to bring to our generation the life-giving and transforming touch from above that accompanied his own dynamic days?

Your question, have I anything to add, reminds me of that Old Testament question: 'Watchman, what of the night?' Yes, I venture into the realm of the prophet. I see the glint of the morning. Zion shall yet see the light of His face. Is not light sown for the righteous? Are all the harvests of light reaped? Is the light of the church to go down in obscurity?

No, for the morning cometh. The darkest hour before the dawn is wrapping us round. The thick blackness is a mixture of materialism, militarism, bolshevism, socialism, pharisaism, indifferentism, devilism, spiritualism, arising from the bottomless pit. The night is dark, but the morning cometh. Children of light, listen. Bend your ears down to the promises of God. They throb with meaning and with hope.

> It must be the breaking of the day,
>   The night is far spent;
>   The day is at hand,
> It must be the breaking of the day.[28]

A contemporary wrote:

Seth Joshua is an optimist ... in this he follows the illustrious Israelite whose name he bears, and who brought back the glowing report of the Promised Land. Perhaps the dominant note of his character is force. He is indeed a Joshua, a man of might and determination, who would not hesitate to command the sun and moon to stand still, should he deem the occasion required it.

CHAPTER THIRTEEN

POSTSCRIPT AND PRELUDE

When Seth died, the elderly Dr Cynddylan Jones, perhaps the leading theologian-preacher in Wales at the time, ventured this verdict. 'Seth Joshua was, in my opinion, the best all round missioner I have ever known. John Pugh took the lead in building mission halls, but it was Seth who filled them. You may find others to occupy his place. I know of none to fill it.'[1]

Late in 1926, some eighteen months after Seth's passing, a young man left on a train from Paddington station to keep a first preaching engagement at Sandfields Forward Movement church in Aberavon. It was eight miles or so from the Neath Hall, but in dire financial straits and with a low congregation. The area was 'wrapped around with the thick blackness' of 'isms' that Seth had listed. It was also putting its hopes in a political shift. Aberavon had elected Ramsay Macdonald in 1922 – a sign that 'Welsh working class people were departing Liberalism for good'. The Sandfields estate now had a population of five thousand, living for the most part in sordid and overcrowded conditions. 'The bookie, the publican and the prostitute prosper here and directly challenge us,' the secretary of the church wrote to the young visiting preacher, Dr Martyn Lloyd-Jones. He was about to resign from medicine and a prestigious position at Bart's and become a Forward

Movement pastor. His ministry was once again to put the Forward
Movement in the limelight as the gospel cut new ground among
working people. Martyn Lloyd-Jones had been preoccupied with
the need for evangelism among poorer working-class people since
June 1926.

> He was persuaded that modern Christianity seemed to appeal to only
> one social group. That was evidence to him that the transforming
> power of real Christianity was largely absent. He wanted to see the
> message tested in a place in Wales where social habits did not support
> church going.... His Charing Cross minister saw that if these particular
> hopes were to be realized it was the Forward Movement that provided
> it.

How much Lloyd-Jones knew of Seth is not clear. But in a
sermon preached in May 1927, Lloyd-Jones put Seth in company
that shows how highly he esteemed his ministry. The sermon is
making the point that true conversion is not the work of men but
of God. 'St Paul did not convert a single person, he was God's
agent. John Wesley, Daniel Rowland, General Booth, Seth Joshua
and all these glorious men did not save a single soul or defeat a
single enemy.' Those words indicate the source of Seth's power –
he was God's agent. They indicate too something of his stature –
'all these glorious men' – what company to keep! Events were to
prove that Martyn Lloyd-Jones himself was to join such ranks and
for the same reason – he was God's agent. The story of his days at
Sandfields are as dramatic as any earlier Forward Movement tale.
When Cynddylan Jones said he could see no-one to fill Seth's
place the young Martyn was not yet above the horizon. It is
interesting that Howell Williams' *The Romance of the Forward
Movement*, the official history of the Forward Movement, and
written in 1946 or 47 (undated), makes an anachronistic reference
to Lloyd-Jones. In discussing the continuing evangelism of the
Movement it remarks: 'That connexional service is being most
effectively continued by the ministry of the Rev. Dr Martin (sic)
Lloyd-Jones.'[2] That of course was true in the 1930s, but it is an
editing slip up. The writer had not noticed it was from a source
written in the 1930s. By 1946/7, Lloyd-Jones ministry was

becoming world-wide in its impact as it radiated out from Westminster Chapel in London. As we shall see that was to include Wales in a significant way.

But first, his Sandfields ministry, in an important sense, effectively continued that of Pugh and the Joshuas, though in a profoundly different way.[3] There are, for example, similarities in the kind of person that was reached through his preaching, such as raw working men who frequented fairs and lived for drink. Some of the characters converted in Sandfields such as Mark McCann and Staffordshire Bill, or Billy Fair Play, sparkle with the transforming grace of God in the same way as Dan the Beer Cask and Tom Pigeon. It is interesting that Lloyd-Jones reached the same kind of people, since his method was also different. The open-air strategy of the three great Forward Movement evangelists that so thrilled and awed people in the streets that they would follow those holding the meeting back to the church services, was not the style of Lloyd-Jones. His voice, his training and professional background did not fit him for the outdoor hurly-burly (though he was of course a great debater!), whereas Seth took to the open air like a lion after its prey. 'The Doctor' gave himself almost entirely to traditional church preaching services. His strategy was that preaching in the manner and power which he did would bring the people in. It did bring the people in. Maybe the decision not to espouse street preaching put the church behind walls when it was becoming less visible in the world, but he saw a sparse congregation fill up with local people including a good sample of characters. The church became a household name. So his ministry very definitely demonstrated what he had longed for and what the Forward Movement pioneers stood for – reaching the neglected who had no church orientation whatever.

Secondly, Lloyd-Jones and Seth both saw revival as the hope of the church. Seth had a lecture which thrilled its hearers: 'The world owes everything to the church and the church owes everything to revival.' Increasingly Lloyd-Jones became preoccupied with that belief. If the condition of the church was truly to improve, revival was a prerequisite.

Next, in terms of preaching power, the earlier Forward Movement evangelists stressed the need of a baptism of power if preaching was to be effective. They witnessed that effect as our story has demonstrated. That emphasis, much more theologically presented and with discerning historical backing, was a heart theme of 'the Doctor' and also demonstrated in his ministry.

But Lloyd-Jones' significance is not so much as a postscript or even pinnacle of the early Forward Movement days of power, rather it is a pointer and prelude to a new evangelical church orientation in Wales which has a measure of continuity with the Forward Movement concerns and was continued in some former Forward Movement centres. This came after Lloyd-Jones had left the Principality.

In 1946, the centenary of Pugh's birth, open-air meetings were held at the spot where Pugh first preached near Tenby. This was something of a token act. More significantly it was a time also when a renewed post-war student verve for open-air preaching – part of a renewed confidence in the biblical gospel – grew among many soon to take charge of Forward Movement churches or to be closely linked with their evangelism. There were, for example, Gwyn Walters, Glyn Owen and Wynford Davies. Then a little later, John Thomas, Hugh Morgan, Vernon Higham, Bill Steed and Mark Pierce joined older men such as A. L. Hughes, I. B. Davies, W. K. Sharman, John G. Roberts, D. C. Rowlands, Mark Pierce senior and others who were already in Forward Movement churches. These older men had tenaciously 'held on' to the evangelical faith in the 1930s, when others had let go of gospel preaching.

Many of the younger men had been given a boost through hearing Martyn Lloyd-Jones, by then at Westminster Chapel, London, at wartime student conferences of the Inter Varsity Fellowship (now UCCF) and then later at the Welsh Conferences of the IVF. Walters and Owen met Lloyd-Jones at the IVF conferences at Trinity College, Cambridge, in 1942. Both later took Forward Movement churches in Cardiff. During the war and later these students were committed to summer evangelism with the IVF during which open-air work was prominent and sometimes potent. The pattern of the day's activities in these campaigns followed precisely that of John Pugh in his evangelistic vacation gatherings for Bala and Trevecka students at the turn of the century. At the Llanelli IVF campaign of 1945 two future Forward

Movement pastors, John Thomas and Hugh Morgan, were converted. Then from the later 1940s Lloyd-Jones' presence at the Welsh IVF Conferences reinforced his ties with Wales and with theological students in particular. During this time, too, the origins of the Evangelical Movement of Wales can be traced and Dr Lloyd-Jones led its ministers' conferences at Bala. The following years saw its identity as a confessional body focus evangelical allegiance across the denominations. Later there were secessions from the Presbyterian Church of Wales on the grounds that the church had ceased to maintain a biblical evangelical stance. Many of those churches were former Forward Movement halls which had retained their biblical roots.

This quick attempt to thread a line through Pugh via Seth and Lloyd-Jones to the continuing remnant of today is partly, of course, the line of fidelity to the gospel which endures in days of God's right hand and days of dearth. In Wales we are now in an era of church closing rather than building. It is a time of crisis of unparalleled dimensions for the future of the church in our land. But Christ still says, 'I will build my church and the gates of death shall not prevail against it'. Our crisis is not John Pugh's. But grit, gumption and the grace of God are still needed. And while grace abides there is hope for the church in any and every area and in any era, ours included.

The seaport towns revisited

We are now some one hundred years on from the first great building and evangelizing decade of the Forward Movement. By now the Forward Movement has been dissolved. Time machines play no part in reality, but it may help to intensify our sense both of loss and gain if we invite 'the Three' – John, Seth and Frank – to accompany us through some of the seaport towns of South Wales at the turn of the new millennium.

They would stop in their tracks as they made their way towards familiar haunts. Pugh would grieve at the loss of prime sites, chosen with vision and won through perseverance. He may have seen the charge that he was building too many halls in a new light. Seth would not believe his eyes as he gazed at empty spaces or redeveloped properties in the places where the gospel blazed forth in packed and enormous halls. 'Where has Central Hall gone?' Frank and Seth would ask as they went through Newport, recalling the pioneering days when they had placarded the town with 'The Joshua brothers are coming.'

So let's take them quickly to Malpas Road, Newport. There's a very encouraging sight for them here. After many years of decline following the Second World War, the Forward Movement hall began to fill again as people were converted in goodly numbers under the long and fruitful ministry of the Rev. Hugh Morgan. It has recently enjoyed its centenary with an evangelistic venture that the Three would have delighted in. Pugh would be impressed with the splendid modern extension styled in a way that blends so well with the old building. The Three would definitely ask questions about the notice board which now reads Malpas Road Evangelical Church. An explanation about how the church seceded from its denominational links because it wanted to be clearly defined as an evangelical witness would no doubt satisfy them. Seth had seen clearly before his death the way liberal trends were developing.

But there are many more bitter moments ahead as well as some consolations. 'Let's see the first ever hall at East Moors near where Pugh and I pitched the tent – that time old Beelzebub went over the ropes.' On we go to Cardiff. As we turn off the Newport Road we pass Pugh's old pulpit at Clifton Street, now the Inkspot Arts Centre. East Moors building is still there but acts as a community centre now. Worse is to come.

Near despair would invade their spirits as they went on to Canton. Another prime site would look so different to them. No sign of one of the jewels in the Forward Movement crown – Memorial Hall, built in memory of David Davies, Llandinam, and filled to the rafters in its early years as Seth preached Christ. The demolition contractors have done their obliterative work. Gone, despite the post-war gospel efforts of Rev. Dr Gwyn Walters, Rev. Dr Eifion Evans, Rev. Mark Pierce and faithful laymen. Changing population patterns were among other factors that led to closure.

It is time for some relief for these stalwart but downcast men.

Time for some evidence, however modest, that what they stood for is truth unchanged, unchanging and that there are old buildings that still hear the same gospel sound as they proclaimed. A quick trip over to Saltmead Hall, where Pugh had cleared the ground with his own hands and made the definite effort to invade hostile territory. Prostitution stared them in the face then. It led to the start of the Sisters of the People. Here at least a witness has persevered with years of gifted ministry from Revs. I. B. Davies, Jack Sharman, A. L. Hughes and Mark Pierce.

A real smile of relief and recognition would break across their faces as we travel down Whitchurch Road. Why even some of the shops and houses looked familiar, and 'there it is!' – ahead are the familiar twin towers of Heath Hall, completed when Pugh came back from America and the scene of his welcome home. The tale here is of an unending line of faithful ministry – beginning just after Pugh's death with that of the Rev. F. W. Cole. A Cardiff newspaper noted its 'remarkable growth' in 1921. That was to continue through the Revs. J. W. Owen, Glyn Owen, Jack Sharman and Vernon Higham. But again, though the old foundation stones spell out names dear and familiar to the Three, the notice board reads 'Heath Evangelical Church'. In times of turmoil the church had seceded on doctrinal grounds. Since its early years Heath has been something of a flagship of evangelical life and now has probably the largest congregation in Wales.

An added pleasure awaits our reviving band. A trip back west across the city and the massive Ely housing estate, built with an attempt to give more space and comfort to its residents than the Three ever saw in their day, spreads itself for miles. Here is something unexpected. The age of strategic building had not ceased entirely with Pugh. Mountpleasant Hall put up by the Forward Movement, and then an independent church holding an evangelical reformed position, had gained in stature and credibility over the years, especially with its respected Christian school playing its part in the witness of the Christian community. It was the concept of the Rev. Don Hooper and the Rev. David Lock and others on the leadership team.

We were now heading out for the west, so we continue on along the coastal plain to the old steel town of Port Talbot, still boasting a huge steel plant able to compete in the modern economic climate. The Sandfields housing estate was another attempt to improve the industrial worker's lot with a clean and spacious environment. Seth's expressed wariness in 1925 as to how much such social developments would improve morality and real well-being have surely borne him out. The broken homes and drink and drug-related problems there would probably surpass his worst fears. But it was here, for more than a decade, between the wars, that the extraordinary ministry of Lloyd-Jones had seen the gospel dynamic break the trends of the times and rescue lives from hopelessness and put them on the road to holiness and heaven. The Sandfields 'Forward' is now an independent evangelical church. The successors of Lloyd-Jones battled in their different ways to exercise their own ministries under the huge shadow of 'the Doctor'. The Revs. Emlyn Jones, John Thomas, sadly cut down at the peak of a young ministry, Gwynn Williams, Peter Jeffery, have seen the church through good days and better. On the estate too is another latter day Forward Movement building under the ministry of Bill Steed. A few miles more and there is Neath Mission Hall, still standing, a group still persevering, but now hugely and excessively too large; a silent monument to the days when crowds thronged to go up to the house of the Lord to hear his servants Frank and Seth.

Our tour, positive though it has been in part, was no triumphal journey. There has been so much to shock the Three, accustomed though they had been to towering problems in their own day. The sheer reduction in the numbers of Christians and the devastating evidence of so much building initiative returned to the dust means the journey back to Cardiff is one of earnest prayer that God would strengthen the remnant and revive it.

We have two final calls, both at recent developments, with hopeful indications for the future. The reality of much modern church life in Wales – closure– occurred at the Monthemer Road site of the Crwys and Pierce Halls in 1996. It had long since failed to retain any clarity of evangelical witness. The massive building complex was in a state of disrepair. Were the labours of Pugh, whose tombstone lies in Cathays cemetery, a few streets from the building (reminding us that our tour has taken liberties with time!)

to fall into oblivion here too? No. He, being dead, still speaks, even in days of gospel decline far darker than any he could have envisaged. Pugh had been the preacher at the opening of the Crwys-Pierce Halls in 1900. His funeral had been held at Crwys in 1907. In 1997 the building was reopened when Highfields Evangelical Free Church took it over.

Highfields had begun in 1986 as a result of a sad contention in the Heath church. By 1996 Highfields had run out of space and, on completion of phase 1 of its redevelopment, moved to the Pierce Hall in July 1997. (The final stage of reconstruction, incorporating the larger Crwys Hall, was completed in 2003). The author, part-time minister at Highfields since 1987, had been joined in November 1994 by Rev Peter Baker, converted at Malpas Road Evangelical Church and son-in-law of the late Hugh Morgan, its much loved former minister. From this point growth accelerated rapidly. Rescue of the splendid though dilapidated site has placed in the area another growing evangelical church, with a congregation of 400 when the university students are in term. The late Lord Tonypandy, who died a few weeks before the reopening of the building, had preached there back in the 1940s, and sent congratulations for the reopening. 'Hallelujah for the resurrection of the preaching of the gospel in Monthemer Road,' he wrote. The Anglican evangelical hymn writer Christopher Idle (echoes of John Griffiths in a different guise?) wrote two hymns for the opening service.[4] One of them, 'Come hear the Gospel word', subtly captures some of the early history of the church and picks up Tonypandy's 'Hallelujah!' and resurrection theme.

> Come, hear the gospel word
> The truth of God made plain;
> Sing hallelujah, praise the Lord
> Dry bones are risen again.
>> By field and tent and inn
>> God brings his plans to be
>> And makes a stable, hall or mine
>> Fulfil his sure decree.

And God who makes things new
Has given this open door,
A time to build, a time to grow
And trust our saviour more.
>   Come wonder at the tree;
>   No leaf it bears, nor fruit,
>   But carries our iniquity
>   In Christ our substitute.

Come, tremble by the grave;
The stone is rolled away!
He came to serve, he died to save;
Raised up, he lives today.
>   Come meet the saviour here,
>   For he will not condemn;
>   Repent, believe in faith and fear,
>   And learn to love his name.

Enjoy this meeting place,
And do not count it strange
If God who gives unchanging grace
Requires his church to change.
>   Lord God, this house is yours;
>   May we your people be
>   Renewed in Christ with all our powers
>   For Christ eternally.

Our final call is at The King's Way Hall in Cardiff, where, once more, closure has given way to a newly opened door for the gospel. The story of this church underlines that there is a resilience and perseverance about the Christian faith which even its more desperate days cannot snuff out. This Mission, situated on the corner of Rhymney and Harriet Streets, has a heritage deriving from the efforts of English, Scots and Welsh Presbyterians! It was originally built in 1887 as a mission hall of city centre Windsor Place Presbyterian Church of England. As was often the case, a goodly proportion of the Presbyterian Church of England were Scotsmen. Contributions for the new hall came mainly from the Cardiff Caledonian (Scots) Society, a member of which laid one of the foundation stones. Nearby, John Pugh began the Fitzroy Street Mission of the Forward Movement in 1898 which later came under the oversight of Crwys Hall. In 1930 the increasingly inadequate Fitzroy Mission closed and the congregation took over the more spacious King's Way Hall. That closed in 1993 with the retirement of Sister Heulwen, the last of the Forward Movement Sisters of the People, who had kept the faith in a determined rearguard battle, with over thirty-five years of unbroken service from 1957.

The reopening in 1998 has bucked the trend in a pleasingly ironic way. A Welsh-speaking evangelical church now owns the building. Under the notably gifted preaching of former Forward Movement minister Gwynn Williams, it serves as a reminder to John Pugh that, even though he was so right to see the urgency of witness in English, Welsh is still a matter of the heart for many! And there are many who pray, preach and labour that the gospel of the grace of God may take hold once more of the Welsh-speaking community.

In three of the great conurbations that John Pugh was most concerned about – Newport, Cardiff and Port Talbot – the former Forward Movement halls bear a solid and reassuring witness to Christ at the second millennium of his coming into the world.

The watchword is still Forward.
The onward thrust still calls for grit and gumption.
And amazing grace will abound till Christ comes again.

APPENDIX 1

Edward Davies, Llandinam

The Park Hall, Cardiff, which held nearly 3,000 people, was filled to overflowing for the memorial service of Edward Davies on 16 January 1898. Hundreds had to stand both on the floor and in the balcony. John Pugh, who was to give the memorial address, 'was too deeply affected to stand during the singing of some of the hymns, but was wonderfully helped when he rose to deliver his address'. The address is given in full below, as it conveys so much of Davies, of the Forward Movement, of Pugh himself and of Christian priorities, both earthly and heavenly, at the close of the Victorian age.

John Pugh's Memorial Address
'The question asked by David, King of Israel, after the tragic death of Abner, the noble and the brave – "Know ye not that there is a prince and a great man fallen this day in Israel" came forcibly to my mind when I read in one of the papers on New Year's day of the sad death of Mr. Edward Davies, of Llandinam. Mark, David did not say "Know ye not that there is a *prince* fallen this day in Israel?" for a mere prince in name, and nothing more, would be no loss to anyone except a few courtiers and dependants, who

flattered him for what they could get; but "a prince" plus *greatness* falling meant national loss and consequently national sorrow. This David felt, and we feel sure this is the heartfelt expression of every fair minded person in Wales over the death of Mr. Davies, who passed away before he had scarcely reached the meridian of his days. If ever a true prince fell in our fatherland, he certainly was one. He was an all round prince.

'First, *he was a prince in our world of commerce*. In this sense he was a born prince, for his father was a commercial prince before him. He inherited from his father large and rich coalfields. Also, large interests in Welsh railways and in the great Barry Docks. He also inherited thousands of acres of fertile soil in his native county of Montgomery. The rule, as you know, is for the sons of rich men to spend what their fathers have toiled for faster than they made it. I remember the late Henry Ward Beecher saying from this platform that the rule in America was to toil hard to make money for the sons to squander it, and for the third generation to begin life over again! Mr. Davies was an exception to that rule. The princely fortune which fell to him as the only child of his parents did not get less in his hands but greatly increased. He held his vast wealth as a solemn trust from God for the good of humanity; and looked upon himself as a steward who would one day have to give account of it all. This conviction made him play the true man in all his business transactions. He knew that His Master was holy and no shady transaction was acceptable to Him. He carried on his vast concerns with *clean hands* and *clean lips*, for he was never known to take a mean advantage of anyone. He was a model to his class. His *good name* is today of greater value to the business man of this country than all the vast wealth of his coalfields. It is men of this stamp who make us trusted by the nations of the earth. Business men of Mr. Davies' character do more for us than all our costly fleets and armies, and spirited foreign policy so called.

'Second, *Mr. Davies was a prince in our education world*. In this sense too, he was a born prince, for his father was such before him. Those of us who remember Wales – whose education had been wickedly neglected for centuries, before our University Colleges were established – know well that the late Mr. David

Davies did more than any other business man to establish the University College at Aberystwyth. To accomplish that he left no stone unturned. He gave his best in mind, energy, time and money to bring it about. And his son soon followed in his footsteps in this as in every other respect. He was one of the hardest working men in the kingdom, yet he was Treasurer of the University College at Aberystwyth and the Trevecka Theological college, as well as being a member of the County and National bodies for regulating intermediate education. And he was no mere figurehead in these things, for he entered into the minutest detail of everything he put his hands to. The hopeful young of Wales owe the Llandinam family a debt which they cannot well comprehend, but which those who lived before the dawn of our national Colleges can well understand. The time, attention and money given by the Davieses towards advanced education should ever endear them to the inhabitants of the Principality. They have left an example worthy of the emulation of all our men of wealth – for wisdom is more precious than gold; and the advancement of a nation, intellectually and morally, is of far greater importance than material prosperity, for wealth without knowledge and character only helps to degenerate and ruin the man.

'Third, *Mr. Edward Davies was a prince in our religious world.* In this respect, also, as far as things human can go, he was a born prince, for his parents were devoted Christians. His mother was one of the most Christian women Wales has seen. The vast wealth which rolled at her feet was kept at her feet. It never corrupted her heart or hardened her spirit. That mother, who thought more of the salvation of her boy than any earthly gain or glory, brought him up in the nurture and admonition of the Lord. Her faithful training, through the blessing of God, produced one of the humblest, and yet one of the strongest Christian characters of this age. His beautiful life was "rooted and grounded in love" and hence was strong enough to overcome the temptations of wealth and to breast and brave the torrents of iniquity which ever beat upon men in his position. This, too, accounted for the deep interest he felt in the salvation of his fellow creatures at home and abroad. When the deplorable moral and spiritual condition of tens of

thousands in Cardiff, and the great mining centres of Glamorgan
and Monmouth was almost crushing me, and when God laid it on
my heart to take Christ to the people, I poured out my heart to Mr.
Davies at the beginning of 1891 and told him all that was in it on
this important matter. He sent me a most kind letter asking what
he could do for me. To which I replied – "Please act as treasurer
for the enterprise." This he consented to do, and that before there
was a church or committee at my back. He was more than a friend
to the Forward Movement, he was the brother born of God to
back it up in every way. He never faltered – for he was a man of
grit, grace and gumption; that is, a man with a grand moral
backbone, with a sound Christian heart and with a sound, clear
head. This all Welsh Wales well knew, hence he gave thousands
of people confidence in the Movement right away. He was too
upright a man, and too sincere a Christian to give countenance to
any shady thing.

'Until recently he attended the Committees of the Movement
and entered into the detail of the work. The part that moved him to
the depths and lit up his eyes like the midday sun, was to hear of
sinners turning to God and submitting to Jesus Christ. This was
clear evidence that he was more than a moral man, and that he
was a regenerated and Christ-possessed man, for what moved the
heart of Jesus moved him the greatest, and what moved heaven
most, moved him the greatest; and we know what does that! It is
not financial prosperity, it is not great victories on the battlefield
or the triumph of a party at an election, but the conversion of a
sinner to God. "For there is joy in the presence of the angels of
God over one sinner that repenteth." The salvation of a soul makes
God to sing, and gladdens the heart of the crucified but now
enthroned Christ to overflowing. And as the principalities and
powers of the glory land see His cup running over with joy, they
are moved from centre to circumference, until heaven's concentric
ranks are one great sea of song and gladness. The conversion of
sinners enhances the joys of earth and heaven. Some who passed
to glory through the Forward Movement have already welcomed
Mr. Davies in that land where God has wiped away the tear from
every eye, and where there is fulness of joy and pleasure for ever

more. When the sowers and reapers shall gather round the throne, Mr. Davies will share in the joy of the Harvest Home.

'But the question now is – "Who will be baptised for the dead?" Who will serve the king? Who will step into this great breach which death has made in our princely ranks? But another question goes before that, that is, Who will surrender himself to Christ our saviour, and consecrate himself to Christ our king? No one can fill this void unless he first commits himself to Christ and is possessed by his Spirit. The breach is too great for any Christless soul to fill. But with Him, every gap can be filled, every difficulty overcome and every good accomplished. For one who knew this by experience said: "I can do all things through Christ who strengtheneth me" – I can live right; I can do right; I can suffer; I can die! This is the one thing needful to make burning and shining lights of our princes of commerce, of our landed proprietors, and of all classes and conditions of men. This is what our country needs to make it pure and truly great.

'May God who made such a Christlike man of Mr. Edward Davies, make many more, who, like him, shall adorn the doctrine of Christ our saviour in all things, and become a blessing to their race and a glory to the gospel which he believed and practised. *Amen.*'

APPENDIX 2

Temperance

The attitude to the Temperance Movement was never, of course, a united one among Christians in the nineteenth century. Many, out of principle, opposed it. But it is difficult today, where the pendulum has swung almost entirely towards complete personal liberty among Christians, to realize how powerful were the convictions and how determined was the campaigning of those who argued for total abstinence. We have pointed out the legalistic dangers of this campaign. But, as we have seen, the Forward Movement, labouring to deal caringly with the personal debris caused by poverty and drink, were prepared to be mocked by many local political leaders for their stand on the issue. An example occurred in August 1900 when *The Torch* carried a *Western Mail* editorial on the matter headed: 'Christian Charity at Cardiff'.

The Forward Movement in Cardiff is engineered by a set of men whose policy it is hard to understand. A few days ago the mayor of Cardiff, as the representative of Grangetown on the town council, gave a treat to the Sunday School children of the ward. The mayor, Mr. Brain (of Brain's Brewery), is a Churchman, but as chief magistrate of Cardiff for the time being he is all things to all men, and this treat of his was given indiscriminately to the children of all the churches and chapels in the district. It was a very fine affair, for when the mayor takes anything of that kind in hand he does it handsomely. Here however the Forward Movement people stepped in, and said they would not allow their children to partake of tea and cake and toffy at the mayor's hand, because – will it be believed? – they said he was a brewer. Fortunately on this occasion the children showed greater wisdom and more Christian charity than their elders and went on their own account to the treat. They did not march, of course, from the great ugly brick temple in Penarth Road to where the tea kettle and tea pot were, but adopted the politic policy of identifying themselves with other contingents from neighbouring places of worship. It goes without saying that they were not disappointed when they turned up at the tables, for there the motto was 'Liberty, Fraternity, Equality'. It has not transpired whether the young recusants have been hauled over the coals or not. Now this is a very curious policy on the part of the Forward Movement, and it is difficult to foresee, if carried to any lengths, where it will end. When the Labour representative is mayor, and gives a treat, are we to suppose that employers of labour in Grangetown will prevent their children from attending? When a strong Nationalist becomes chief magistrate, and gives a treat to the rising generation in his ward, will all the English and Scotch children be ordered not to attend? If the Forward Movement policy is carried to its logical conclusion, matters will arrive at that point, and we shall be landed in a state of confusion worse than the primeval chaos.

'The first feeling we are conscious of is that of thanksgiving,' replied *The Torch*, in its editorial reply, written we assume by Pugh, going into the attack with relish. 'We feel thankful to God that the *Western Mail* does not praise us. We prefer being bruised rather than praised by some people.' The article then continues:

The next feeling that we are conscious of is the sense of honesty and fair play. The mayor is the chief magistrate of the whole town; he did not give the treat as the mayor of Cardiff, or else the offer should have been made to all the Sunday Schools in Cardiff, but the offer was given in the year in which his contest takes place as the representative of Grangetown to the town council. As our two Forward Movement Halls are in the ward that he represents, the workers felt that it was neither right nor fair for their Sunday School children to enjoy his treats whilst the very same Sunday School teachers may think fit to oppose his return to the town council. Our centres fight the Trade, and therefore, they intend entering the battle-field with clean hands and clear consciences. While they have no fault to find with the Mayor as a citizen, they felt grieved that he threw in his influence in his speech against the Children's Bill to prevent publicans selling intoxicants to children, and they are against the liquor traffic to such a degree that they will not compromise themselves in going to a brewer's treat. To us it is a matter of conscience. The *Western Mail* advocates the opening of public houses on Sundays in Wales, has opposed the extending of the Sunday Closing to Monmouthshire, and is loyal to the Trade, hence its opinion about the Forward Movement and 'its ugly temple' in Grangetown. We have no money for external decorations and high spires, but we do adorn the inside of our halls with men and women who have been rescued from the demon drink. These who were once ruined through the drink are our ornaments and jewels. And, we do not want their children to think that traders in intoxicating drinks are their benefactors.

And, lastly, we feel grieved that other workers and leaders in the Band of Hope work did not join us in the refusal, and thus impress the district that they are in earnest against the drink. The temperance cause has often been wounded in churches and in the houses of its friends. But this is a matter of conscience and there are consciences that need enlightening. It is not a class question, as that of employers and employed, as the *Western Mail* suggests in its illustration of the point, but a Moral Evil. 'The Trade' as it is called, is the politics of the brewers and publicans, and not the good of the state. It is the serpent that swallows all the rest, and we believe that it is a great national evil, and we long for the people to have the power to remove this gigantic evil which undermines the greatness of our country from within.

If the Forward Movement policy be carried to its logical conclusion, we would not be landed in a state of confusion worse than the primeval chaos, but in a world of righteousness, peace and joy in a creation of light, life and love. We have no policy but to teach our members by the grace of God to live soberly, in relation to themselves, righteously in relation to their neighbours, and godly in relation to their Creator, in this present world (The Forward Movement Magazine entitled *The Herald*, August, 1897 – July, 1899, continued in *The Torch*, August, 1899f; August, 1900).

A CENTENNIAL APPENDIX

Burning Hearts

Revival people I knew and treasured

The 1904/05 revival is important to the story of this book. Though I have not lived through revival, I have lived among people who have lived through it – and that in itself was a rare treat. It reminds us that there is a direct continuous link of one hundred years between today and people of the revival. Memory of them prompts me to pay a personal tribute.

I was born in Gorseinon in 1935 and grew up there and in Loughor,[1] the home of Evan Roberts. These two townships were the first to witness the public outbreak of the revival. There, and in the Gorseinon suburb of Penyrheol, I knew several men who had experienced the visitation of God upon them and the community. I count myself privileged to have gained early impressions of how God had visited a people in an extraordinary way by the outpouring of his Spirit in '04/'05. These men, most of them with roots in the local industries and business, still had a residual touch of the afterglow of the revival upon them and I knew moments of awe when they retold some of the stories and especially when they laid hold on God in prayer. Although I was third generation I was aware that something very special indeed had happened in the chapels and in the streets and homes of the townships where I grew up because these older men were a constant reminder of it. These men had known intense, disturbing feelings about their own sin, uplifting, overwhelming feelings regarding salvation from sin, overflowing joy in the Saviour, and sometimes a heightened consciousness under the Spirit's influence on them that made them 'see visions'.

Now some regard revival experiences as emotionally superficial, spurious, loaded with religious fanaticism. It's a truism that some level of bizarre excess has always accompanied times of great religious stirrings. But trying to interpret these people in that light just will not do! As a teenager and a young man I think I could have become very cynical if the wonderful testimonies I heard had come from men who were really only victims of intense excitement. I can affirm that for me they were a model and an inspiration. Their very existence and attitude made me realize that they had engaged a dimension of the spiritual heights and depths of the love of Christ that any normal believer would delight in, were God to grant it. My aim is simply to give a glimpse of my acquaintance with several of these people and quote some as they recall the ways God dealt with them. They all come from the towns of my upbringing, which happen to be where the clouds burst!

In both locations I lived less than half a mile from Moriah Welsh Calvinistic Methodist Church in Loughor where the revival under Evan Roberts broke out. There is a bust of Evan Roberts outside the church. People from all over the world visit the church and their number increases substantially as the centenary of the revival is upon us. Within a mile is Brynteg Congregational Chapel where many of the long term leaders of evangelical life in the area were converted during '04 and who, some years later, carried on their witness at Penyrheol Gospel Hall, Gorseinon where I attended Sunday school. It's a similar distance to Seion Welsh Baptist Chapel, Gorseinon where my mother was converted and less to Caersalem Evangelical Free church[2] founded by revival stalwarts.

My first awareness of the longer term influence of the revival was through my mother. The story of her conversion shows the kind of Christian presence in post revival Gorseinon during her teenage years in the mid 1920's. She had left school to work in a local ladies-wear shop owned by a Christian business man named George Bassett of Bassett's Bus Company, a man with a great Christian influence upon her life. Every day she would go home to lunch and one day, while walking along the High Street, began to notice that she did not meet a single Christian. This was so unusual in view of the number of Christians in the town that she suddenly panicked. Supposing Christ had returned! What if all the Christian's had been taken to heaven in 'the secret rapture!' (This teaching had taken a strong hold during the revival period). Had she been left behind? She knew she was not ready to meet Him. In her concern she knew there was one way to tell. She knew her mother was a Christian and if she was still at home all was well. She dashed into the house and found her mother there. The immediate relief was enormous but the longer term impact was to lead her to seek Christ for herself and yield to Him.

My first awareness of a church leader who had come out of the fires of revival was John Morgan, owner of the local music shop in the High Street which was opposite Basset's shop. He was the church song leader of my childhood at Caersalem. He had previously been a coal miner in one of the local pits, working with pit ponies. Miners customarily gave their animals rough and sometimes violent treatment to goad them into heavy work. From him came the story of how confused and passive the ponies became when such men as he were converted and stopped beating the creatures. The men changed to trying to cajole the ponies to work during the shift. Their charges did not know what to do! He would tell us this with tears in his eyes.

Another leader with direct experience of the early days on the revival was Johnnie Webb. He was for a while one of my Sunday school teachers at Caersalem. I well remember my delight when he told me that a talk on the life of Paul the Apostle I gave as a young student to an OAP meeting at the Gorseinon Institute was the best he had ever heard on the subject. I cannot but feel he was being kind to a former Sunday school lad! But the encouragement

I felt from 'a 1904 man' knew no bounds. Brynmor Jones in *Voices* from the Welsh Revival quotes Mr. Webb's experience of conversion during the early days of the revival. Mr. Webb was a youth worker in the church but not born again. His words show very clearly the felt power of the Spirit which is such a feature of revival:

'What came about was that the Holy Spirit revealed to me that I was a lost sinner. A very big shock it was, and there was no one there to tell me things or to lead me. The Holy Spirit was glorifying the Son and showing Jesus crucified on Calvary for me – he did it all.... I remember going into Old Seion (chapel) and as I was opening the door to go into the old chapel from the lobby, the Holy Spirit met me like the wind. I'll never forget that coming across us: the place was full of God. You ask why I saw myself as a lost sinner although I had been such a religious man. It was sin in another sense and it looked different because I had been stripped of everything. Before the revival, if you went to meetings and did the Lord's work, you were all right. But the Holy Spirit had given a new revelation: it is not through such things that one is saved, but through faith and grace. It's nothing of self, but is God's gift' (*Voices*, p. 194).

As with many others he tried to be committed to his daily shift, but work times and night times were transformed under the sense that worship of God was of supreme worth:

'How remarkable that (when the revival broke out) we should be at meetings all through the night and then return home about 5 am so as to be at work by 6 am. Every dinner hour, directly on the hooter, dozens would wend their way to the carpenter's shop to praise and thank God for his free gift of salvation through his matchless grace. It was as the psalmist wrote, 'As the hart panteth after the water brooks, so panteth my soul after thee'. To seek the living God and to know more about Jesus came before meals and sleep' (*Voices,* p. 34).

The powerful presence of God and the joy of salvation transformed evangelism into an urgency. My mother had a vivid memory – twenty or more years after the revival – of the open air meeting that was regularly held on the steps of Seion Church.

Strong men abounded and the witness out into the High Street was robust. Her favourite speaker was Titus Jones, the father of three exceptional Welsh sportsmen.[3] Mr. Webb's recorded memories of the early days of this and other open air meetings shows how the period '04/'05 invigorated believers to engage in real battle with the world:

'Open air meetings were held in every street every Saturday night for years. The saved would assemble at Seion, High Street for an hour's prayer before appearing on the steps outside. At that time there was very little traffic, so people assembled on the road to hear the gospel preached. There was a drunken man in the midst of the crowd and he was always in opposition. After much prayer on his behalf he at last repented and believed and changed sides and joined the company of believers and testified.

'We were storming the force of sin and we were trying to gain an entrance to the Mardy Hotel one night (just further down the High Street) when we were met by pints of beer thrown over us. After a while the drinking bars were empty and the publicans born again.

'I well remember during an open air meeting in Lower Lime street, Gorseinon (where Titus Jones' family lived) with the Rev. M J Jones speaking, a certain man was standing on his doorstep. He rushed through the ring and gripped the speaker with both hands round his throat. With much difficulty we released Mr. Jones from his clutches.' Mr. Webb was himself caught by the throat and threatened with violence at work after he had named five of his workmates as being in particular need of prayer (*Voices,* p. 102).

Meanwhile other churches had their share of blessing. Up a hill and away from the town centre in a northerly direction was Brynteg Congregational Chapel, Gorseinon. Brynteg caught the fire very early on in the revival and, being in an elevated part of the town, became a kind of beacon at night – some drawn to it, others afraid to go in. Large in my memory are four men under whom I learned the fact of past divine intervention and who possessed in their hearts a deep longing for God to return among us as the years of dearth came upon us. They were Tom Watkins, Thomas (Tommy) Shepherd and two brothers Henry Rhys Penry and John Penry. I have great satisfaction in remembering them as men with a heavenly dimension whose blood ran bibline. They were also sane, balanced, upright, rational men, cultivated gentlemen in their working class way.

Tom Watkins impressed my young life immensely and made me think what a wonderful time the revival must have been. He had been a collier but when I knew him he was an Inspector on the buses. To a strong voice and a cheerful heart and a commanding presence he joined an uplifting power in prayer and he was not ashamed of the gospel in any company. One of his stories that particularly struck me was that of his conversion. He was a member of a dance band who, very early on in the revival, was returning home in the early morning hours after a concert. He noticed the lights still on in Brynteg chapel and thought they had been left on by mistake. He went over to investigate, not knowing what was going on, opened the door and immediately on entering the building was overwhelmed with a conviction of sin and the reality of hell.

Tommy Shepherd was altogether a different personality. He was one of the very first converts of the revival. He was a gentle person with a touch of drama. When he prayed in public it was not long before he was weeping copiously before the Lord. It laid bare the genuine longing that these men had for a return of the Lord's presence among them and reflected how they missed Him. And above all it shows a burden that God would bless with salvation those who were increasingly showing an indifference to Christ. Tommy's burden for the lost was wonderfully answered. His son, David Shepherd, became an evangelist of widespread impact. David gave his heart and life to getting through to the younger generation with the love of Christ. He died in 2002 being active almost to the end . He gave his final years to ministry at Pisgah, Loughor a little chapel near to Evan Robert's family home at Island House.

The Penry brothers both lived on to a ripe old age and left a sense of the prophet upon us youngsters. I joined John Penry's young men's bible class when I was 17. He had previously held the Sunday afternoon class in Welsh. But when he knew I was looking to join he changed it to English with the occasional relapse into his beloved Welsh. Here we have an example of an old gent prepared to put the priority of sowing for the future of the kingdom of God before his very strong Welsh speaking traditions. Though he was entirely bilingual he would have been much more fluent in Welsh and he would have been much more conversant with his Welsh Bible. I don't think I realized what a cross cultural Christian act this was. The class was composed mainly of sixth formers and university students. His formal education was restricted. He had been a tin-plate worker. But he held the group in rapt attention week by week. He sat among us in the back two seats. He kept us to the scripture and, though he was so full of the years of visitation, he did not live in the past. To hear him preach and pray at the graveside was to be summoned into the reality of eternity and the judgement. There was only one occasion when I shared a ministry with him. When I was a ministerial student an aunt was dying of cancer. She requested that I join John Penry in praying and anointing her with oil. I was 25 and he was 75. His brother Henry Rhys was older than John. He was generally regarded as the leader of the fellowship. He was not quite as readily accessible to young people as John was though he had a nice touch of humour.

In taped recollections Henry Rhys and John have passed on their memories of the impact that their close friend Evan Roberts had on them very early on in the revival – just a few days after Evan Roberts had seen blessing break out in Moriah on the last day of October 1904. Striking visionary elements occur in both.

First Henry Rhys:-

'I was not satisfied with my moral and spiritual state – many times praying for something more. I wanted to be better. I remember a Sunday morning when we were praying in the young people's meeting and I could not express myself except through the hymn:

O! Jesu mawr, rho d'anian bur...
('Oh great Jesus, give me your pure nature').

'I was praying that morning, not just reciting the verse.
'Two girls were on the way to a Saturday night oratorio practice in Brynteg Chapel [on 5th of November] when Mari, an old woman, met them in the road and said "Do you know about these remarkable meetings in Moriah? Since Evan Roberts came back, there are extraordinary meetings." Meanwhile Evan Roberts had met Thomas

(Tommy) Shepherd, who played the organ at our oratorio practices and had spoken earnestly to him and told him about the Moriah meeting. After practice we young people were minded to go down.... It was about nine so we pushed into the gallery so as not to disturb the meeting. We felt there was something different about this meeting.' (They heard Evan Roberts speak from his open Bible on 'the white horse striding through the land and his gospel is going to triumph in this land and we will see wonderful things happening'.)

'Then Evan asked "Is there anyone here ready to confess Christ?" I was debating up in the gallery and I said to myself that I could stand up to confess since I had been faithful to the chapel meetings and was morally upright. I did stand up to confess Christ, and immediately I was under conviction, especially of smoking.

'They decided to ask Evan Roberts to Brynteg Chapel on Wednesday evening. I had been working the afternoon shift from 2 pm to 10 pm, and as I came home from work there was a crowd out on the road and a great crowd going down from the top towards the (Gorseinon) Police Station. I asked them why all the people were out on the roadside. They told me to run home as quickly as possible and have a bath and go back to Brynteg. There are remarkable happenings at Brynteg. I was back in Brynteg by 11 pm. I was in the meeting till after midnight. No one had announced this meeting yet the crowds had packed the place. Many people who hadn't spoken to each other for years were reconciled. A policeman came up from Gorseinon to see what was happening and was saved in the meeting. There were others who did not know what was going on and had left their pints in the pubs and come up to see.

'On Thursday the new chapel was full to overflowing. I came under conviction during the meeting and Evan Roberts came up to me and asked what was the matter. I said "I don't know", and he said "Come on your knees". So we prayed. We went home at about four to half past. At the end a reporter came up to Evan and asked, "What can I put in the Western Mail?" Instead of answering him, Evan prayed "O Lord, save the reporter" – and he was saved and went home. Yes, those were strange meetings: Penyrheol and Gorseinon were filled with the Spirit of God. People had to run to the meetings, being made conscious of God. The roads were packed and everyone crowded into Brynteg every night for weeks.

'On the Sunday afternoon, 13 November 1904, the chapel was overflowing and the meeting going on with no preaching (Evan had gone) and people standing up to testify and confess Jesus Christ.

Suddenly I saw – I was awake and conscious of everything – I felt Jesus coming to me and I was going to Him (very much like John Bunyan), and as he came towards me – He was on the cross – He moved his hand and pushed me away. "If God has deserted me" [I thought] "only a lost state awaits me." That thought was too terrible to bear and I stood up and said "Dear friends , God has departed from me; I have no hope; only total loss awaits me; pray for me". It made no difference to me how many people heard me. Well, the only one I knew nearby who could pray for me was my brother John, but John was in the same condition. It was extraordinary. People said, "Rhys if you are lost, where are we others", for conviction had gone through the congregation' (*Voices,* p. 28-30).

We now have John Penry's fuller recollections of the events at the Moriah meeting of Saturday November 5th and the Brynteg meeting of Sunday 13th:

'After Evan Roberts took charge of the meeting he went from seat to seat and asking everyone personally whether they were willing to stand up and confess Jesus Christ. He started at the pulpit on the right hand side. I had a seat next to the door and he came to the seat and said "will you stand up to confess?" "Yes" I said and I stood on my feet. I said to myself, "Why can't I? I am religious" I stood up to confess – but not everyone stood. It was now about 11 o'clock and Evan went back to the big seat and said, "we are going to finish this meeting now for there are children here and some want to go home to their children. But I want those who can stay to stay. The majority went out till there were about fifty young people left under forty years of age.

'The doors were locked and he said "We are not going to leave this meeting tonight till the Holy Spirit is poured out. I want each one to pray this short prayer, "O Lord, send the Holy Spirit now, for Jesus Christ's sake". We began and went from each to each till everyone had prayed. "The Holy Spirit has not come," Evan said, "so we must ask again". We prayed again all the way round. "Well, the Holy Spirit still has not come. We are not leaving this meeting tonight until the Holy Spirit has descended. We will start again." As we came to half way down the second row of chairs a young woman broke into tears calling on the Lord. Then someone was praying elsewhere, and then another was sighing and weeping profusely.

"That's it," said Evan Roberts," the Holy Spirit has come. We can now go home from the meeting happy and rejoicing.""

When the discussion got round to revival in our Sunday school class, one of the factors that fascinated us most was John Penry's attempt to describe the sense of God that prevailed in the area and the way it would affect non Christians. Here is an example of that as experienced down in the town's tin plate works from where Brynteg chapel was visible:

'I am sorry to say that I wasn't able to be in the Brynteg meetings the following week on Tuesday and Wednesday evenings, because I was in work. But when I was in work I could see the chapel, and there was much excitement among the night shift workers. They were going out every now and again to see if the lights were still on in Brynteg chapel. We all of us went out in turns and there was a real stirring up in the tin works because the ungodly were fearful and amazed to see the lights in the chapel at three and four and five in the morning. It was 5.30 am before the lights went out. My father was at that meeting until 5.30 am. My father, a man of great piety before the revival, stayed throughout the meetings and never wanted to go home.'

Another of the effects of the outpouring of the Spirit upon the people was that the power did not depend upon the presence of Evan Roberts. Whether he was there or not the meetings were conducted with complete spontaneity. People would pray, testify, confess, or sing as the Spirit moved them:

'On Sunday morning' says John, 'I went as usual to the 9.30 am meeting at Brynteg, but this Sunday there was no preacher. Mr. Stephens had been obliged to stop preaching because people who had been saved and sanctified during the week wanted to take the meeting themselves. [There was no Sunday school that afternoon, but rather another revival meeting.] At that meeting I had a vision of Jesus hanging on the cross. My head was in my hands and I was in tears for about an hour. My sister had been blessed that week and she said "John, come on your knees here. Pray." I went on my knees and prayed "God be merciful to me a sinner" Sin had come home! As God sees sin, not as we see it. I rose to my feet. That's all! That's all!

The tears stopped and joy came in. That night, before going to the (evening) meeting, I went to the bottom of the garden to pray, asking God to be in the meeting that night. As soon as the meeting started I went to the big seat to try to tell what God had done for me that afternoon, but other people were queuing up to speak from the big seat and there was no opportunity for me, yet I did tell them what happened that afternoon. I said "Look here! I went through a wonderful experience this afternoon, I saw myself a great sinner and you know, Jesus Christ has forgiven my sin and I love him with all my heart. My heart was like flint, now it is like a lake of water. The Lord has done great things" You know, the glory of the Lord and the joy of the Lord came into my life to such a degree as to be indescribable, until I felt I was a new man in body, soul and spirit. The only verse that came to me at that time was "Put off thy shoes from off thy feet, for the place whereon thou standest is holy ground"' (*Voices,* p. 30-32).

It is little wonder that we young men had the sense that here were leaders whose hearts had been touched in a special way. I cannot but repeat that it is one of the crucial factors in my life that these men's testimonies were backed by a lifetime of quality Christian living. The stories fitted what we saw and heard!! And the revival shoots have continued to run by grace into the present century. One of the students at our Penyrheol Sunday school class was Oswald Penry, a nephew of Henry and John. Now in his seventies he is vice chairman of the Llandrindod Wells Keswick in Wales Convention. In August 2003 I was one of the speakers at the Convention's Centenary. The first Llandrindod Convention in August 1903 was one of the streams out of which flowed the Revival in the following year.

There were others living in the immediate neighbourhood around us who triggered thoughts of the revival. There was Sidney Evans of Loughor who had been a very close friend of, and ministerial student with, Evan Roberts. He was, as Brynmor Jones describes him and as I remember him, quiet, studious and seemingly shy, in no way a charismatic figure. To my knowledge, he did not share to the same extent in later days the burden of those old stalwarts who still longed for revival. But if the fire seemed to have burned low he continued a quiet gospel ministry to the end. He had probably been closer to Evan Roberts than anyone when the Holy Spirit began his special work. He had been present during Evan Robert's critical experience of 'bending to the Spirit' (see *Grace, Grit and Gumption*, p. 124). The two friends were convinced that 'the wheels of the gospel are to be turning rapidly before long. The night is beginning to vanish and the dawn extending gradually but certainly'. Because of this he and Evan engaged together as students at Blaenanerch in planning evangelistic missions and seeking the guidance of the Spirit as to their next move. He and Roberts prayed that 100,000 souls be won for Christ. He then had for a while a very powerful ministry indeed, the quiet, shy man being given, for a period of time, a rare authority. He shared much of that ministry with Sam Jenkins, the 'Sankey of the Revival' and was used in the conversion of many.

And then I recall the lady walking along our road with the aid of a stick – Miss Hughes 'the chip shop' – she ran a fish and chip shop 200 yards from my home in Bryn Road, just around the corner in Woodlands Road. Hannah Hughes remained all her life in membership in Moriah. She was the youngest to be dealt with by God in that first night Evan Roberts ministered in Moriah. Her life had a sense of presence that lingered from those days and everyone knew her revival story. That story reflects how young she was at the time and how ordinary patterns of life changed so quickly and dramatically for young people, causing confusion in their homes as to what was going on. Here is how Hannah Hughes reflected on it:

'Evan Roberts was in a preparatory school intending to enter the ministry, but he received this call. He had a message to come to the young people of Moriah. He came of course. He answered the call. I was in that meeting, the usual prayer-meeting, but after that ended, Mr. Jones said that Mr. Evan Roberts wanted to speak with the young people. I thought that I was too young. "If she can stay I can stay", I thought ... (the tape is unclear at this point) We all went to the front, about 16 of us. He asked us to confess Jesus Christ as our Saviour. The thing was entirely new to me. I did not understand it, but I accepted everything from him because I looked up to him as a boy out of the ordinary, and he meant everything he said. The meeting went on until 10.30 pm and there was much concern in our house because I had not arrived home. I went with the other girls to the house across the road to tell my mother where we had been and what had happened. My mother came over to ask if I was there, and Mrs John said "It gives me the shivers".

The following day there was a meeting in Pisgah (a small chapel near Evan's home). We had a remarkable meeting there with a number taking part. That meeting continued to 10.30 pm. My mother could not understand why these meetings continued so long, and what the young man had to say to us all the time 'Well, come and see' I said, 'but remember the meeting is for the young people' 'Young people or not' she said. 'I'll be there tomorrow night'...

Soon the big showers came of course, with people crying for forgiveness, making up old quarrels, paying their debts. It was a pleasure to hear the children singing hymns on their way to school. The pubs were emptied. The whole community was changed. You realized that God took a personal interest in you. I think it was the confession that you took Jesus Christ as your personal Saviour. That came to your mind all the time. That we had an interest in heaven' (*Voices*, p. 32-33).

On October 30th and 31st 2004, two local boys who used to buy chips in Hannah Hughes' shop – Owen Milton and Geraint Fielder – will preach at Moriah to commemorate the day one hundred years before when the heavens rent and blessing flowed down.

Standing back after 100 years it strikes me there are two other tentacles of revival associations (though not revival conditions) visible down the years in Gorseinon.

Firstly, on Monday and Tuesday, October 14th and 15th 1946, Gorseinon was the first host in Britain to Billy Graham's powerful evangelistic preaching. His slogan on the poster advertizing was – 'geared to the times, anchored to the rock'. His rallies followed directly on from a campaign David Shepherd was running in Caersalem. David himself, as we have seen, was the son of a revival convert. He believes that Billy left the area with a larger view of the Spirit's work after his contact with some '04 converts.

I was converted at the closing Graham rally. It took place at Seion Baptist Church, Caersalem proving too small for the crowds. It was a return of the gospel to a revival venue which had gone cold. The overflowing congregations at the Graham rallies, stirred memories among those who recalled those days. Earlier I quoted Mr. Webb's recollections of Seion in 1904: 'I remember going into Old Seion (chapel) and as I was opening the door to go into the old chapel from the lobby, the Holy Spirit met me like the wind. I'll never forget that coming across us: the place was full of God.' I cannot but compare and contrast that with the moment, forty two years later, when I followed up Mr. Graham's invitation and he opened the door into the old chapel at Seion and prayed with me in the minister's vestry. However, there was not the sense of the place being 'full of God' that Mr. Webb experienced. The intensity of his revival experience gives unmistakeable evidence of the difference between revival and evangelism.

A second continuity with revival days came in the marking of its 60th anniversary in 1964, held again in Seion Chapel, Gorseinon, because it was the largest church in town. The chairman was David Shepherd, I led in prayer and Dr Martyn Lloyd-Jones preached. David had a gift for rousing congregations into song with his piano accordion. But he quoted his father's attempt to define how different was the responsive spontaneity in revival congregations: 'My late father,' he said (that is Tommy, an accomplished organist himself), 'used to tell me, "We didn't need such things (i.e. piano accordions) in the revival Davydd. The Spirit was in sovereign control of the singing and congregations were in His hands."'

The hymn 'Here is love vast as the ocean', the love song of the revival as it was called (it closes with the words – 'Heaven's peace and perfect justice, Kissed a guilty world in love') was often the theme of those outbursts of praise. Thankfully it has become an increasingly precious hymn in our day. It could well be the best echo of 04 to conclude on, teaching us that at a time of subjective emotions of the deepest kind it was the objective truths of Christ and His cross that filled the mouths of his people with praise. Such commitment to the Word wedded to such experience of the Spirit could well be the lesson we could most profitably learn from the children of the Revival.

Here is love vast as the ocean
Loving kindness as the flood,
When the Prince of life our ransom
Shed for us His precious blood.
Who His love will not remember?
Who can cease to sing His praise?
He can never be forgotten
Throughout heaven's eternal days.

On the Mount of crucifixion
Fountains opened deep and wide
Through the floodgates of God's mercy
Flowed a vast, a gracious tide.
Grace and love, like mighty rivers,
Poured incessant from above,
And heaven's peace and perfect justice
Kissed a guilty world in love.

BIBLIOGRAPHY

Copies of the Forward Movement Magazine entitled *The Forward Movement Herald*, August 1897–July 1899, continued as *The Torch*, August 1899–December 1900, also other occasional numbers up to September 1905.
The Life of Faith, July to September 1905
Letters of Seth Joshua to Mrs Jessie Penn-Lewis, April to September 1905
Swansea Evening Post 15th September 1945, 'It started at the Neath Fair.'

Dictionary of Scottish Church History and Theology.
Dictionary of Welsh Biography Down to 1940, 1959
Roger Brown, *Eminence Grise, John Griffiths, Archdeacon of Llandaff,* 1995
Keri Evans, *My Spiritual Pilgrimage*, James Clarke, 1961.
Eifion Evans, *The Welsh Revival of 1904*, EPW, 1969.
Geraint D Fielder, *Excuse Me, Mr Davies, Hallelujah*, Bryntirion, 1983
E. Griffiths, *Calvinistic Methodist Historical Handbook*, 1735–1905
Carl Henry, *Confessions of an Evangelical Theologian*
R. B. Jones, Rent Heavens, *The Revival of 1904*, Stanley Martyn, Paternoster Row, 1930.
Brynmor P. Jones, *The King's Champions, 1863–1933*, 1968.
Brynmor P. Jones, *The Spiritual History of Keswick in Wales, 1903–1983*, 1989.
Brynmor P. Jones, *Voices from the Welsh Revival 1904–5*, Evangelical Press of Wales, 1995.
Buick Knox, *Voices from the Past*, Gomerian Press, 1969.
Bernard W. Matthews, *Jessie Penn-Lewis*, A memoir.
Kenneth O. Morgan, *Rebirth of a Nation, Wales 1880–1980*, OUP, UWP, 1982.

NOTES

Introduction

1. T. Mardy Rees, *Seth and Frank Joshua, The Renowned Evangelists*, p.57.

2. David Davies, Llandinam 1818–90. M.P. Cardigan District. His Ocean Coal Company in the Rhondda was so productive that the Bute docks in Cardiff could not cope with the volume of exports. Davies, originally a humble sawyer, (though always 'top sawyer' he claimed!), promoted a new dock in Barry with a railway connexion of its own from Rhondda only after severe battles in parliament. Always rather rough hewn he became a founder and treasurer of University College, Aberystwyth. A 'self made' capitalist he was 'unspoilt by the great wealth he acquired. He distributed it to religious and educational causes and deserving individuals with a generous hand. A Calvinistic Methodist by upbringing he was imbued with a deep religious sense and was a Puritan in his attitude to drink and Sunday observance. His speech was untutored but with a homely eloquence and a native humour' (*Dictionary of Welsh Biography Down to 1940* [D.W.B.].) He had one son – Edward, 1855–99 who suceeded him as head of the business empire.

A memorial statue to David Davies also stands by the A 470 roadside in Llandinam, Montgomeryshire, the village home of Davies (a few miles from New Inn, Pugh's birthplace.) The statue is by Alfred Gilbert known for his statue of Eros (or more correctly Christian Charity!) in Piccadilly.

3. John Cory (1828–1910) and his brother Richard Cory (1830–1914), of Cory brothers, were ship owners, coal owners and philanthropists. 'With the universal demand for Welsh steam coal for shipping in all parts of the world the firm established coal depots, offices and agencies along all the great trade routes of the world.' They were also coal owners in their own

right. John was a Wesleyan Methodist and Richard a Baptist. 'Both gave unstinted assistance to all evangelical movements, especially the Salvation Army. Both assisted the temperance movement. For many years before his death John's benefactions amounted to nearly £50,000 a year. He was held in such esteem in Cardiff that they erected his bronze statue outside the City Hall during his lifetime' (D.W.B.).

John is buried at St. Nicholas church in the vale of Glamorgan. He was lord of the manor of St. Nicholas. Richard is buried in Cathays Cemetery, Cardiff.

Chapter 1: The Clock Strikes for Pugh

1. *Hanes Symudiad Ymosodol*, J. Morgan Jones, ch. 2, p.16 [trans.]

2. Thomas Charles Edwards (1837–1900). A scholar of Lincoln College, Oxford, with First Class honours in Lit. Hum. Received honorary doctorates of divinity from the University of Edinburgh in 1887 and the University of Wales in 1898. He was powerfully influenced by the 1859 Welsh Revival. (See the remarkable story in *Preaching and Preachers*, D. M. Lloyd-Jones, Hodder and Stoughton, 1971, pp. 322-23.) He became a Calvinist Methodist minister at Liverpool. 'An exceedingly powerful preacher, combining the fiery zeal of an evangelist with the highest culture of a scholar.' He preached all over Wales year in year out. His standard commentary on the Greek text of 1 Corinthians appeared in 1885 and on Hebrews (for the 'Expositors Bible') in 1888. As first Principal of University College, Aberystwyth, in difficult days, 'it was his magnetic personality and his eloquent advocacy that brought it triumphantly through its trials' (D.W.B.). In 1891 he resigned to become the second Principal of Bala C.M. College. His health broke down some time before his death. The first Bala principal had been his father, Dr. Lewis Edwards (1809–1887). Lewis had studied at Edinburgh University. He married the granddaughter of the famous Thomas Charles of Bala, a founding father of the British and Foreign Bible Society. Lewis Edwards became the undisputed leader of C.M. in Wales especially in intellectual matters. He persuaded his denomination to adopt a modified form of Presbyterian government. He wrote books on the person of Christ, the doctrine of the Atonement and a brief history of theology. He sought to evade controversy while 'maintaining a somewhat modified Calvinism' (Dr. Tudur Jones).

3. Howell Williams, *The Romance of the Forward Movement,* p.26.

4. Williams, p.27.

5. Williams, p.35.

6. Williams, p.36.

7. Williams, p.37.

Chapter 2: The Drinking Dens

1. Edward Matthews (1813–1892). Calvinistic Methodist minister and

popular author. His reputation as an imaginative and dramatic preacher and author stands high. He entranced his congregations, was full of the unexpected, and was 'for a long time uncrowned king of the Calvinistic Methodists' (D.W.B.).

2. Howell Williams, *The Romance of the Forward Movement,* p.38.

3. *Atgofion am y Dr. John Pugh,* Annie Pugh Williams [private translation])

4. *Atgofion am y Dr. John Pugh,* Annie Pugh Williams [private translation] ch. 1, p.14.

5. D. L. Moody had a big influence on Pugh. Moody's powerful campaigns drew the strong support of men like C. H. Spurgeon in England and Horatius Bonar in Scotland: firstly because they saw in them a special touch of divine blessing as crowds turned to Christ; and secondly, because Moody preached the simple gospel of conversion and forgiveness without showing any distinctly Arminian tendencies in his preaching. However, Spurgeon and some of the Scottish Calvinists were uneasy about the implications of the new appeal system which had been developed in the United States. Moody used this method in his campaigns, where seekers were called forward for counselling and decision. In keeping with their theology Spurgeon and others (who would have included the Welsh forebears of Pugh and Seth) had exhorted seekers after God to deal directly with Him through Christ. They saw the introduction of counsellors and enquiry rooms as a failure to understand the Holy Spirit's primacy and sovereignty in the work of regeneration.

Both John Pugh and Seth Joshua remained moderately Calvinistic all their days but did not seem to share these misgivings. As we shall see, in their eagerness to get to grips with the unchurched, they quickly took over the new method of counselling along with the tendency to count the numbers of those responding. They also picked up from the Moody/Sankey approach a strong emphasis on lively instrumental music to 'brighten up' services for ordinary people, though music, of course, in the form of the powerful draw of hymn singing on crowds, had also been at the heart of the eighteenth and nineteenth century revivals in Wales. So the Forward Movement men took their momentum from two sources. The contemporary example of Moody stirred them, while, at the same time, they were deeply conscious that in going to the crowds with the gospel they were running in the tracks of their Calvinist Methodist heritage. Some later Forward Movement men, under the influence of Martyn Lloyd-Jones, were to abandon the methods of the invitation system and return to the convictions of these earlier generations. For a well-argued defence of the old ways, see Iain Murray, *The Forgotten Spurgeon,* Banner of Truth, 1966, especially the last chapter.

6. Though the record of the coal owners in providing housing is hardly a flattering one and the numbers of jerry built terraced housing put up by

speculative builders with a total absence of planning or amenity provision contributed massively to the bleak misery of living conditions, there was a surprisingly high degree of home ownership in the Rhondda and the new wealth constantly pumped in through the agency of the mining industry was shared to a degree by the workers. It is gratifying to note that some of the new terrace housing provided by colliery companies, such as David Davies constructed at Ton Pentre and Treorchy, was in advance of its time (see K. O. Morgan *op. cit.* p.72). The better employer realized that, over and above benevolence, he had a direct interest in the health of his experienced workmen. The author's personal research into the earliest of Welsh industrial environments – the copper industry in Swansea – affords a prime example of this in the Vivian family, the main copper magnates. In 1848 Vivian wrote to the Treasury concerning the alarm of rate payers at the likely cost of public health works proposed by the new health bill. He proposed that by constructing drains for his own industrial cottages at Hafod on the most improved plan, the local health authority could then have them as a model to refer to and be able to calculate the outlay required for its own works. The government inspector examined those model cottages. He found a long garden behind with a privy and pigstye to each house situated at a distance from the house. The road in front was neatly formed and a footway paved and flagged. Each house contained five rooms, the windows being made to open. Nothing could have been cleaner, more comfortable or in more contrast to the usual pattern, concluded the inspector. In 1854 the local health officer reported that the ample room, sound structure, dry brick floor, tiled roofs and convenient partitions characteristic of the newer Vivian houses contrasted in almost every detail with the old miners' cottages that were numerous in the area. This observation cautions against the mistake of accounting the industrial revolution responsible for nothing but unmitigated suffering to the labouring population. Those who settled in Trevivian did not have to wallow in the cellars of a city slum. The copper workers enjoyed a good standard of living. One of the effects noticed independently by the government inspector and the local health officer was the change of health and prospects evident in 'the improved countenances and happy ruddy faces of the children in this area. They seemed to speak eloquently of the care bestowed on them by their wealthy Christian employer.' This is a welcome relief to the picture painted of the new towns as a breeding ground of 'a pallid, sullen, twisted stock of humanity' (G. D. Fielder, 'Public health in 19th century Swansea', M. A. Thesis, University of Wales, 1962).

7. The Welsh Sunday Closing Act when passed in 1881 was endorsed by Gladstone himself. 'It was constitutionally significant in being the first distinctively Welsh act of parliament.' It was for the first time 'pronounced by parliament that Wales had a separate political identity.... With all its

flaws ... the Welsh Sunday Closing Act was a testimony to the identity of the nation' (K. O. Morgan, *Rebirth of a Nation*, pp. 36, 37).

8. *Hanes Symudiad Ymosodol*, J. Morgan Jones, ch. 2 p.23.

9. Cowper-Temple. He was the author of the Cowper-Temple clause in the Education Act of 1870 whereby unsectarian Christian teaching was provided in Board schools.

10. T. Mardy Rees, *Seth and Frank Joshua, The Renowned Evangelists*, pp. 4, 5.

11. T. Mardy Rees, p.5.

12. T. Mardy Rees, p.6.

13. T. Mardy Rees, p.7.

14. T. Mardy Rees, p.8.

15. T. Mardy Rees, p.9.

16. T. Mardy Rees, p.9.

17. T. Mardy Rees, pp.10-11.

18. T. Mardy Rees, p.11.

19. *Atgofion am y Dr. John Pugh*, Annie Pugh Williams [private translation], ch. 2, p.16.

20. *The Calvinistic Methodist Historical Handbook*, 1735–1905, E. Griffiths.

21. ibid.

Chapter 3: The Joshuas at Neath

1. T. Mardy Rees, *Seth and Frank Joshua, The Renowned Evangelists*, p.13.

2. T. Mardy Rees, p.15.

3. T. Mardy Rees, p.16.

4. *South Wales Evening Post*, September, 1945.

5. Seth never lost the instincts of the boxer! Many years later, in 1900, when introducing a reply to the Forward Movement's critics, he could not resist, it seems, making his point, with some sarcasm, via the latest boxing topic i.e. the Queensbury rules: 'It may be news to many that the title Forward Movement creates vexation of spirit in some, even within the borders of Methodism. The danger, however, lies in the fact that the criticisms are far too polite, apologetic and softly feminine in tone. The old pugilistic attitude is gone, to make room for the new Queensbury rule, in order to lift criticism into the sphere of a "noble art". The gloves must be of the specified weight, just and true to the very ounce. To strike out in the old way would be considered uncultured enmity, but under the new regime it is good breeding. An up-to-date critic must not slog now; he must only tap smartly, lightly and gain on points.'

6. *South Wales Evening Post*, September, 1945.

7. T. Mardy Rees, p.53.

8. A search around the walls of Llandaff Cathedral revealed no tablet.

After enquiries with the Cathedral archivist it appears that it was one of the casualties of the bombing the Cathedral suffered in the Second World War. I am grateful to the Rev. Roger Brown, Vicar of Welshpool for the information on Griffiths. It is taken from his article entitled *Eminence Grise: John Griffiths, Archdeacon of Llandaff.*

9. Roger Brown.

10. Roger Brown.

11. Roger Brown

12. T. Mardy Rees, pp.23, 24.

13. Iain Murray, *The Forgotten Spurgeon*, p. 3.

14. T. Mardy Rees, p.18.

15. T. Mardy Rees, p.18.

16. T. Mardy Rees, p.21.

17. T. Mardy Rees, p.22.

18. T. Mardy Rees, p.22.

19. T. Mardy Rees, pp. 22, 23.

20. T. Mardy Rees, p.23.

21. T. Mardy Rees, p.23.

22. T. Mardy Rees, p.54.

23. T. Mardy Rees, p.19.

24. 'The money we had saved for our wedding was spent on mission work in Blaenavon,' Mary recalled (T. Mardy Rees, p.22)

25. T. Mardy Rees, p.54.

26. T. Mardy Rees, p.54.

27. T. Mardy Rees, p.23.

28. T. Mardy Rees, p.26.

29. T. Mardy Rees, p.27.

30. T. Mardy Rees, p.29.

31. T. Mardy Rees, p.29.

32. T. Mardy Rees, p.29.

33. T. Mardy Rees, p.50.

34. T. Mardy Rees, p.30.

35. *South Wales Evening Post*, September, 1945.

36. C.M. Archives, National Library of Wales, HZ1/17/4

37. T. Mardy Rees, pp.31, 32.

38. T. Mardy Rees, p.32.

39. T. Mardy Rees, p.33.

40. T. Mardy Rees, p.33.

41. T. Mardy Rees, pp.33, 34.

42. T. Mardy Rees, p.98.

43. T. Mardy Rees, p.28.

44. Roger Brown.

45. Roger Brown.

46. Roger Brown.
47. T. Mardy Rees, p.17.
48. T. Mardy Rees, p.36.
49. T. Mardy Rees, p.45.
50. The Forward Movement Magazine, Dec. 1898, p.54. Seth touched a deep chord of protestant distinctiveness here and may perhaps be reflecting his reading of the Puritans. Instead of choral singing or organ playing, which they believed distracted the attention from the intellectual content of worship, the Puritans advocated congregational singing – which was a more radical protestant innovation. The Puritan Bishop Jewell in 1559 thought that the 'kingdom of the mass, priests and the devil ... is weakened and shaken at almost every note uttered' by large crowds singing together after the sermon at Paul's cross. Hymn singing was regarded by the authorities as potentially dangerous, associated with the lower classes. Jeremy Collier, an Anglican with Romish sympathies who supported James II, feared hymn singing and said that 'music was almost as dangerous as gunpowder and it may be requires looking after no less than the press or the mint.' Seth's words, 'the whole church is a royal priesthood and every priest may minister with singing', though unremarkable at first sight, breathes the vitality of reformation radicalism!

Chapter 4: Glasgow, Cardiff and The Forward Movement.

1. Dr. Cynddylan Jones (1840–1930). Educated at Bala and Trevecka Colleges. Minister at Pontypool, London, and chiefly Frederick St., Calvinist Methodist church, Cardiff. For twenty years he was deputation secretary for the Bible Society. He was a prominent preacher in both Welsh and English. While minister in English causes he published a number of expository works which attracted much attention e.g. Studies in Matthew, in Luke, in John, in Acts, in Romans. The latter was entitled *Eternal Truth in the Eternal City*, a book described by Dr. T. L. Morgan as 'the sunset splendours of a great ministry, unclouded by shadows of modernism'. Later in a very long life he wrote in Welsh.

2. *Atgofion am y Dr. John Pugh*, Annie Pugh Williams [private translation], ch. 2, p.17.

3. *Atgofion am y Dr. John Pugh*, Annie Pugh Williams [private translation], ch. 2, pp.18, 19.

4. Not long after the death of Seth the young Jack Sharman from Neath was persuaded to attend the Mission Hall. He was reluctant. He was especially put off by the rousing type of tunes. During the singing of 'Come ye that love the Lord and let your joys be known' he refused to join in partly because of its swinging chorus, 'marching to Zion'. But when he came to the verse 'Let those refuse to sing who never knew their God' he was hit by the real reason why he was refusing to sing. He did not know

God. His conversion led to service with the China Inland Mission in mainland China and then as minister of two Forward Movement churches in Cardiff.

5. *Atgofion am y Dr. John Pugh*, Annie Pugh Williams [private translation], p.20.

6. Howell Williams, *The Romance of the Forward Movement*, p.52.

7. Ross' success was achieved by concentrating on those in his surrounding territory and not by attracting people who liked his style from elsewhere in the city. He appreciated that a congregation could only become a focal point for the local community if it offered a vibrant and attractive range of agencies. Within a short space of time Ross' church offered a wide array of organizations: church choir, children's classes, boys' and girls' industrial societies, Boys Brigade, mothers' meetings, Sabbath schools, Bible classes, Christian Endeavour societies, literary societies, prayer meetings, medical mission, communicants classes, office bearers and workers meetings.

8. Howell Williams, p.54.

9. J. M. E. Ross, William Ross of Cowcaddens, p.280.

10. J. M. E. Ross, p.155.

11. J. M. E. Ross, p.186.

12. *Atgofion am y Dr. John Pugh,* Annie Pugh Williams [private translation].

13. The question arises of how much this means in contemporary terms. Experts estimate the figures should be multiplied by 60. I am grateful to Sir Fred Catherwood for this information. So the equivalent cost for First Hall, East Moors, built for £2,000, holding 1,000, would be £120,000. The debt of the Forward Movement when Pugh died (£86,000) must read £5,160,000. This was eventually paid off through the generosity of the Davies family.

14. *Atgofion am y Dr. John Pugh*, Annie Pugh Williams [private translation].

15. The Forward Movement Magazine.

16. Howell Williams, p.66.

17. The Forward Movement Magazine, July, 1892.

18. Howell Williams, p.76.

19. T. Mardy Rees, *Seth and Frank Joshua, The Renowned Evangelists*, p.58.

20. T. Mardy Rees, p.59.

21. Howell Williams, p.85.

22. Davies took a keen interest in the churches of Montgomeryshire and was in demand, among other things, for Sunday school prizegivings where his ability to have his eye on the detail led to this story. At one such occasion in Montgomeryshire he spotted among the prize books a 'Life of Darwin'. He checked the minister who was about to pass it on. 'What's the

matter with it? Darwin was a good man.' 'No doubt – but his writings are not the kind of literature to put into the hands of young Sunday school scholars.' And the book was kept out off the list. With all his immense backing of the development of the university and secondary education in Wales, Davies was not in the business of making thoughtless shipwreck of young faith.

23. Owen Prys (1857–1934). Studied at Peterhouse, Cambridge in 1883 but on winning a scholarship of £100 he migrated to Trinity College. He graduated with first class honours in Moral Sciences Tripos and did further study under the conservative scholar F. Delitzch in Leipzig. He was Principal of Trevecka and then Aberystwyth Theological College until 1927.

24. Howell Williams, p.88. 'What do our critics mean by outsiders?' asked a perplexed Seth. 'Outside of what? Is it someone outside the Church of Christ, outside the family of God, outside the Christian fellowship?'

25. Williams, *The Romance of the Forward Movement,* p.90.

Chapter 5: Grace, Grit and Gumption

1. Howell Williams, *The Romance of the Forward Movement*, p.94.

2. Howell Williams, p.94.

3. Howell Williams, p.95.

4. This pattern was taken up almost exactly by the church student campaign teams from the university Christian Unions in Wales (IVF/UCCF) from the mid 1940s. In the 1960s, for example, IVF missions were held in Gabalfa FM Hall, Cardiff, led by Rev. Gordon McDonald, and Fitzclarence FM Hall on the Sandfields estate, Aberavon, led by the Rev. Gareth Davies and others. See G. D. Fielder, *Excuse Me, Mr. Davies – Hallelujah!*

5. J. M. E. Ross, William Ross of Cowcaddens, p.283.

6. J. M. E. Ross, p.283.

7. *Atgofion am y Dr. John Pugh*, Annie Pugh Williams [private translation], ch. 1, p.13.

8. ibid., ch. 9.

9. ibid, ch. 9.

10. ibid, ch. 9.

11. *Hanes Symudiad Ymosodol*, J. Morgan Jones, ch. 4, p.45.

12. Howell Williams, p.111.

13. Compare another writer: 'In invective and sarcasm we know few to equal him. He has reminded us of Disraeli's description of Salisbury – a master of flouts, and jibes and jeers!'

14. The Forward Movement Magazine, Jan., 1899, p.65.

15. The Forward Movement Magazine, Oct., 1905, pp.50, 51.

16. Howell Williams, pp.135-136.

17. Howell Williams, p. 136.

18. Howell Williams, p. 136.

19. A distinctive feature of the building is that it has a street corner open air pulpit entered via the gallery of Crwys Hall. A Cardiff man, now a member of Heath Church, recalls stopping in the street to listen when it was used sometime in 1933. It was used again after many years at Christmas time 1998.

20. *Atgofion am y Dr. John Pugh*, Annie Pugh Williams [private translation] ch. 8, p.40.

21. The Forward Movement Magazine, June, 1900.

22. *Hanes Symudiad Ymosodol*, J. Morgan Jones, ch. 4, p.42.

23. Ibid.

24. The Forward Movement Magazine, October, 1905.

25. The Forward Movement Magazine, October, 1905, p.54.

26. *Hanes Symudiad Ymosodol*, J. Morgan Jones, ch. 4, p.49.

27. *Atgofion am y Dr. John Pugh*, Annie Pugh Williams [private translation], ch. 8.

28. *Hanes Symudiad Ymosodol*, J. Morgan Jones, ch. 4, p.50.

Chapter 6: Poverty and Prostitution

1.At*gofion am y Dr. John Pugh*, Annie Pugh Williams [private translation], ch. 7, p.37.

2. Ibid, ch. 7, pp.37, 38.

3. Howell Williams, *The Romance of the Forward Movement*, p.158..

4. Howell Williams, p.159.

5. Howell Williams, p.159.

6. Howell Williams, pp.159, 160.

7. Howell Williams, p.160.

8. The first Sisters appointed were Sister Lloyd, Saltmead; S. J. Jones, Grangetown; Alison Jones, Merthyr; Ellen Watkins, Wrexham; Sister Walker, Memorial Hall; Gertrude Davies, Porth, Rhondda.

9. The Forward Movement Magazine entitled *The Herald*, August 1897–July, 1899 continued in *The Torch*, August, 1899f; August 1905, pp.39, 40.

10. Letter from Seth Joshua to Mrs. Jessie Penn-Lewis, April 1905.

11. The Forward Movement Magazine, July 1905, p.35.

12. The Forward Movement Magazine; August, 1905.

13. Because they were in areas that suffered quickly from industrial distress or slump, some of the Halls became very inventive in their endeavours to raise funds for relief for their own communities. This is an example from July 1898: 'During the severe distress resulting from strikes in the coalfields, the East Moors Choir and Orchestra, realizing it would be useless to endeavour to raise funds by concerts in their own area due to lack of emloyment, decided to ask the Mayor of Cardiff for permission to visit other more prosperous areas for fund raising purposes. The Choir of 100 plus the Orchestral Band visited the principal streets in Roath. It is not

every day one hears Handel's Hallelujah Chorus, Worthy is the Lamb, and Gloria etc sung in the streets of Cardiff. In this manner they collected £16.8s.8d in aid of relief.'

14. *Atgofion am y Dr. John Pug*h, Annie Pugh Williams [private translation] pp. 61, 62.

Chapter 7: Seth – Wales For Christ

1. T. Mardy Rees, *Seth and Frank Joshua, The Renowned Evangelists*, p.61.
    2. T. Mardy Rees, p.62.
    3. T. Mardy Rees, p.63.
    4. T. Mardy Rees, p.64.
    5. T. Mardy Rees, pp.64, 65.
    6. T. Mardy Rees, p.65.
    7. T. Mardy Rees, p.69.
    8. T. Mardy Rees, p.66.
    9. T. Mardy Rees, p.67.
    10. T. Mardy Rees, p.67.
    11. T. Mardy Rees, p.68.
    12. T. Mardy Rees, p.69.
    13. T. Mardy Rees, p.70.
    14. T. Mardy Rees, p.70.

Chapter 8: The Full Tide of Revival

1. T. Mardy Rees, *Seth and Frank Joshua, The Renowned Evangelists*, p.72.
    2. T. Mardy Rees, pp.72, 73.
    3. T. Mardy Rees, pp.73, 74.
    4. T. Mardy Rees, p.74.
    5. T. Mardy Rees, p.74.
    6. T. Mardy Rees, p.74.
    7. There were many Christian leaders who, though they were very ready to see God's hand in the ministry of Evan Roberts, and themselves experienced extraordinary blessing, were given cause to wonder at the way the revival developed. This is commented on by the Rev. Eliseus Howells, whom the author heard preach in his old age. He was, like Seth and many others, prepared to see God's overruling in Roberts being the main agency of blessing. A group of able and dedicated ministers had begun organising, many months before the revival, a series of conventions for the deepening of spiritual life. The first two were at New Quay and Aberaeron. The third, at Blaenannerch, was the one Seth spoke at and which was the cradle of the revival. Howells gives an honest personal comment on the varying reactions – 'As the revival proceeded Joseph Jenkins and the other brethren who had been concerned with these conventions were worried because they thought that the Word was being dethroned and that men were readier to speak to

God rather than to listen to what God had to say to them through the preaching of the Word.... The leadership passed into a young man's hands, to the hands of one considered less suitable than themselves, but "my thoughts are not your thoughts". The revival took a very different path from the one they wished to take.... Among Calvinistic Methodist leaders the older members were thinking of a revival similar to that they had seen in 1859, while others among us wished to devise means to deepen the spiritual life of our people. But "your ways are not my ways," saith the Lord' (David Jenkins, Agricultural Community in S. W. Wales, pp.231, 226). What we might call the 'articles of faith' of the revival, which were common whether Roberts was present at meetings or not, were these: a confession of all sins not previously confessed to Christ, dissociation from all doubtful pursuits, a public confession of Christ and a ready obedience to the promptings of the Spirit.

8. T. Mardy Rees, p.77.

9. T. Mardy Rees, pp.77, 78.

10. T. Mardy Rees, p.78.

11. T. Mardy Rees, p.78.

12. T. Mardy Rees, p.79.

13. T. Mardy Rees, p.79.

14. T. Mardy Rees, p.80.

15. T. Mardy Rees, p.80.

16. T. Mardy Rees, p.80.

17. T. Mardy Rees, p.80.

18. T. Mardy Rees, p.80.

19. The Forward Movement Magazine, August, 1899.

20. T. Mardy Rees, p.81.

21. See Brynmor Jones, *Voices from the Welsh Revival*.

22. T. Mardy Rees, p.81.

23. T. Mardy Rees, p.81.

24. T. Mardy Rees, p.82.

25. T. Mardy Rees, p.82.

26. T. Mardy Rees, p.82.

27. T. Mardy Rees, p.84.

28. See *The Confession of Faith of the Calvinistic Methodists* 1823, Article 33, 'Of the Assurance of hope': 'The assurance of hope follows upon true peace of conscience and a strict walk with God by faith. Hypocrites may deceive themselves with a false hope and a carnal presumption of being in the favour of God and in a state of salvation, but their hope shall perish. But all that believe in Christ, and love him in sincerity, and endeavour to walk before him in all good conscience, may, in this life, be certainly assured that they are in a state of grace, and may rejoice in the hope of the glory of God; and their hope shall never be put to shame. This is not a

doubtful conjecture, grounded on a false and a feeble hope: it is "the full assurance of faith", resting on the blood and righteousness of Christ, as revealed in the gospel; an inward evidence of saving grace in the soul, and the witness of the Spirit to their adoption ...'

29. The Forward Movement Magazine, August, 1899.

30. T. Mardy Rees, p.83.

31. T. Mardy Rees, pp.83, 84.

32. T. Mardy Rees, p.84.

33. T. Mardy Rees, pp.84, 85.

34. Letter from Seth Joshua to Mrs. Jessie Penn-Lewis, 12 July, 1905.

35. The Forward Movement Magazine, August, 1899.

36. The Forward Movement Magazine, August, 1899; July, 1905.

37. Letter from Seth Joshua to Mrs. Jessie Penn-Lewis.

38. Letter from Seth Joshua to Mrs. Jessie Penn-Lewis, 12 July, 1905.

39. Letter from Seth Joshua to Mrs. Jessie Penn-Lewis, 8 April, 1905.

40. Dr. J. Edwin Orr tells us that one of those converted through the ministry of Seth Joshua was Donald Gee, who became an outstanding leader in the Assemblies of God church (*The Light of the Nations*, p.241).

Chapter 9: Revival Repercussions

1. Dr. Andrew Bonar (1810–1892), brother of the hymn writer Horatius Bonar and the great friend of Robert M. McCheyne. Involved in the Kilsyth revival of 1832–39 with which McCheyne was associated. Bonar died a year after the Forward Movement got going and would have delighted its leaders in that he spent some of his early ministry preaching in a tent in Collace, Perthshire until a Free Church was built. Preaching was the necessity of his life. 'I long,' he says, 'to speak to the troubled soul about Jesus the Peace-maker, saying to the waves and storm, "Be still".' In a letter to the Rev. D. M. McIntyre in June 1891 he writes, 'I am not and never was, a great or popular preacher. I have been only an earnest expounder of God's Word, longing to save sinners and edify the saved.' His *Diary and Life* is a devotional classic. It contains the interesting information that the young Bonars worshipped in Lady Glenorchy's Chapel, Edinburgh – 'a church which enjoyed the powerful ministry of Dr. Jones, a Welshman, trained at the Countess of Huntingdon's College at Trevecka....' There is little doubt that under the ministry of Dr. Jones, Trevecka, Andrew Bonar and his brothers learned much of former revivals in England and Wales and this subject became their lifelong interest (Andrew Bonar, *Diary and Life*, Banner of Truth, 1960, pp ix,x).

2. The Forward Movement Magazine, September 1905, p.43.

3. Buick Knox, *Voices from the Past*, p.58.

4. The Forward Movement Magazine, September 1905, p.43.

5. The Forward Movement Magazine, September 1905, p.43.

6. Before Spurgeon, in ill health, left London for the last time in the autumn of 1891, he had arranged for Dr Pierson, a Presbyterian minister from Philadelphia, to occupy the pulpit at the Metropolitan Tabernacle. Pierson had first preached there in 1889 and when Spurgeon had a serious health breakdown in 1891 Spurgeon took advantage of Pierson's availability and left for Europe to convalesce. Spurgeon died there four months later.

7. *My Spiritual Pilgrimage* (English translation) James Clark, 1961, is the peerless autobiography of the first Professor of Philosophy at University College, Bangor, who had been previously lecturer in Glasgow University under the great Caird and who resigned his Bangor chair to enter the Christian ministry. He was both richly blessed in the revival and a perceptive judge of many of the revival experiences. What he says there of his own experience of the Spirit's outpouring (p.64) is a valuable example of what many Christians were being granted in these days, and which Seth Joshua in less detail tells of himself:

'A saying of Reader Harris came back to me – a saying which had not made any particular impression upon me at the time – and demanded my attention: "Conquer the devil where he has conquered you." There is nothing extraordinary in the sentence, but it is of practical importance, stressing the human side.... As I looked around, I saw that there was one thing at least that called for improvement. Though my sleep had been greatly restored this was my weak point, or at least one of them, and when I failed to sleep I would come to the breakfast table irritable and bad tempered. Well, I went to my study one morning before breakfast, going as a matter of will, and against my desire, and engaged in prayer with wholly unexpected results. As far as I can recall, the most I had expected was some help to overcome my bad temper, or to keep it from troubling me; but instead of that I was baptized with streams of life giving, cleansing, transforming power for about half an hour, that made me feel clean and healthy and joyous to the very depths of my being. And I had no need of tea or coffee to clear my head! It was an experience so wonderfully delightful and refreshing that I sought it again on the morrow, with the same results; and so it continued for twenty years till my health broke down in 1924. It was sometimes more powerful, sometimes less, sometimes freer sometimes less free, but as a rule it richly rewarded faith and perseverance. I was sometimes kept on my knees for an hour, occasionally for hours, and they were without question the golden hours of the day for me....'

On page 67, he details his memories of the Keswick platform ... swept by the influences of the Welsh revival.

8. R. B. Jones, *Rent Heavens, The Revival of 1904*, pp.109, 113.

9. R. B. Jones, p.102.

10. The Forward Movement Magazine, September, 1905, p.43.

11. R. B. Jones, pp.105, 106.

12. R. B. Jones, p.111.

13. The Forward Movement Magazine, September, 1905, p.43.

14. Another of the platform speakers records, first, Pierson's words and then the impact: 'It will add a great deal to the power of the simple address I am giving if we take one step before that. I solemnly say in the presence of God, that while our brother's address was being delivered, the refining fire went through my soul, showing me an immense amount of what does not please God. Every one of us, on the platform and in the audience, who can solemnly say to God – "Let this refining fire go through my being" – I wish you would stand before Him while we pray.'

'It was the writer's seventh Keswick and in the course of his professional work there he has received much personal blessing; but never before has he witnessed or heard anything to equal the never-to-be-forgotten sights and sounds that followed the close of Dr. Pierson's confession. For more than two and a half hours there was a stream of broken hearted confession of sins on the part of people from the platform and the floor of the tent.'

15. R. B. Jones, pp.112, 113.

16. The Forward Movement Magazine; September, 1905, p.43.

17. Letter from Seth Joshua to Mrs. Jessie Penn-Lewis, July 31, 1905.

18. Letter from Seth Joshua to Mrs. Jessie Penn-Lewis, 8 April, 1905.

19. Letter from Seth Joshua to Mrs. Jessie Penn-Lewis.

20. The Forward Movement Magazine, July, 1905, p.35.

21. Brynmor Jones, *The Spiritual History of Keswick in Wales*, p.14

22. The Forward Movement Magazine, September, 1905, p.42.

23. The Forward Movement Magazine, September, 1905, p.42.

24. The Forward Movement Magazine, September, 1905, p.43.

25. R. B. Jones, p.118.

26. R. B. Jones, p.110.

27. The Forward Movement Magazine, September, 1905, pp. 43, 44.

28. The Forward Movement Magazine.

29. T. Mardy Rees, *Seth and Frank Joshua, The Renowned Evangelists*, p.87.

30. Alun Ebenezer of Caersalem Church, Gorseinon has this as a family heirloom!

31. T. Mardy Rees, p.87.

Chapter 10: A Great Victorian and his Lieutenant

1. The Forward Movement Magazine, September, 1905, p.41.

2. Howell Williams, *The Romance of the Forward Movement*, p.148.

3. The Forward Movement Magazine.

4. The Forward Movement Magazine.

5. The Forward Movement Magazine.

6. Evidence for this can be found in G. D. Fielder, *Excuse Me*, pp. 20-21.

7. The Forward Movement Magazine, August, 1905, p.36.

8. The Forward Movement Magazine, August, 1905, p.36.

9. The Forward Movement Magazine, August, 1905, p.39.

10. K. O. Morgan, *Rebirth*, pp. 134, 135.

11. The Forward Movement Magazine, October, 1905, p.50.

12. The Forward Movement Magazine.

13. *Atgofion am y Dr. John Pugh*, Annie Pugh Williams [private translation] ch. 9, p.50).

14. Howell Williams, pp.198, 199.

15. *Atgofion am y Dr. John Pugh*, Annie Pugh Williams [private translation] ch. 12, pp.62, 63.

16. *Atgofion am y Dr. John Pugh*, Annie Pugh Williams [private translation], ch. 13, p.68.

17. Howell Williams, p.202.

18. Howell Williams, p.204.

19. Kensit, John (1853–1902). Protestant preacher and controversialist. From his youth an ardent Protestant he was deeply incensed by the Romanizing trends within the Anglican church. He founded the Protestant Truth Society in 1890. The anti ritualist agitation of 1898–1900 led him to establish the Wycliffe preachers to bear staunch witness to Protestant principles. While conducting a Protestant crusade in Liverpool in 1902 he was assaulted by a Catholic mob and died in hospital a few days later (*The New International Dictionary of the Christian Church*, Paternoster 1974). Remembered in the founding of Kensit Memorial College in London.

20. The Forward Movement Magazine, September, 1898, p.18.

21. The Forward Movement Magazine, September, 1898, p.18.

22. Pusey, E. B. (1800–1882). One of the leaders of the Ritualist movement that Kensit fought. Professor of Hebrew in Oxford. His own desire for reunion with the Roman Catholic Church led to his publishing his *Eirenicon*. A man of great personal devotion, he lost his wife after eleven years of marriage and all his children but one predeceased him. *New International Dictionary of the Christian Church*. Pusey House, Oxford was founded after his death.

23. The Forward Movement Magazine, September, 1898, p.18.

24. Howell Williams, p.211.

25. F. Dummer, The Forward Movement in Wales 1890–1914, M.A. Thesis, University of Wales.

26. Howell Williams, p.235

27. T. Mardy Rees, *Seth and Frank Joshua, The Renowned Evangelists*, p.113.

28. T. Mardy Rees, pp.112, 113.

29. T. Mardy Rees, pp.111, 112.

30. *Atgofion am y Dr. John Pugh*, Annie Pugh Williams [private translation], ch. 9, p.45.

31. The Forward Movement Magazine, December, 1900.

32. *Atgofion am y Dr. John Pugh*, Annie Pugh Williams [private translation], ch. 9, p.48.

33. T. Mardy Rees, p.112.

34. T. Mardy Rees, pp.113, 114.

35. The Forward Movement Magazine, April, 1909.

36. The Forward Movement Magazine, April, 1909.

37. T. Mardy Rees, pp.116, 117.

38. T. Mardy Rees, p.117.

39. The Forward Movement Magazine.

Chapter 11: 'Saint Francis of Neath'

1. Howell Williams, *The Romance of the Forward Movement*, pp.44, 45.

2. T. Mardy Rees, *Seth and Frank Joshua, The Renowned Evangelists*, p.45.

3. T. Mardy Rees, p.47

4. T. Mardy Rees, pp.51, 52.

5. T. Mardy Rees, p.52.

6. T. Mardy Rees, p.53.

7. T. Mardy Rees, pp.53, 54.

8. T. Mardy Rees, p.49.

9. T. Mardy Rees, p.49.

10. T. Mardy Rees, p.48.

11. T. Mardy Rees, p.48.

Chapter 12: The Return of Seth

1. Letter from Vernon Mills, Neath.

2. T. Mardy Rees, *Seth and Frank Joshua, The Renowned Evangelists*, p.94.

3. T. Mardy Rees, pp.94, 95.

4. T. Mardy Rees, p.105.

5. Letter from Vernon Mills, Neath.

6. T. Mardy Rees, p.102.

7. T. Mardy Rees, p.103.

8. Letter, Carl Henry.

9. Professor Carl Henry, Th.D., Ph.D. Personal communication with the author, 19 April, 1999. When professor of Christian Philosophy at Fuller Seminary, Dr. Henry observed: 'Twice – at least once in Chicago and again

in Los Angeles seminary life I have seen the power of God break through under Dr. Joshua's ministry with such force as the flame of awakening hovered over the student body.'

10. T. Mardy Rees, p.114.

11. T. Mardy Rees, p.116.

12. T. Mardy Rees, p.98.

13. T. Mardy Rees, p.99.

14. T. Mardy Rees, pp.99, 100.

15. T. Mardy Rees, p.100.

16. T. Mardy Rees, p.100.

17. R. J. Rees. Born in Cardiganshire, but brought up in the East End of London where Welsh remained the language of the home. He attended Moody missions while a lad and was also interested in the work of Fred N. Charrington, the converted son of the wealthy brewer. Charrington's Gospel Mission was close to his home and he would slip in to the services. Went to University College, Aberystwyth. While there he came under the power of the ministry of Henry Drummond during his mission to the university at which time he seems to have been called to the ministry. He studied in Oxford under A. M. Fairbairn and took a first in theology, one of the first Welsh Calvinistic Methodists to attain that distinction in Oxford. He succeeded to Clifton Street, Calvinist Methodist Church, Cardiff when Pugh resigned to take up the Forward Movement full time (H. Williams, *The Romance of the Forward Movement*, pp. 258-9).

18. (Lionel), Beatrice Mary, Florence, Gladys, Peter, Seth, Lyn, Phyllis. Lyn became an actor on BBC Wales. He wrote the very popular song 'We'll keep a welcome in the hillside' which became for a time a kind of National Anthem for Welsh emigrants. In July, 1944, he received an affectionate and appreciative letter from Evan Roberts, writing from Beulah Road, Cardiff.

19. T. Mardy Rees, p.106.

20. National Library of Wales, Calvinistic Methodist archive, HZ1/17/10-13. By kind permission.

21. Letter, Seth Joshua to daughter Phyllis.

22. Letter, Seth Joshua to daughter Phyllis.

23. Mardy Rees in *The Renowned Evangelists* leaves us with an insoluble mystery regarding a further family letter. He quotes a letter of Seth (there is no copy of the original) written to his son Llewelyn who was in the army in France. Seth had no son called Llewelyn. The circumstances behind the letter, however, suggests that this letter was to Peter, though the internal evidence of the quoted letter is against this as Seth addresses his son as Llew! In the National Library is Peter's army New Testament. Inside the cover are written the following details: 'Isaiah 26:3 World War 1 Entered the Army 1 Aug. 1914 Private Peter Joshua 1914 my first army New

Testament. Served in France-Belgium (Ypres), Middle East, Salonika –
Bulgaria. Gassed Ypres Sept. 7 1916, Salonika June 30 1917. Capt. Peter
R. Joshua 11 Royal Welsh Fusiliers Combat.'

Whilst on a Mission at Rhayader in March 1919 Seth wrote, according
to Rees, to his son, Llewelyn, then in the army. With the memory of Flanders
mud still not far from people's minds, it captures Seth's view of post war trends
and also shows his warm father's heart. But which son is he writing to?:

'Have an eye on your future, lad. Keep your chin up and out of the mud.
The world seems to be three parts mud now. Mud brains, mud manners,
mud politics, mud everywhere; even religion has become muddy, sloppy
and adulterated ... life is in Christ. It is in a Person, not in the tapestries
of religion. He is the Life, the Truth and the Way. I notice that men's
objections are thrown at religious shams, and not at the Christ. God
bless you, Llew. How I wish you could run home and see your brothers.
I would bring home a goose or some other animal, that we might have
a club feast together.'

24. Letter, Seth Joshua to son Peter.
25. R. B. Jones, *Rent Heavens, The Revival of 1904*, p.115.
26. R. B. Jones, p.118.
27. R. B. Jones, p.115.
28. R. B. Jones, p.119.

Chapter 13: Postscript and Prelude

1. Howell Williams, *The Romance of the Forward Movement*, p.60.

2. Howell Williams, p. 181.

3. D. Martyn Lloyd-Jones, *The First Forty Years*, Iain H. Murray, Chapter
6 and subsequent chapters.

4. See 'Light upon the River', Christopher M. Idle, St. Mathias Press,
1998, hymn numbers 277 and 278. A sample of his notes reveals some of
the careful research, as well as the inspiration, that goes into the writing of
a hymn! 'Letters and papers sketched the history of Highfield Evangelical
Free Church, soon to open a new home in buildings dating from the Welsh
"Forward Movement" around 1900. Highfields church, whose history
included the places I later listed in verse 2 of the hymn, kept outgrowing its
premises; in September they would start at Monthemer Road. Lord
Tonypandy (formerly Speaker of the House of Commons) had exclaimed
"Hallelujah for the resurrection of the preaching of the Gospel there!" I
had just read his biography "Order, order" (by Ramon Hunston) and seen
the huge part the coal mines played in the story of his family, and this
community.... At the September services David Jackman preached, but for
George Thomas heaven had truly drawn nearer. Before the new beginnings
in Cardiff, he went to be for ever with his Lord.'

A Centennial Appendix

1. Loughor held a significant position historically, the River Loughor being an important stage in travel to West Wales. In Roman times it went under the name of Leucarum. It was the 5th station of Antoninus on the Via Julia. Archeological investigation at the site of the Roman camp near the old river bridge have yielded interesting finds. Nearby is a Norman Castle, further witness to the importance of the estuary. It had two coal mines. Evan Roberts was born in Loughor in 1878 and worked as a collier from the age of twelve and later as a blacksmith. He lived close to the river at Island House which now bears a plaque in his memory. See p 119-120 'GGG'

Gorseinon is a much younger town. It grew up fast in the Industrial Revolution and became host to a vigorous tin plate industry and also had several coal mines. It had a High Street of bustling prosperity in the good times when coal and tin offered secure employment.

2. Both Penyrheol Hall and Caersalem Church were founded as a result of later resistance to and compromise of the gospel in Brynteg and Seion. It is important to note that the exceptional spiritual 'highs' of joy experienced did not leave people indifferent to objective biblical truth. In fact, just the opposite as far as these men were concerned. I judge that this was partly the result of there also being such a profound sense of sin and hell and their overwhelming awareness and gratitude that the blood of the cross was the only place of forgiveness – 'When the Prince of life our ransom shed for us his precious blood' was the keynote hymn of the people. Their experiences reinforced the doctrines of sin, judgement, atonement, grace and holiness. Because of a later hardening against the need of conversion by the minister and some traditional church members after the revival power subsided, many of the converts were obliged to leave Brynteg to pursue their concerns in worship and witness unhindered. They built Penyrheol Gospel Hall, Gorseinon, which began in 1910. This has retained its biblical testimony and liveliness down the years, while the Congregational church has sadly but predictably declined.

Caersalem Evangelical Free Church was founded in 1931 by strongly evangelical men, many of them men of the revival, who had been previously pillars of Seion Welsh speaking Baptist Church. These leaders were distressed to discover that their respected minister was a Free Mason. He refused the request of church leaders to resign from the Lodge. Many were convinced that this was a compromise of the gospel. It is often asserted that the gospel truths of revival times ebbed away. But here we have an example, thirty years after the revival, of evangelical convictions being so strong among the people that they took the huge decision to secede. My mother recalls, as a young Christian woman, the sense of deep grief they had in leaving, yet aware that there was a principle of gospel faithfulness at its root. Her own memory was of the vivid picture presented in the final church meeting that the vessel of the Lord was going down in a troubled sea. As it turned out my parents' wedding was the first to take place in the new Caersalem church in 1933. It is worth recording that Caersalem, of which my brother Godfrey is at present the minister, has continued over the years to maintain a lively witness, whereas the Baptist church is just about keeping its doors open.

3. One of his sons, Lewis Jones, became the 'Golden Boy of Welsh rugby' in the fifties. (He had taught me to play the viola in Grammar school!!) Titus Jones' eldest son, Cliff, who was the youngest full back ever to play for Llanelli Rugby Club, was an elder at Caersalem till recent retirement in old age and is still a member there.

INDEX

◆

Person's index

Barnardo, Dr 26
Baxter, Richard 41
Beecher, Henry Ward 210
Bonar, Andrew 136, 230
Bonar, Horatius 219, 230
Booth, General William 78, 199
Booth, Richard 27
Bunyan, John 177
Calvin, John 163
Campbell, R J 146
Cole, F W 157
Colwill, Colonel 27, 31
Cory, John 11, 59, 61, 77-9, 106, 154-5, 218
Cory, Richard 59, 60, 61, 77-8, 218
Dale, R W 41
Davies, Charles 80, 84, 124
Davies, David 11, 23, 79, 98, 203, 209, 218, 220
Davies, Edward 23, 34, 61, 79-80, 94, 98, 164, 209-13
Davies, I B 201, 204
Davies, Llewellyn 36
Davies, Mark 209
Davies, Richard 154
Davies, Mrs Richard 105, 156
Denney, James 35, 160
Edwards, Ellis 150-1
Edwards, Lewis 87, 219

Edwards, T Charles 16, 24, 61, 71, 80, 87, 98, 149-50, 218
Evans, Eifion 203
Figgis, J B 138, 139
Forsyth, P T 35
Gibson, Monro 81
Graham, Billy 185
Griffiths, Griffith 98
Griffiths, John 39, 42, 54, 62, 71, 75-6, 130
Harris, Howell 11, 17, 21, 54, 163, 169
Henry, Carl F 185, 234
Higham, Vernon 201, 204
Hill, Rowland 178
Hooker, Richard 99
Hopkins, E H 145
Howe, John 41
Howells, H G 67, 73, 150, 189
Howells, William 17, 21
Hughes, A L 201, 204
Hughes, Hugh Price 78
Huntingdon, Countess of 11, 17
Idle, Christopher 206, 236
Jeffery, Peter 176, 205
Jones, Cynddylan 58, 198, 199, 224
Jones, Emlyn 205
Jones, Heulwen 96, 207
Jones, John 16, 96

Jones, John Morgan 97, 99, 152, 159, 163-5
Jones, Thomas 86
Jones, W S 138
Joshua, Clifford 184
Joshua, Frank 30, 36-57, 89-91, 96-7, 175-80
Joshua, Lionel 190
Joshua, Mary 42-3, 46, 66, 115, 126, 183, 190
Joshua, Peter 184-7, 190-1, 194
Joshua, Phyllis 191
Joshua, Seth 29-32, 36-57, 65-6, 89-91, 111-49, 165-74, 181-90, 220, 222, 235
Kensit, John 161, 233
Knox, John 163
Lloyd-George, David 11, 153-4
Lloyd-Jones, Martyn 92, 119, 150, 198-205, 219
Luther, Martin 162
Macdonald, Ramsay 198
MacIntyre, D M 136, 142, 230
Manton, Thomas 41
Matthews, Edward 21, 219
Meyer, F B 26, 35, 86, 116, 146
Mills, Vernon 181-2, 189
Moody, D L 23, 26, 60, 63, 78-9, 83, 219, 220
Moore, E W 140
Morgan, Campbell 35
Morgan, Hugh 201, 203, 206
Owen, Glyn 201, 204
Owen, John 41
Parker, Joseph 99
Penn-Lewis, Jessie 107, 122, 130-4, 136, 141, 142, 143
Pierson, A T 133, 137, 139-41, 145, 230, 232
Phillips, Ieuan 119
Prys, Owen 62, 80-1, 159, 225
Pugh, Ann 22, 67, 108, 155, 157, 166
Pugh, John 15-35, 58-82, 86-88, 99-100, 157-70, 220, 235
Pusey, E.B. 233
Rees, Evan 53
Rees, R J 189, 235
Roberts, Evan 87, 119-25, 130, 144, 153, 228

Ross, William 33, 58, 62-5, 70, 85-7, 101-2, 111-3, 116, 143, 224
Rowland, Daniel 199
Ryle, J C 116
Sankey, Ira 60
Sibbes, Richard 41
Simpson, A B 147
Smith, Gypsy 129
Spurgeon, Charles H 26, 41, 83, 178, 219, 220, 230
Stalker, James 35
Stanley, H M 32
Thomas, John 75, 153, 201, 205
Tonypandy, Lord 206, 236
Torrey, R A 129
Wesley, John 11, 41, 167, 199
Williams, Glanmor 12
Williams, Gwynn 96, 205, 208
Williams, Howell 159, 164, 199
Williams, William 16
Whitefield, George 11, 29, 63, 163, 167
Whyte, Alexander 113

Subject Index

Aberavon 65, 119, 198
Abercynon 172
Abergavenny 22, 23
Aberporth 131
Aberystwyth 86, 210
Acrefair 156
America 27, 147-8, 161
Amlwch General Assembly 104
Ammanford 123-4
Assurance 128, 131-2, 149-50, 160, 229
Bala College 83, 150, 201
Band of Hope 216
Barry 11, 12, 98-9, 126, 209
Begelly Presbyterian Church 17-18
Blaenannerch 119-22, 125, 131, 133, 144
Bradford 172
Bridge of Allan 142
British Weekly 112
Brynmawr 172
Brynteg Chapel 125
Cadoxton 47
Caersalem 171
Calvinistic Methodism 10, 11, 15, 17, 35, 59, 61, 64, 70, 86, 92

Cambridge Settlement, London 83
Canton 67-82, 105, 126, 127
Capel Dridod 133
Cardiff 9-12, 23, 39, 43, 58-61, 66-82, 84, 89, 92-97, 101-110, 122-3, 126-7, 152, 157, 162-3, 171-2, 181, 194, 201, 203, 208, 211, 214-5
Cardiff Prison 59-60
Cardigan 119, 127-8, 131-2, 133, 172
Cathays 93-5, 158, 205
Central Hall, Newport 90
Christian and Missionary Alliance 147
Christian, The 81
Church Army 54
Church Pastoral Aid Society 40-1
Cilgeran 133
Cinderford 115
Confession of Faith 128
Cornwall 47
Counselling 87-8
Cowcaddens 33, 62-4, 101-2, 111-3, 116
Crwys Hall 93-5, 96, 126, 158, 205, 226
Cwmdare 172
Dinam Hall, Barry 98-9
Dowlais 107
Drinking dens 21-35
East Moors 9-10, 66-8, 94, 203
Ebenezer Welsh Church, Newport 90
English Conference of churches in South Wales 33
English medium preaching 33-5, 75-6, 79
Evangelism
  fair 37-9, 50
  open air 19-21, 24-5, 36-7, 44-7, 51-2, 56, 62, 65, 67, 73-4, 96, 115, 118, 144-5, 167, 201
  tent 38-9, 47, 49, 62, 65-8, 93, 96
Finance 55, 76-7, 81
First South Wales Conference 34
Forward Movement
  aims 83, 109
  beginnings of 33, 65, 67
  church building programme 61
  decline of 98, 151-80
  finance 55, 76-7, 81
  growth 67-110
  recognition 71
  regeneration 198-208
    training 83
    weakness of 67
    Women's Branch 103
Free Church Council 78
Gelligwastad 31
Glamorgan 21, 79, 81, 89, 151, 211
Glasgow 58, 62-4, 70, 101-2, 112-3, 116
Gorseinon 124-5
Gower 118
Havelock Street Presbyterian Church, Newport 89
Hayes 74
Heath 93, 95-6, 155, 157, 204
Hertfordshire 172
Highfields Evangelical Free Church 205-6
Hotel de Marl 72-5
Hoylake 127, 129
Independent Labour Party 153
Ireland 171
Joshua, Frank
  conversion 30
  death 181
  ministry in Neath 36-57, 96-7, 175-80
  ministry in Newport 89-91
Joshua, Seth
  at Keswick Convention 136-41
  at Keswick in Wales 143-6
  conversion 30-2
  death 189-90
  early days 27-30
  in America 147-8, 184-5
  in Scotland 141-3
  leaves Forward Movement 165, 169-70
  ministry in Neath 36-57, 65-66, 118
  move to Cardiff 66
  ministry in Newport 89-91
  preaching and preparation 113-5, 172-4
  return to Neath 181-9
  wider ministry 111-49, 190
  with Federation of Evangelical Free Churches 165-174
Keswick Convention 130, 136-141
Keswick in Wales 111, 130, 143-146

Kingsway Hall, Cardiff 96-7, 207
Life of Faith, The 122, 137
Liverpool 129, 189
Llandaff 171, 194
Llandeilo 124
Llandrindod 111, 116-8, 143-6, 189
Llandudno 123
Llanelli 171, 201
Llanrwst 103
Llantrisant 27
Llechryd 133
London 83, 171, 199
London West End Mission 78
Loughor 122, 124, 125
Machynlleth 115
Maerdy 194
Maesycwmer 171
Malpas Road, Newport 92, 202, 203, 206
Melbourne Hall 133
Memorial Hall, Cardiff 152
Merthyr Tydfil 69, 106, 107, 195
Methodist Chapel, Tonypandy 165
Mid Granville 147
Model of Prayer, A 113
Modernism 151, 186
Monmouthshire 21, 81, 211, 215
Montgomery 112, 210
Moriah Chapel, Loughor 125
Moserah Calvanistic Methodist Church 22
Music 55-7, 60, 63-4
National Temperance League 27
Neath 12, 36-57, 84, 96-7, 118, 124, 130, 147, 175-97, 205
Newcastle Emlyn 119-21
Newlyn 170
New Mills 12
Newport 89, 111, 202, 208
New Quay 119, 121, 129, 134
New Theology 146
Newtown 112
Overcomers Movement 130
Pantycelyn 16
Park Place, Tredegar 22
Penbrokeshire 15, 18
Pembroke Terrace Church, Cardiff 127
Pentyrch 27
Penydarren 107

Pierce Hall 95, 156, 205, 206
Pontnewywydd *115*
Pontypool 27-32, 65, 108-9
Pontypridd 9, 12, 23-7, 32, 33, 34, 61, 74, 114, 129, 133, 150
Porthcawl 49
Portsmouth 172
Port Talbot 65, 204, 208
Poverty 101-10
Prayer 47-8, 51, 55
Preaching 85-6
Presbyterian Church of England 81
Presbyterianism 163
Presbyterian World Alliance 99
Prestatyn 115
Prostitution 53, 93, 101-11, 203
Protestantism 163
Pugh, John
  conversion 15-7
  death 157-9
  preaching 86-8
  training for the ministry 17-8
  marriage 22-3
  ministry in Cardiff 58-82
  ministry in Pontypridd 23-35
  ministry in Tredegar 18-23
  overseas 99-100
  overview 159-170
Puritans 41, 84, 113
Raglan 22
Revival 119-135, 149-51
     and evangelism 134-5
Rhondda 23, 66, 69, 115, 172, 194
Rhyl 127, 172
Ritualism/ists 161-2
Rogerstone 171
Roman Catholicism 162-163
Romance of the Forward Movement, The 199
Rothesay 62
St David's, Pontypool 108
Salem Church, Canton 126, 127
Saltmead, Cardiff 92-3, 104-5, 158, 203
Salvation Army 30ff, 51, 78, 95, 104-5
Sandfields 92, 198, 199, 204-5
Scotland 58, 62-4, 70, 85-7, 101-2, 112-3, 116, 141
Second baptism 149-5

Sheffield 189
Shewsbury 112
Sisters of the People 87-8, 96, 101-110, 203, 207
Skewen 47
Social care 59-60, 69-70, 101-110
Society for the Aid of Released Prisoners 59
Splott 9, 47, 61-4, 66
Sunday Closing /CommissionAct 53, 72
Sunday School 53
Swansea 53, 153-4, 188, 194
Tabernacle Church, Cardigan 128
Tabernacle Welsh Baptist Church, The Hayes 124, 126
Temperance 26-7, 30-1, 38, 39, 53-4, 78, 90, 109
Tenby 16, 17, 18
Torch 62. 70, 90, 95, 97, 103, 106, 128, 132, 136, 143, 145, 149, 150, 152, 156, 161, 162-3, 168, 170, 214, 215, 216
Treborth 105-6
Tredegar 9, 12, 18, 20, 21-3, 27, 32, 60, 86, 99, 150
Treforest 29, 53, 69
Treherbert 114
Trevecka College 17, 81, 83, 150, 201, 210
Trevithan 114
Watford 172
Welsh Church, General Assembly of 64
Welsh Free Church Council 86
Welsh Presbyterian English Conference 136
Welsh Sunday Closing Act 23-4
Westminister Chapel, London 199
Wilkesbarre 147
Women's Training Institute 95
Wrexham 115
Y Drysorfa 15
Y Goleuad 123
YMCA 78, 89, 133
YWCA 78, 130

Revival Man

The Jock Troup Story

George Mitchell

Jock Troup's story is quite simply extraordinary. From a childhood in the Far north of Scotland he went to work in the fishing industry and then on to service in the First World War. It was during the war that the major turning point in Jock's life arrived - his conversion.

Jock went on to become an Evangelist, but no ordinary Evangelist. To quote a neighbour *'he had huge hands. He could pick up a fully inflated football easily with one hand. He had sixteen-inch biceps, un-expanded, and a neck like a prize bull'*, and to match this formidable physical presence he had a fire for reaching the lost with the Gospel.

George Mitchell gives fascinating insights into the lives of the fisher folk on the East coast of Scotland, and Glasgow life in Jock Troup's time. He includes many testimonies of those influenced through the ministry of Jock Troup and looks at the ingredients of revival, providing a useful lesson to the Church today.

'From one who has gained so much from the legacy he left in my own life, I can do no better than recommend this book to all, praying that the passion and fire for souls that he had for his day, will once again be experienced in our day.'

Bill Gilvear, Evangelist

Dr. George Mitchell is pastor of Castle Street Baptist Church in Inverness, Scotland. Author of *Chained and Cheerful: Paul's Letter to the Philippians* ISBN 1-85792-666-8, his autobiography, *Comfy Glasgow* ISBN 1-85792-444-4, was published in 1999 and was a best seller.

ISBN 1-85792-728-1